FOOD HYGIENE

A Study Guide

By the same author

Food Hygiene Manual (H.K. Lewis & Co., London)

Food Poisoning (H.K. Lewis & Co., London)

Also published by Stanley Thornes and Hulton:

Jill Trickett *The Prevention of Food Poisoning 2nd Edition*

Janet Hughes and Brian Ireland *Costing and Calculations for Catering*

Julia Reay *A Guide to Catering Organization*

Chris Ryan *An Introduction to Hotel and Catering Economics*

Iris Jones and Cynthia Phillips *Commercial Housekeeping and Maintenance*

FOOD HYGIENE

A Study Guide

P.A. Alcock Hon MIHI (NZ), FRSH, MIEH, MRIPHH, MISTC, MBIM

Principal Environmental Health Officer, City of Manchester

Stanley Thornes (Publishers) Ltd

First published in 1986 by:
Stanley Thornes (Publishers) Ltd
Old Station Drive
Leckhampton
CHELTENHAM GL53 0DN
England

British Library Cataloguing in Publication Data

Alcock, P. A.
Food hygiene: a study guide.
1. Food service — Sanitation
I. Title
363.1'927'024642 TX911.3.S3

ISBN 0-85950-607-X

Typeset by Tech-Set, Gateshead, Tyne and Wear in 10½/12½ and 11½/13½ Garamond
Printed and bound in Great Britain at the Bath Press, Avon

Contents

Introduction

Note: All readers are advised to study this introduction carefully before reading the rest of the book.

Who should use this book?

This book is perhaps a little different from many you have seen before. It has been carefully designed and tested in order to perform one very important function — to help readers learn and understand the essential principles of practical food hygiene. The book deals with fundamentals (key facts), and avoids unnecessary and often confusing details. It is, therefore, addressed to all those who wish to acquire such knowledge or who wish their staff to acquire it. In particular, the following people will find this book of special interest and importance.

- **Food workers** of all grades. It is of immense importance that such workers know and apply the very highest standards of food hygiene. This book tells you exactly what you really need to know.

- **Caterers and catering managers.** The book is designed to enable you to teach your own food hygiene course to your staff with the least possible effort on your part — in fact, the book does the job for you. Simply give each member of staff a copy of the book and it will do the rest.

- **Students** — especially those taking catering or allied courses (e.g. bakery, butchery etc.). The book will be especially useful for students sitting the Royal Society of Health (RSH) or Royal Institute of Public Health and Hygiene (RIPHH) examinations in food hygiene, as well as for those taking the Institution of Environmental Health (IEH) courses in food hygiene.

- Anyone interested in food hygiene for whatever reason. Even if you have already read something about the subject, this book will help you to test your knowledge, and may even surprise you sometimes.

What does the book cover?

The book has been edited to contain only essential, key material. It is, nevertheless, comprehensive. The essential facts of the subject are dealt with in detail but all non-essential frills have been removed. This makes the book especially easy and quick to use. Volumes could be written on the subject of food hygiene but most people are not interested in very technical matters. Only the essential facts will be found within these pages, selected on the basis of the author's experience and the comments of readers of previous works.

How do I use this book?

This book has been designed to be a workbook. It is intended that you take an ACTIVE PART in it. Do not simply read it from cover to cover; you will need a pen and paper to use the book properly.

The text you are about to read has been developed from many prototypes. It can help you to learn AND understand the essential principles of food hygiene *but* it can only do so in the fastest, most interesting and most painless way possible, if you use it carefully.

You will find that the text is divided into a number of programmes (not chapters). Each programme contains short sections, at the end of each of which is a question (Q). The questions either relate to what you have just read in the section above, *or* are designed to get you thinking. Have a go at each question in turn immediately after having read each paragraph. A 'model answer' (A) appears after each question. As you read each section, cover up the model answer below the question with a piece of paper or card. DON'T 'CHEAT': have a go at answering each question yourself, in your head, and only then compare it with the model answer.

You will also find that a series of questions appears at the end of each programme in a progress paper. Write down your answer to each question on a separate sheet of paper. You should attempt to answer the questions in your own words BEFORE looking at the model answers.

At first, you will probably find that you cannot answer some questions or that you get some wrong. When this happens, don't worry. If you could get all the questions right all the time, you would not need this book. If you do get any wrong, and if you don't understand the model answers, go back to the beginning of the programme and read it all again. You will be surprised just how quickly you learn. BUT this will only be true if you follow the above instructions carefully. If you attempt to press on regardless — not bothering with the questions, 'cheating' (you can only be cheating yourself), or do not re-read the parts you get wrong — the book cannot do its job properly. This really is the best, most painless way to learn. Trust the book: it WILL help you if you use it correctly.

Near the end of the book there is a collection of test papers which (if you complete them carefully) will help you to revise the main points in the book. As before, you should answer each question in turn. Write your answers on a separate sheet of paper, and then (and ONLY then) compare your written answers with the printed model answers that follow.

A word of warning: The model answers given throughout the book should be read carefully. Many of them contain additional information, further explanation of major points and so on. This is intended, once again, to help you to learn quickly and effectively.

Your written answer does not have to be exactly like the printed model answer.

As long as you include the essential elements of the answer — the 'gist' of it if you like — you may mark your answer as correct. Always take special note of the model answers however, as the additional points which some of these contain are important to you.

A glossary is included (just before the index) which explains a selection of the more important and frequently used technical terms found in the text. It is intended for quick, convenient reference, and does not pretend to be comprehensive.

The book has been designed to be interesting as well as useful. It is hoped that you will enjoy using it. Learning need not be a drudge, and as long as you use this text carefully, learning food hygiene most certainly will not be.

What is 'food hygiene' and why is it important?

'Hygiene' is a term which originally described the science of infectious disease prevention. Unfortunately, it is a term that is much misunderstood and often misused. Most people equate hygiene with cleanliness. You will discover as you read this book just how wrong they can be.

The subject of food hygiene concerns all theoretical and practical considerations in the study of the prevention of food-borne infectious disease. Because of its inherent usefulness, its exact boundaries have become blurred and extended over the years so that it now encompasses quite a lot more than its main aim alone. You will learn more of the scope of food hygiene as you read this book.

The importance of food hygiene as a subject cannot be overstressed. You should be in no doubt that the consequences of poor food hygiene can be, and often are, dire. Unfortunately it is not a fashionable subject and therefore does not receive the publicity it really deserves, except at a very elementary level. People do die as a consequence of poor food hygiene, and many thousands are made ill each year. To be responsible for the death of a customer is a frightening prospect, but this is the risk you run if you do not ensure that your food hygiene practices are correct.

Even if you have never had anyone die in your establishment, could it be that your time and luck are running out? Hadn't you better ensure that it never happens? It is not suggested that your establishment or your practices, are 'dirty'. Not a bit of it. In fact, safe food could be produced in 'dirty' premises. Dangerous food is FREQUENTLY produced in 'clean' ones. You will have to study the rest of this book very carefully to appreciate just why this apparent paradox is true. You will soon discover that all is not what it may seem as far as food hygiene is concerned.

In general, food hygiene is important for three main reasons. These are also the reasons why you should be interested in this book. They are:

1. Good food hygiene (which, remember, does NOT mean 'cleanliness'), can prevent food consumers from becoming infected with various food-borne diseases, many of which can be fatal. Good food hygiene protects the food consumer; mere 'cleanliness' never does.

2. Correct food hygiene design and practice can protect both a business AND individual food handlers from possible prosecution by Local Authority Environmental Health Officers. (Currently the maximum penalties are either an unlimited fine or two years' imprisonment.)

3. Good standards of food hygiene (not just 'cleanliness') can enhance and protect the reputation of a business (which, remember, can lead to increased profits and increased job security for all concerned).

You, no doubt, are interested in food hygiene because you are professionally concerned with food preparation and service. You must have a good knowledge of food hygiene if you are to be truly professional. This book will help you to acquire such knowledge; it is up to you to put it into practice after that.

Hints on study (and exam) techniques

You may be reading this book because you will be sitting an exam on, or containing parts with, food hygiene. If so the following hints will be of value to you. Even if you will not be sitting an exam, much of the advice which follows will help you to get the very best from this book.

To learn anything requires the expenditure of effort. Sometimes it requires very hard work indeed. Some things, however, we can learn very effectively even when we are not aware of it. We learn to speak our native language without being aware of the fact. If you doubt your ability to learn, just remember that fact, and things will not seem so bad. Think of ANY subject or topic you know already — (it could be anything from sewing skills to mathematics). Recall how very difficult it seemed at first. Remember how very hard learning to read was. The mysteries of 'sums' at school must be a memory for everyone. Yet — and this is a most important point — once we have mastered a topic, it seems so easy doesn't it? We wonder just why we had any difficulty at all.

You may well find much in this book that is new to you. Don't expect to be able to learn or understand all of it overnight. Very few could do this, and those who could probably know something of the topic to start off with. Nothing that is worth doing is ever easy — you will only every get out what you put in. This book has been designed (and the manuscript has been tested) to make your learning task easy, but no one has a magic formula. You will have to work at it, and it will take time, but the time you spend should be enjoyable — so relax and be patient; you WILL learn in the end.

Don't try to do too much at once. This is a common mistake. Set yourself a target for each session of study. Make yourself comfortable and ensure there are no distractions — no noise around you. This may be difficult in some cases, but always try to study in a quiet place whenever possible. The 'target' for each study session should NOT be time based. To say to yourself that you will do 'one hour's study' tonight is WRONG. Instead, set yourself the target of doing ONE programme at a time. Each one should take from thirty minutes to one hour to complete. This is long enough. The real secret of studying is to do a little, very often. If you really don't feel like doing it one day or evening, then don't. Forcing yourself to learn will not work at all. You may have to discipline yourself of course, but don't be too strict.

There is a very common, and very wrong, impression in the minds of most people which causes them to equate 'intelligence' with 'education'. Many people presume that someone who has passed a certain number of O-levels, A-levels, or other exams, must be clever and that someone who has never passed an exam in their life is not. This conclusion is neither true, nor fair. Some people are better at exams than others, some had more chances than others, and so on. Have faith in yourself. This text has been used, successfully, to teach university graduates but it has also been successful (on more occasions) with people who left school over forty years ago!

What matters more than anything else is that you really want to learn the material in this book. When you think just how important food hygiene is, you will want to learn more about it. The text will show you how beneficial such knowledge will be.

Success in learning anything also depends on technique. Many people who believe they cannot learn a particular topic are frequently mistaken. Often they have had bad experiences with 'learning'. They may well have been taught very badly. This book uses a well-tried and tested method of helping you to learn. Have faith — even if you couldn't do it before (or thought you couldn't), you will almost certainly be in for a pleasant surprise.

It is important for you to have a reward in mind when you study. It may be that you promise yourself a box of chocolates, a bottle of whisky or whatever, if you pass the exam (or get all the test papers at the end of the book right). The exact nature of the reward doesn't matter, but reward yourself when you have done well, look forward to the reward and remember, if you do happen to fail, there is always a next time.

It is no good at all just to read a book and hope that you will learn the material in it as if by magic. You must take an active part in the process if you are ever to succeed. That is why this book has a series of questions throughout the whole of the text. Only by having a really good try at all of these will you be able to learn efficiently. This really IS the most painless way to learn. Effort is still needed, but it will be less effort than would otherwise be required.

Another way of taking an active part in the learning process is to read a programme, answer all questions (check your answers with the model answers), and then read the programme again if you get anything wrong. There is a tendency in most people to try to skip through a book at the greatest possible speed. Such people, and such a technique, usually fail. Be patient, and re-read any passage or section you are unsure about.

Whether or not you are reading this book for the purpose of an exam, you MUST revise the material within it once you have completed the whole book. Learning depends to some extent upon repetition but pure parrot-fashion memorising is no good at all. Always try to UNDERSTAND what you read; think about each new point carefully.

As far as revision is concerned, it is essential to remember the phrase 'a little, often'. Cramming the night before an exam is of no value to anyone. Revision should be a gradual process, do a little at a time and plan the revision so that is is spread over many weeks. One useful trick is to write down little 'key facts' from the text on to postcards (the kind that are used in box files and index files — they are readily available from large stationers). You can carry these cards around with you and read a few of them when you are on the bus, having a coffee break or during any free moment.

Exams

Some of you reading this book will be sitting an exam with food hygiene either as the main subject or as part of the syllabus. The following advice is offered to you.

Many people who fail exams do so either because of 'nerves' or because of an incorrect exam technique. The 'nerves' you feel before an exam actually help you, so don't be afraid of them. Only if you get yourself well and truly 'worked up' will 'nerves' spoil your chances. As long as you have prepared for the exam sensibly, and have studied and revised properly, you can do no more — so why get so het up about it?

When you start a WRITTEN EXAM (advice regarding oral exams appears below), you will stare at a blank piece of paper. The distance between you and that paper can seem like miles. Remember, however, that you will be starting with no marks at all. As soon as you start to write, you will automatically be improving the situation. The moment you start to write you will start to score points.

Always arrive for the exam early, don't get het up before you even start. NEVER revise anything on the day of the exam. In fact, you would be well advised to go out the evening before. You can do little to improve your chances at this point: all depends upon the work you have done previously. If you try any last minute cramming, you will be more likely to reduce, rather than increase, your chances of success.

As soon as the exam begins, DON'T pick up your pen and start to write immediately. Nearly everyone does, and it is always the wrong thing to do. Be calm, take a few deep breaths (this nearly always helps people to relax a little) and read through the question paper. Spend about five minutes familiarising yourself with it. If you have to answer, say, six questions out of ten, choose the best six from your point of view. START with a 'good' one, and FINISH with a 'good' one. Be careful to work out how much time to allow for each question (always take a watch with you). If you must answer ten questions in an hour, you have about six minutes per question. Allow yourself just five minutes in such cases for each one. This will leave ten minutes at the end for checking through the paper.

Read ALL the instructions on the exam paper most carefully. If you must answer two questions from Section A and three from Section B for instance, it is no use doing it the other way round. Once again it is essential to stay calm: don't panic, don't act like a bull in a china shop. Read all instructions carefully and make sure you follow them.

It is equally important to read each question CAREFULLY. Many examinees get questions wrong merely because they did not bother to read them properly. THINK about each question: try to see what the examiner who wrote it actually wants in the answer. Don't jump in with both feet. It is no use finishing an exam in record time only to find that you misread the questions. Always answer the questions that are asked — read each one carefully; think about each one carefully.

It is very easy to be thrown if you meet a question you cannot answer. If you find that you cannot answer the first three or more, panic will set in. The rest of the questions could be 'right up your street', but once you panic, once you feel your heart sink, you will be lost. If you cannot answer a particular question, leave it until the end then go back to it. Go on until you find one that you CAN answer. NEVER allow yourself to be thrown out of step. A good guess is better than nothing and, if an answer doesn't readily spring to mind, use common sense. Have a good guess at least — you *may* guess right.

Always remember that no exam requires you to get every single answer right. Usually you will need about 50 percent of the marks to 'pass'. This means that you could get half the questions wrong and still pass. Looked at in this way, the one or two out of fifty or so that you cannot answer simply do not matter at all!

Use ALL the exam time available. When you reach the end of the exam paper, go back and attempt any questions you could not answer. Check through ALL your answers, but be warned, never, ever change any answer unless you are sure it is wrong. Very often, your first thoughts will be the correct ones. If an answer is definitely wrong, then change it, but not otherwise.

Always write legibly. Print your answer if you have to. Remember that the examiner who marks the paper cannot give you any marks if your answers cannot be read. Few of us have really neat handwriting, especially if writing at speed, but we can all try to make our written words as legible as possible.

It is a good idea to take a spare pen with you — having checked to make sure it works. Panic will set in again if your pen runs out half way through the exam. It is usually best to use a ball-point or a fountain pen (not a felt-tip). Blue ink is preferable to any other colour.

Once the exam is over, don't engage in a 'post-mortem'. It is over; you can only wait for the results. If you have failed, so what? You can always have another try next time.

ORAL EXAMS may be taken by some of you. Remember the following points with regard to these:

Always look smart; first impressions often count. Listen to the examiner carefully and answer the question that is actually asked. If you do not understand the question, say so. The examiner will repeat it or elaborate on it. If you do not know the answer, say so. The examiner will go on to the next question.

Treat each question separately. Do not be put off if you cannot answer the first few that are asked. Once again it is essential to avoid panic. Keep calm, speak in a clear voice, don't whisper your answer, but don't shout either!

Don't be put off by the examiner's manner. Most are friendly and kind, but some are a little gruff by nature. Don't let this put you off, just answer the questions calmly and sensibly. Calm, cool and collected is the attitude you want for all exams. Keep your head and you will have the best chance of passing.

After this book, what then?

In a book of this type, it is impossible to cover all possible topics in the vast subject of food hygiene. Any reader who has any queries or would like more advice, or who has a comment on the book, is cordially invited to write to the author (who can be contacted through the publishers). He will be pleased to hear from you. Please enclose a stamped, self-addressed envelope for a reply.

MOST IMPORTANT OF ALL, however, is that you apply in practice all that you learn from this text.

You may feel that some of the advice contained in this book just cannot be applied in practice. Be assured that it can. Each piece of advice is based on the author's many years of experience and much research in this field. You can rely on the information herein, it is not 'pie in the sky', but good, honest, down-to-earth practical advice.

You may meet with many difficulties. You will meet some 'doubting Thomases' who tell you not to bother — "Don't worry — nothing has happened yet!" Perhaps their time and luck is running out too. Be determined, believe that what you are doing is right, and you will overcome the opposition and all the difficulties. You are asked, begged even, to do this — the people who consume your food are relying on you and your knowledge and skill. They may not realise it, but their health and perhaps even their lives, may depend on it.

Food Hygiene Theory

PROGRAMME 1
Microbiology

1 Microorganisms, or microbes, are very simple creatures. They are extremely small living things, so small that they cannot be seen without the aid of a microscope capable of magnifying about 1000 times. Microbiology is the study of all microbes. Not all microbes cause disease. (Those that do are often called 'germs'.) In food hygiene we use the theory of how harmful microbes behave in order to prevent food-borne illness and to help us to extend the keeping qualities (shelf-life) of food. Microbiology is therefore essential to any study of food hygiene.

Q Bacteria and fungi are two of the three main groups of microorganism — do you know the name of the third?

A The viruses.

---

2 Microbiology is a science (it is a branch of biology). We will be studying it in some detail in the pages that follow. Don't let this bother you, even if you haven't studied any biology before (or were not very good at it when you did). The material in the following pages will be easy to learn, and it is essential to learn it if you are going to understand just how food hygiene principles work.

Q Why do you think that it is so necessary for anyone wishing to learn something about food hygiene to study something about microbiology?

A It is necessary because food hygiene is the practical application of microbiology. We use the theory of how microbes work in order to help prevent food poisoning and to increase the keeping qualities (shelf-life) of food (see paragraph 1).

---

3 We know that for the purposes of studying food hygiene, the three main types of microbe are fungi, bacteria and viruses. Each of these is different as regards general shape, the way they live, etc.

Q Which of the groups do you think are of most concern to food hygiene — fungi, bacteria or viruses?

A It depends whether we are concerned with food-borne illness or shelf-life. Bacteria and viruses produce the majority of diseases which can be transmitted to us via food. Bacteria and fungi are responsible for food spoilage.

---

4 We know the names of the main groups of microbe, but we still don't know any particular, specific names of any of them. Scientists use Latin or Greek names for animals and plants because this enables them to understand which creature is being referred to, no matter what language they may speak. Usually two names are used — the **genus** name and the **species** name. Pet dogs are members of the canine family of animals. Wolves, foxes, jackals, domestic (pet) dogs, belong to the genus *Canis.* This tells us they are all related to each other. The domestic dog belongs to the species *familiaris,* so a pet dog is *Canis familiaris.*

Q Do you think it is enough to have just two names for organisms (like *Canis familiaris* for pet dogs)?

A No, it is not. There are many different types of dog — spaniels, terriers, hounds, etc. There are even different types of terrier — cairn terrier, Airedale terrier, bull terrier and so on. If we are to be able to refer to different microbes in sufficient detail, we need more than two names for them.

5 In microbiology we use two main names (genus and species) and then, in addition, we use **type** names to further distinguish things. The table below will make this clearer with a bacterium as an example.

Dog	=	terrier	cairn	black
Bacterium	=	*Staphylococcus*	*aureus*	type I

The name *'Staphylococcus'* (pronounced *staff-i-lo-cock-us*) gives us the genus of bacteria involved, *'aureus'* (pronounced *ore-re-us*) refers to the species. 'Type I' tells us that we are talking about a *Staphylococcus aureus* that is a type I.

This method of description is just like having a black cairn terrier, which distinguishes it from other types of dog (it is a terrier), from other types of terrier (it is a cairn), and from other types of cairn terrier (it is a black one).

Q Why do you think it is necessary to have so many names for one microbe?

A Well, part of the reason is that scientists always try to be exact. A very practical reason also exists however. If we can identify specific types of microbe, we can distinguish their habits, characteristics, weaknesses, etc. more easily. For instance, *Staphylococcus aureus* type III, can produce a particular kind of food poisoning whereas *Staphylococcus aureus* of other types (I, II and IV) cannot.

NOTE: It is common practice in bacteriology, which is the study of bacteria, to shorten the names of bacteria. For example, the genus name *'Escherichia'* can be shortened so we have *E. coli.* It is a convention that the genus name is written with a capital letter first — *Escherichia,* not *escherichia* — and the species name with a small letter — *coli,* NOT *Coli* — hence we have *Escherichia coli.* It is also a convention that the whole name is printed in italics or, if handwritten, is underlined.

6 Bacteria and fungi are usually given both genus and species names (and type numbers or letters perhaps) in most cases. Viruses tend to be described by group or by a general name relating to the disease they cause (for example 'smallpox virus').

Q Why do you think that viruses are given only general names?

A The answer is that they are so simple in design that it is hard to distinguish one from another, and also there are far fewer types of virus than of fungi or bacteria.

---

7 We can now go on to describe fungi, bacteria and viruses. We will talk about them in very general terms at first, and consider a little more detail later on. Fungi are multi-celled OR single-celled organisms. A **cell** is a bag of chemicals from which living things are made. They are like building-bricks if you like. Humans are made up of billions of them. Some fungi (the yeasts) are made of only one cell — others are made of many.

Q Do you know the name of any type of fungus that you can find very commonly in the kitchen? (HINT: there are two main types that could be found; both are actually visible to the naked eye).

A Moulds and mushrooms are both types of fungus. Although most microbes can only be seen with a microscope, many types of fungus are exceptions to this. In fact, the mould that you can see on bread, cheese and so on, does not consists of one organism but of a large number of them clumped together.

---

8 Fungi usually consist of long thin tubes which ramify (branch) through a food on which they are feeding. The parts that are usually visible are the **fruiting bodies** whose purpose is to make **spores** which are the 'seeds' of the fungus. This is what a mushroom is — the gills on the underside of the mushroom hold the spores which, when the time is right, fall out and are blown around by the wind. (The spores of fungi are extremely small.)

Q If the mushroom that we can see is the fruiting body of the fungus, where do you think the rest of it is?

A The rest of the fungus is below the ground. The thin tubes which form the fungal body are called **hyphae** (pronounced high-fee), whereas the whole mass of hyphae together are called **mycelium** (pronounced my-see-lee-um).

---

9 Yeasts are fungi, but they consists of only one cell. They do not have hyphae and do not form fruiting bodies, although they can turn themselves into a resting type of cell in order to help them survive some unpleasant conditions in their environment.

Q Do you know what some yeasts are used for?

A Yeasts are used in bread-making, in the fermentation processes for making beer and some wines, and in some other fermentation food producing processes.

10 Bacteria are simpler organisms than fungi. Their cell structure is less complex. They ALL consist of only one cell, although in some species, several individual cells usually clump together in one place. Even so, each of the cells is capable of living an independent existence.

Q What is a cell?

A A cell is essentially a bag of chemicals. It is the smallest unit of life and cells act as building-bricks from which the bodies of most organisms are built. The majority of life forms on Earth are made up of many, many cells — they are **multi-cellular**. Bacteria are **uni-cellular** ('uni' means one, i.e. they are one-celled, or single-celled).

---

11 The general names given to certain groups of bacteria tell us what their overall shape is. For instance:

Streptococci — round organisms, like beads on a necklace, several cells aggregated together.

Staphylococci — several round cells aggregated together like a bunch of grapes.

Bacilli — single cells, sausage shaped.

Cocci — spherical, therefore streptococci are spherical cells aggregated together like beads on a necklace.

Vibrios — single cells, shaped like a comma.

Q How many bacteria (single cells) do you think you could fit on this page? Have a guess.

A In fact, the number is too large even to write down. You could fit about 100 000 of the average-sized ones on the head of a dressmaker's pin! To see one in any real detail, we would need to use an electron microscope which could magnify about 250 000 to 500 000 times.

---

12 Viruses are perhaps the strangest living things of all. They don't consist of cells. In fact they are really clumps of chemicals which form crystals (like crystals of salt or sugar): some are contained inside a bag (like a cell), some are not. They are even smaller than bacteria (about one thousand times smaller) and, as we shall see later, they have a peculiar style of life.

Q Can you guess what shapes viruses can be?

A Viruses come in some very odd shapes indeed. Some are spirals (like corkscrews), some are bullet shaped, some are twenty sided (looking very much like a lunar landing module), while others are more or less spherical.

KEY FACTS

1. Microbiology is the scientific study of microbes.
2. Food hygiene is the practical application of microbiology. By applying good food hygiene practices, we can help to prevent food poisoning and increase food shelf-life.
3. There are three main groups of microorganism ('germs') — bacteria, fungi and viruses.
4. Bacteria and viruses are the most common food-poisoning organisms. Bacteria also spoil (rot) food. Fungi are principally of interest to us because they cause food spoilage.
5. Bacteria usually have two scientific names — a genus name, (e.g. *Salmonella*) and a species name (e.g. *typhi*). (Occasionally a bacteria is further specified by a type number, added after the genus and species.) This example's full name is *Salmonella typhi.*
6. Cells are 'bags of chemicals'; they are the smallest units of life. Bacteria consist of only one cell and are therefore very small (thousands would fit on the head of a pin).
7. Yeasts are types of fungi. They consist of only one cell. Moulds and other fungi (besides yeasts) are multi-celled. Viruses are not really made of cells at all — they are 'alive', but resemble dried crystals.

PROGRESS PAPER 1

This is the first progress paper in the book. Remember that it is designed to help you, not to criticise you. Different people learn at different speeds. DON'T worry if you cannot answer all the questions below, or if you get any wrong. If you do get them wrong, make sure you understand the answer given in the answer pages following the questions. If you don't, then read the programme again from start to finish. Don't cheat — you will only be cheating yourself. Answer each question below as carefully as you can (make a guess if you don't know a particular answer) and only after you have attempted each question should you mark them by looking at the model answers on page 9. Take your time, read each question carefully, and think carefully about your answer. Write down your answer to the questions on a piece of paper. Answer all the questions you can before looking up the answers. Keep your answers brief.

1 What is microbiology?

2 Why should we study microbiology if we are really concerned about food hygiene?

3 Name the three main groups of microbe of greatest concern to us in food hygiene.

4 Describe in a very general way what fungi are (e.g. single-celled or multi-celled, shape, size, etc.)

5 Describe in a very general way what bacteria are.

6 Describe in a very general way what viruses are.

7 How small are bacteria? (e.g. about how many would fit on the head of a pin?)

8 What is a cell?

9 Describe some of the shapes of bacteria. (Spheres, round, etc.)

10 Describe some of the shapes of viruses. (Spheres, round, etc.)

ANSWERS

1 Microbiology is the scientific study of microbes. It is a branch of biology.

2 Food hygiene is the practical application of microbiology. By using its theories we can help to prevent food poisoning and increase the shelf-life of food.

3 Fungi, bacteria and viruses.

4 Some fungi are single-celled and very small (the yeasts). Many are made up of hyphae (thin tubes made up of several cells laid end to end) which when aggregated together are called a 'mycelium'.

5 Bacteria are single-celled organisms which are microscopic (cannot be seen with the naked eye).

6 Viruses are very small organisms which are rather like chemical crystals (like sugar or salt crystals).

7 You could fit about 100 000 average-sized bacteria on the head of a pin.

8 A cell is a bag of chemicals which acts like a building-brick. Multi-celled organisms are made up of very many of these bags (building bricks); uni-cellular organisms consist of only one cell.

9 Bacteria shapes can be spherical, spheres strung together like beads on a necklace, spheres aggregated together like a bunch of grapes, or sausage shaped.

10 Viruses come in some very odd shapes. Some are spiral, some bullet shaped, some are twenty-sided (almost like a lunar landing module), and some are more or less spherical.

PROGRAMME 2
Life Processes

1 Before we can go on to consider just how microbes live, what they can and cannot do, how resistant they are to adverse conditions and how we may control them, it is essential that we know a little of how general life processes work.

Q Why do you think it is necessary for us to know about the processes of life?

A Because if we know what makes microbes 'tick', we can control them and kill them. Microbes work in a very similar way to other living things, and therefore we need to know what 'life' is all about so that we can help control the microbes which threaten our food.

---

2 Have you ever thought about the differences between a lump of rock and a worm? Apart from the obvious fact that they look very different, what is it that makes one 'alive' and the other not. For that matter, what is the essential difference between a wriggling worm and a dead worm? In other words, what does a 'living' thing do that makes it 'alive' and special?

Q Can you think of what makes 'living things' (such as ourselves) alive? (HINT: for instance, you may say that living things breathe.)

A Essentially, living things perform a combination of the following: they eat, drink, breathe, move (and grow), and reproduce themselves.

---

3 In fact, only one of these processes is unique to living things. It is the ability to produce more of their own kind that distinguishes living from non-living things. Viruses for instance, do nothing but reproduce. Although all the other processes such as eating, breathing, etc., are displayed by most types of living things, it is the ability to reproduce which makes living things unique.

Q Not all living things move. Many plants are literally 'rooted to the spot'. Do you think that microbes move?

A Some can, some cannot. Many rely on the fact that they can be carried about by humans and animals, or in air currents (especially when we sneeze for example). No microbes can 'fly' of their own free will, and those which can move about by themselves (rather than being carried by air or water) can only do so when they are inside a liquid of some kind (e.g. water, soup, gravy etc.).

---

4 Now that we know just what the special characteristics of 'living things' are, let us look a little more closely at what each of these processes actually mean and what their significance is.

Q To get us started on this discussion, can you think why living things have to eat food?

A Living things 'eat' in order to do two things. Firstly, they must obtain energy — they use food as a 'fuel' in the same way that a car uses petrol. Secondly, many of the chemical constituents of food are used by living things as building-materials to build up the constituent parts of their own bodies. (NOTE: even single-celled organisms like bacteria have to be built up of some raw materials: they get the raw materials from the food they eat.)

---

5 Even when an organism is 'resting' it still needs energy to stay alive. This fact often puzzles people but it can be explained very easily. The chemical substances from which living things are made are actually very 'unstable'. This means that they are very liable to fall apart (almost like a house made of playing cards). This fact can be explained by laws of chemistry and physics but we need not worry about why it is so; we need only remember that it is a fact. Energy, albeit a small amount when an organism is at rest, is essential to prevent an organism's constituent chemicals from falling apart. Energy is used in this case as a kind of 'glue'.

Q OK, so we know why energy from food is needed even when an organism (a 'living thing') is resting. But does it need raw materials from food all the time? (It certainly does when it's growing, but what about when it's stopped growing?) What do you think — does an organism need raw materials from food even when it isn't growing?

A This is a tricky question. The real answer is best described as yes and no. In the case of a large organism containing many cells (such as a human being), many cells wear out each day, even when the organism is fully grown, and therefore raw materials are needed to make new cells to replace those that wear out. In the case of most simple organisms (such as single-celled bacteria, etc.) raw materials are used only for growth, but such organisms will always be growing to some extent if conditions are favourable.

---

6 The last sentence may have made you think that bacteria grow and grow until they reach a massive size. This is not so. All living things grow to a certain size (within limits) and then stop growing. In the case of bacteria (and as we shall see later, in the case of other microbes), they grow to a certain size and then split into two. Of course, simple organisms don't eat three meals a day like we do. They consume food when it is available and when conditions are right for them to use it so that they can grow and reproduce.

Q We know that when we grow (and when animals, plants, etc., grow), we get bigger. We now know that bacteria grow to a certain size, then split into two. What do you think happens to the two 'halves' of the bacteria then?

A They have become two independent organisms. They will grow to a certain size and then split into two (we now have four independent organisms where we originally had only one). 'Growth' therefore, as far as microbes are concerned, has the same effect as 'reproduction'. In effect, they grow to a certain size and then reproduce themselves by splitting into two.

7 In fact bacteria do this. Fungi (which, remember, apart from yeasts, are multi-celled) grow by adding on new cells (made from the raw materials they get from their food) onto the ends of their hyphae. Yeasts are similar to bacteria: they grow to a certain size and then a 'bud' forms, which breaks off to form a new, independent organism. Viruses are a very special case, and we shall leave consideration of them until later.

Q Not only do complex organisms like ourselves, grow to a certain size and then stop, they also have a limited amount of time in which to live — eventually they all die. Do you think that microbes die of 'old age'?

A In effect, no, they don't. The actual life span of an individual microbe may be very short (usually about a day or so), but they usually 'die' because of lack of food or because something in their environment kills them. They don't just die of 'old age'.

---

8 We have mentioned reproduction and we have seen that simple bacteria reproduce in a very simple manner. No courting, no seduction for them. In fact, they don't even need a mate. They simply grow to a certain size and then split into two. This method of reproduction is called **asexual reproduction** (which means reproduction 'without sex'), whereas more complex organisms engage in **sexual reproduction.** It is all a matter of genes.

Q Do you know what genes do?

A Genes are the 'plans' used by an organism to build a copy of itself. Cat genes contain certain instructions to tell the cat's reproductive cells how to make a kitten; a bacterium's genes tell it how to make another bacterium exactly like itself.

---

9 Sexual reproduction requires that the genes from a **donor** (the 'male'), fuse with the genes of an **acceptor** ('female'). This is an effective method of reproduction but it is slow. It also requires that every male finds a female to mate with, and vice versa. Asexual reproduction on the other hand, is rapid, and the organism concerned does not need to find a mate. Many bacteria, for example, can reproduce themselves once very twenty minutes under ideal conditions. This is a fantastic rate of reproduction. If a human female could reproduce at this rate, she would be capable of producing 788 400 children (seven hundred and eighty-eight thousand, four hundred) during the average span of the child-bearing years.

Q If asexual reproduction is so efficient, why is it that 'advanced', complex creatures like humans don't use it? Have a guess.

A In fact the answer to this one is a bit complicated — we slipped it in here just to get you thinking! Sexual reproduction (where we have genes from male and female) allows for a mixing of genes. Therefore, sexual (male and female) reproduction can create a wide variety amongst individuals. In the case of bacteria, for instance, which reproduce asexually, each 'daughter' bacterium is exactly like its 'parent'. (NOTE: you may be similar in looks, etc., to your mother, but you are not of course, EXACTLY the same — you will have some of your father's characteristics also.)

10 We know that, as far as most microbes are concerned (or at least the simple bacteria, viruses and simple fungi, that we are most concerned with in food hygiene), they can be said to 'grow' and 'reproduce' in a very simple way. We know that most cannot move around of their own free will and that they 'eat' food to obtain energy and to obtain raw materials to make new microbes.

Q Why do you think living things (not just microbes) need to drink. What purpose has water to do with life? (Have a guess.)

A Water has two main uses for living things. Firstly, it helps energy to 'glue' the chemicals of life together. It's strange to think of water as a glue, but as far as living things are concerned, this is exactly what it is. Secondly, and equally important, water acts as a medium through which the chemicals of life can react. The best way to think of this is to look upon life processes as being a series of chemical reactions. They are a type of chemical reaction which requires the presence of water so that the chemicals doing the reacting can move about. They dissolve in water, if you like, and this allows them to perform their life-giving reactions.

---

11 We are familiar with the fact that most complex animals breathe in air through their lungs. Plants breathe air too, even though they do not have lungs. The question is, just what purpose is served by breathing?

Q Air contains mostly the gases nitrogen and oxygen. Which one is necessary for life?

A Oxygen. It works in a very clever way. We know that organisms get energy from food. They do this by breaking down the food's complex chemicals. When this happens, sub-atomic (i.e. smaller than atoms) particles called **electrons** are released, together with a little bit of energy. These electrons must be got rid of if the whole process is to work properly. Oxygen will collect electrons and enable them to be 'breathed out' again.

---

12 In fact, electrons are tagged on to the oxygen molecules which then combine with hydrogen atoms which are also released when food is broken down. This hydrogen and oxygen mixture is actually water; so we, as human beings, breathe in oxygen, it collects electrons and hydrogen from broken down food, and becomes water which we breathe out again. (NOTE: you can easily prove that we do breathe out water as you can see misty steam coming from your mouth on a cold winter's morning.) The reaction can be written:

glucose + oxygen → energy + water vapour + carbon dioxide gas.

Q Microbes do not have lungs. How do you think they 'breathe in' and 'breathe out'? (Have a guess!)

A Oxygen and water merely pass across the microbe's cell membrane. This can happen in liquids very easily which is why microbes do not 'drown' when in water, soups, gravies, etc. They absorb oxygen from liquids, in a similar way to a fish's gills which also absorb oxygen from water.

13 Many microbes have managed to do away with the need to use oxygen as an electron collector. Many can pass on electrons from broken-down food to other substances, or can obtain energy from food merely by breaking down the food into smaller chunks and passing electrons round it in circles. Some microbes can even be killed if they come into contact with oxygen. Others can use it when it is available but can still obtain energy from foods even when there is no oxygen. You should note well that three major types of microbe exist as far as oxygen need/use is concerned. They are:

Aerobes (*must* have oxygen).

Facultative (can use oxygen when available but don't always need it).

Anaerobes never need oxygen and will NOT grow in its presence; some may even be killed by it — *an* means 'without'; anaerobic means 'without air'.)

Q If some anaerobes can be killed when in the presence of oxygen, where do you think they might be found? (HINT: the answer to this question is really rather simple).

A Where there is no oxygen! This will be the case in the centre and bottom of pans of stew, soup etc., in river muds, in the deeper layers of soil and so on. Oxygen from the air will dissolve at the top of lakes (and for some distance below the surface otherwise fish could not live there), but not in the muds at the bottom. Oxygen dissolves at the top few inches of a pan of soup, but not below this level.

14 Living things must 'live' within some form of environment. For birds of the air it is the sky, for fish, the seas, lakes, etc. Even microbes live within particular environments, but, because the majority of them are very small indeed, their immediate environment is very small also. There can be a very considerable difference between different parts of a joint of meat for example, at least as far as bacteria are concerned. Living things can only perform their necessary life functions at certain, rather limited-range, temperatures. Too cold and the chemicals which perform the life processes will not work; too hot, and these essential chemicals will be destroyed.

Q We now know that the temperature at which an organism finds itself can affect its life processes (being too cold or too hot can result in death). What else do you think could affect microbes? (HINT: think of different types of environment — dry, wet, etc., and have a guess.)

A Primarily, the moisture content and the **pH** of the environment are the other factors (besides temperature) that can affect microbes within an environment. The term 'pH' refers to the degree of acidity or alkalinity of the environment.

15 Acidity, and its opposite alkalinity, are measured on a scale called the pH scale. On this scale, pH 1 is VERY acid: the degree of acidity reduces as we go from pH 1, pH 2, pH 3, etc., to pH 6. At pH 7, we have neutrality (which is neither acidic nor alkaline — like pure water). Moving on to pH 8, we are getting slight (dilute) alkali, and the degree of alkalinity increases at pH 9, pH 10 up to pH 14 which is very alkaline.

Q What pH level (roughly) do you think microbes would prefer?

A About pH 7. In other words, at or about, neutrality. Acidic environments seriously inhibit the growth of the vast majority of microbes. They would die in strong acids. Most microbes can tolerate slight alkalinity, but most prefer to be between pH 7 and pH 8.

KEY FACTS

1 Essentially, living things perform a combination of the following things: they eat and drink, breathe, move (and/or grow), and reproduce.

2 The only SINGLE life process that distinguishes living things from non-living things (e.g. a lump of rock) is that living things can reproduce themselves. In fact, this is the ONLY process of life that viruses engage in at all.

3 Food, of some sort, is used by living things as a source of energy (as a 'fuel'), and as a raw material from which the organism can build up its own 'body'.

4 As far as bacteria are concerned, they grow to a certain size then split into two (this is actually how they reproduce). Remember that bacteria consist of just one cell.

5 Most microbes reproduce asexually; they are all one sex. This is an efficient process but does have the disadvantage that a mixing of genes (and therefore a mixing of the characteristics from a 'father' and a 'mother') cannot occur.

6 Bacteria reproduce very quickly. Under ideal conditions, some bacteria can split into two once every twenty minutes.

7 Water is needed by living things because it forms a kind of chemical 'glue'. In addition, the chemicals of life dissolve in it. It allows the chemicals of life to move about and to perform the chemical reactions that go to make up life processes.

8 As far as oxygen breathing is concerned, some microbes do not need oxygen at all. (Air is made up of $\frac{1}{5}$ oxygen. It is the oxygen in the air that we need when we breathe in.)

Aerobes must have oxygen.

Facultative organisms can use oxygen when it is available, but do not always need it.

Anaerobes do not need oxygen — they grow and live without it. Some anaerobes could be killed if they were exposed to air and they certainly do not grow in its presence.

9 Microbes can only live and grow at certain temperatures (they don't like it either too hot or too cold).

10 Microbes need to be kept moist and preferably within a near neutral environment (neither acidic nor alkaline), in order to survive.

PROGRESS PAPER 2

Here is another test paper for you to have a go at. If you get any questions wrong, or cannot answer any of them, DON'T WORRY. Just read the programme again and see where you went wrong.

You must always remember that it is hard to learn something that is new to you, but with a little practice, you will improve. Many of the major points you need to know about food hygiene are repeated several times in this book so you will have plenty of opportunity to learn them. Be patient; all will become clear to you in time.

Be brief with your answers. Write your answers to all the questions on a separate sheet of paper before looking at the model answers which follow.

1 Why do we, who are interested in food hygiene, need to know something about life processes in general?

2 What are the main characteristics of 'living things'? In other words, what do living organisms do that make them different from lumps of rock?

3 Can microbes move? How do they get from one place to another?

4 What are the two main uses of food as far as living organisms are concerned?

5 Even when an organism is resting it still needs energy. Why is this so?

6 What is the essential difference between sexual and asexual reproduction?

7 What are the two main uses of water to a living organism?

8 What is the purpose of oxygen to those organisms that use it?

9 What is an organism called that:

(i) uses oxygen as an electron collector?
(ii) can grow either with or without oxygen?
(iii) cannot grow in the presence of oxygen and might be killed by it?

10 Name the environmental conditions (e.g. moisture), which have the greatest influence upon microbes.

ANSWERS

1 If we know what makes living things work, we can control these things and hopefully, we can then kill or inhibit microbes.

2 The main characteristics of living things are that they eat food, drink, breathe, move about (some cannot of course do so, e.g. rooted plants), grow, and reproduce their own kind.

3 Some microbes can move, but only in fluid environments. Most are carried about inside or on animals (including humans), in water, through the air on air currents etc.

4 Food is used by organisms firstly as a fuel to provide a source of energy, and secondly, as a source of raw materials to build and replenish their own life process and 'body' chemicals.

5 Because the chemicals which go to make up the substance of living things and which perform life processes, are very unstable by nature. Energy is needed, literally, to stop them from falling apart.

6 For sexual reproduction to occur, there has to be a fusion of male and female genes. This does, however, provide an opportunity for variations in the characteristics of the offspring. In asexual reproduction, only one individual is involved. It merely makes a copy of its genes and then splits into two. This is an efficient and fast method of reproduction, but each new 'half' of the organism is exactly like its 'mother'.

7 Water is used as a kind of chemical 'glue' to hold an organism's chemicals together, and it forms a medium (or environment) in which life's chemical reactions can take place.

8 It collects (accepts) electrons that are released from the organism's food when it breaks down that food in order to produce energy for itself.

9 (i) An aerobe.
(ii) A facultative organism (sometimes called a 'facultative anaerobe').
(iii) An anaerobe (*'an'* means without, hence an-aerobe means without air).

10 Moisture content, temperature (heat and cold) and pH (degree of acidity or alkalinity).

PROGRAMME 3
Microbial Life

1 Having considered life processes in general in the last programme, we now turn to an examination of microbes specifically.

Q Why, do you think, do microbes require a source of food?

A Because, like all other living things, microbes require both a source of energy and raw materials from which to build the constituents of their cells (or cell) and to provide life-process chemicals. In the case of microbes, food provides these things, just as it does for other types of living organisms.

---

2 Humans eat food by means of cutting it up or biting lumps off, chewing it and swallowing. From the mouth, the food enters the stomach and then on to the intestinal (digestive) tract. Here, chemicals called **enzymes** break down the food substances into smaller chemical 'bits'. These 'bits' circulate in the blood and each cell of the body uses them as fuel and raw material supply. In effect, each of the cells in our body acts like a unicellular organism: each one 'eats food' to obtain its own energy and raw materials source.

Q The enzymes which first break down the large and complex food chemicals that we eat are secreted into our digestive tract. Microbes do not have a tract like ours, so how do they manage to break down the complex food substances they 'eat'? (Have a guess).

A They secrete enzymes out of their cell (or cells) and these liquefy and break down the complex food substances they feed upon (such as stew, lump of meat, inside of an egg etc.), and turn them into smaller, simpler substances which are then merely absorbed into the microbial cell itself.

---

3 When foods rot, they do so because microbes are growing in or on them. The microbes secrete more and more decomposing enzymes into the food and the food becomes progressively 'digested'.

Q Do you think this process goes on and on until no more food is left to rot? (HINT: think of your own experiences with rotting food.)

A No, usually the process stops when the food has become really foul. This usually happens because the most common rotting organisms produce acids as a result of the digestive processes they perform. As these acids accumulate, they suppress any further growth of the microbe. All decomposable foods would, eventually, rot down to nothing, but it would take a very wide variety of microbes to do this. The process of total food decomposition is slow; as some types of microbe become inhibited, others take over. In their turn, they too cease to dominate and another type then completes the process.

---

4 Rot-producing microbes get into our foods in several ways. They may come from the place where the food was collected (the seas, fields, slaughter houses, etc.); be present in a living animal in the first place (which is later killed); be carried to food by animals or people, be carried on air currents or within water used in food processing, or they may contaminate the food during transport, storage, processing, etc.

Q Which types of microbe do you think are chiefly responsible for bringing about the decomposition of foodstuffs?

A The fungi (including, especially, moulds and the yeasts) and bacteria. Viruses do not, and cannot, rot food. (We shall learn much more about viruses in later programmes in this book.)

5 Microbes need water to survive just like other living things do. They don't 'drink' it as we do. However, it is absorbed into their cells.

Q How do you think water can get into a microbial cell?

A It doesn't soak in through holes in the cell (as many people think when asked this question). It enters the cell through a process known as **osmosis** (pronounced *os-mow-sis*). We will now discuss what this involves.

6 We described a cell earlier in the book, as being a 'bag of chemicals'. This is a very simple description but it is very close to the truth. The chemicals inside the cell are called the **protoplasm** and the 'bag' consists of a **membrane** (cell membrane) which is semi-porous. It is like a bag made of cotton rather than a plastic bag (which is non-porous). When a concentrated fluid is separated from a fluid which is less concentrated, by a semi-porous (or semi-pervious) membrane like a cell membrane, the less concentrated fluid passes across the membrane towards the concentrated fluid. When microbes are surrounded by fluid which is less concentrated than their protoplasm, the fluid is drawn into the cell as it is drawn across the cell membrane. This is the process of 'osmosis'.

Q What do you think happens if the microbe is surrounded by a fluid which is more concentrated than its own internal protoplasm?

A The fluid in the protoplasm passes out of the cell, across the cell membrane. This can be a very serious problem for the microbe — it could result in its death. It will certainly stop the microbe from growing.

7 Jam, and similar preserves, can prevent the growth of many types of microbe because the sugars within them make them very concentrated. Although a lot of water is contained in jam, many microbes cannot suck it into their cells because the jam is more concentrated than the protoplasm inside the microbes' cell(s). In other words, the water in the jam is unavailable to the microbes. It has been made unavailable because the sugar in the jam makes it more concentrated than the microbes' protoplasm.

Q How else might water be made unavailable to a microbe?

A By being frozen. There is a lot of water in an iceberg but it is solidified. The water in ice cubes cannot move into microbial cells because an ice cube is solidified water.

8 Microbes therefore, need available water. They also need to obtain energy from the breakdown of food. Some types of microbe obtain this energy by breaking down the food they 'eat' and passing the electrons which are released to an electron-acceptor such as oxygen (aerobic microbes). Others may use electron acceptors other than oxygen or may simply pass electrons around as the complex food molecules are progressively broken down into smaller and smaller molecules (this process is known as **fermentation**). Organisms which do not need to use oxygen but which can use it if available are, as you know, called facultative anaerobes.

Q What is the name given to organisms which do not use oxygen at all?

A Anaerobes. Some of these will be killed if they come into contact with free oxygen. Bacteria of different types may be aerobes, anaerobes or facultative. Fungi may be facultative or aerobes: none of them are anaerobes. Moulds (which are a kind of fungi) are always aerobes. They cannot grow in the absence of oxygen (though unlike ourselves, they will not be killed if it is absent. They cannot be 'smothered' or choked to death).

---

9 We know that some microbes are able to move of their own free will (if within a fluid medium). Growth can be considered to be a form of movement. We know that bacteria grow to a certain size and then divide into two, so that a microbiologist referring to the 'growth' of bacteria, really means an increase in the number of individual bacteria present within a colony.

Q How do fungi 'grow'?

A It depends upon the type of fungus. Yeasts, which are single-celled, grow to a predetermined size, form a 'bud' which breaks off and produces a new yeast cell. Most other fungi 'grow' in the true sense of the word. They elongate their hyphae by adding more cells on to each one.

---

10 You may well have noticed that we have made very little mention of viruses. These organisms are very unusual and for this reason, we shall leave a discussion of them until later in the book.

Bacteria reproduce by growing to a certain size and then splitting into two (asexual reproduction). Fungi reproduce by three possible means. Either they form buds which break away to form a new cell (yeasts), or part of a hyphae breaks off and starts to grow independently, or they form structures called **spores** which are very like seeds.

Q When fungal spores are released from the fungus, what do you think happens to them?

A They get carried away by air currents. They germinate and grow into a new fungal 'plant' when they land upon a suitable medium which will support them (e.g. a loaf of bread or a lump of cheese).

11 We will not consider how viruses reproduce here. We will consider viruses in detail later, as they are different from other types of microbe.

Microbes differ with respect to the types of environmental conditions they like or can tolerate. If they find themselves in an environment which is not to their liking, they won't grow but they are not necessarily killed. They are capable of lying dormant and 'weathering the storm' until conditions which favour their growth arise again.

Q What are the main environmental conditions which can affect microbes?

A Moisture, temperature and pH.

---

12 We know that microbes must have a supply of water that is available to them (i.e. which passes into the cells by osmosis). Microbes differ with respect to the temperatures they need to grow. They are classified into three different groups depending upon the temperature ranges which favour their growth:

Psychrophiles grow from	−5 °C to 20 °C
Mesophiles grow from	5 °C to 65 °C
Thermophiles grow from	40 °C to 90 °C

Most microbes are mesophiles and those which are **pathogenic** (disease producing) to humans usually grow best at 37 °C (which is human body heat).

Q At what temperatures (lowest and highest) do you think the growth of food-poisoning microbes is prevented? (HINT: the microbes which produce food poisoning are mesophiles).

A Below 5 °C and above 65 °C. (NOTE: these figures MUST be memorised as they are important in food hygiene practices — as we shall see later. You can easily memorise them by remembering that we start school at 5 years old and retire, at least many people do, at 65 years old.)

---

13 If microbes are heated to a high enough temperature, they die, but it is the temperature AND time combination that matters. Heat kills microbes by degenerating their life chemicals. This takes time, but will be faster at higher rather than lower temperatures. For instance, most (not all) microbes, can be killed at about 65 °C in about 30 minutes, but many will die in a few minutes at 85 °C.

Q Do you think that low temperatures will kill microbes?

A No, they won't kill microbes with certainty. Many of the individual microbes within a colony will die if frozen but many will only be put into a state of suspended animation to start growing again when it gets warmer.

14 Most microbes cease to grow at temperatures below 10 °C although, to be safe, we can use 5 °C as some pathogenic ones can grow between 5 °C and 10 °C. By using a fridge or freezer carefully, we can stop microbial growth to a great extent. On the whole, fungi are better able to withstand low temperatures (that is, grow at low temperatures) than are the bacteria, although bacteria, on the whole, are more able to resist high temperatures than are the fungi.

Q At what pH do you think most microbes grow best?

A At or near to neutrality. Most prefer from pH 7 to pH 8. In general, fungi are more tolerant of acidic conditions than bacteria. In fact, most fungi prefer their environment to be slightly acidic whereas they generally do not like alkaline conditions. Many bacteria can grow happily under alkaline conditions. (Some types of bacteria can grow in slightly acidic environments, but these are very much in the minority.)

KEY FACTS

1. Microbes need food in order to obtain energy and to build up new cell constituents (viruses do not need food at all as they absorb chemicals from the host cells which they infect).

2. Microbes 'digest' the food they need by excreting digestive juices (enzymes) out of their cells. The partially digested food is then absorbed into the microbial cell. Water enters the microbial cell by the same process of absorption.

3. It is this process of pouring digestive enzymes over food that is responsible for food rotting. Some types of bacteria rot food as do some types of fungi.

4. If a microbial cell is surrounded by a solution that is more concentrated than the solution inside the cell, water passes out of the microbe. This could cause the death of the microbe: it will certainly stop its growth.

5. Jams, preserves, salted meats, etc., are 'preserved' because most microbes cannot grow in them. They cannot grow because the concentration of sugars and salts is too high.

6. Microbes need to have a supply of 'available' water. The water must be capable of entering the cell. Water can be 'unavailable' because it contains dissolved dubstances (it is too concentrated), or because it is frozen, or, of course, it may not be there at all (as in dried foods).

7. Bacteria 'grow' by increasing in size to a certain limit and then splitting into two. Yeasts, which are single-celled fungi, form 'buds' which enlarge and then break away from their mother cell. Multi-celled fungi grow by adding new cells on to their hyphae. (Viruses only grow when inside their host cell).

8. Some fungi form 'spores'. These are very like plant seeds, are released into the air and start to germinate when they land on an appropriate medium — such as bread, cheese and so on.

9. The main environmental conditions that can affect microbes (and which must be favourable for them to grow), are moisture, temperature and pH (acidity/alkalinity).

10. Microbes need moisture, appropriate food, warmth and neutral (neither acid nor alkaline) conditions in order to grow.

11 Most microbes stop growing below 5 °C and above 65 °C. (This is important for food hygiene. Remember these two temperatures. One way to remember is to recall that many of us start school at 5 years old and retire at 65.)

12 High temperatures (at least 85 °C) will kill most microbes if that temperature is maintained for long enough. Low temperatures will not kill most microbes, but put them into suspended animation.

PROGRESS PAPER 3

Have a go at these questions. If you cannot answer any, or if you get any of them wrong, go back and read the programme again to see where you went wrong. REMEMBER, don't worry if you don't do very well at this paper — you are still learning. It won't seem half as difficult when you have revised each programme a few times. As before, write your answers to all these questions before looking up the model answers.

1 Why do microbes need a food source?

2 How does 'food' get inside a microbe?

3 What is the main reason why foods rot?

4 Where do food-rotting microbes come from?

5 Which types of microbe rot food?

6 How does water get into a microbial cell?

7 How can water be 'unavailable' for microbes?

8 How do microbes obtain energy from food?

9 How do bacteria grow? How do fungi grow?

10 What are the main 'environmental conditions' that affect microbes? At which temperature (low and high) will most microbes cease to grow?

ANSWERS

1 As a source of energy and to obtain raw materials for growth and life processes.

2 Enzymes are secreted out of the microbe and then decompose the 'food' material in which they are present into smaller, simpler, chemical substances which are then absorbed into the microbial cell(s).

3 Because food-rotting microbes are growing within them and are secreting decomposing enzymes into the food.

4 They may be already present in the food (e.g. from soil or within a food animal prior to slaughter); they can be carried to the food via animals or humans; they may contaminate the food during transport, storage or preparation, etc.; they may come from food-processing water, etc.

5 Bacteria and fungi mostly; NEVER viruses.

6 By the process of osmosis. If the protoplasm of the microbial cell is more concentrated than the fluid around the cell, it will pass in across the cell membrane.

7 It could be more concentrated than the microbial protoplasm (high sugar concentration for example, as in jam) or it could be frozen.

8 They break down the food and release electrons from it (passing them to electron-collectors such as oxygen) or they remove electrons from the food molecules and pass them around smaller and smaller 'bits' of food. When electrons are removed from molecules, energy is released.

9 Bacteria grow to a certain size and then divide into two. Yeasts grow to a certain size and a bud forms which breaks off. Multi-celled fungi make up new cells and add them to their hyphae.

10 Temperature, moisture and pH (acidity/alkalinity). Most microbes cease to grow below 5 °C or above 65 °C.

PROGRAMME 4
Bacteria I

1 Bacteria are single-celled microorganisms which can only be seen through a microscope with a magnification of about 1000 times. Real detail of the bacteria can only be seen by means of an electron microscope (at magnifications of 100 000 to 250 000 times or more). Many thousands of bacteria could fit on the head of a pin.

Q What are the usual shapes of bacteria?

A Sausage shaped (bacilli), spherical (cocci), spheres chained together like beads on a necklace (streptococci), spheres clumped together like a bunch of grapes (staphylococci), comma shaped (vibrios). Other shapes do exist but they need not concern us here.

---

2 Bacteria are the most ubiquitous forms of life. They come in a vast variety and can be found virtually everywhere. They can be found in seas, lakes and rivers, in soil (in vast numbers and very great variety), in the air (where they simply float around or get carried about on air currents; they do not live in air as such, and may well die there if they become dried), in and on both animal and human bodies.

Q What harm may bacteria do? Are they all harmful?

A Some bacteria (pathogens) produce many types of human, animal and even plant diseases. They cause spoilage and rotting of foodstuffs. Not all bacteria are harmful, however, and in fact many of them are very useful. Some are used in industrial processes (to make drugs, tan leather, cure tobacco leaves and so on). Some varieties that are ordinarily present in or on the human body, actually protect us from more harmful organisms.

---

3 Within the human gut, one particular species of bacterium — *Escherichia coli* (pronounced *esh-sher-ish-ia coal-eye*) is a **commensal.** This term should be remembered. It refers to an organism which lives within or on another, but does no harm whatever. We excrete vast numbers of *E. coli* in our faeces. The *E. coli* type I is found virtually only in humans.

Q If bacteriological analysis discovered that a particular food was contaminated with *E. coli* type I, what would this fact indicate? (HINT: this organism is found in the human bowel.)

A Because *E. coli* type I is found virtually only in human faeces, its presence in a food indicates a poor standard of personal hygiene on someone's part. It is likely that someone who handled the food did not wash their hands after using the toilet.

---

4 Bacteria reproduce asexually. They grow to a certain size and then divide into two. This is called **binary fission** (remember this term — it means splitting into two). Each 'half' of the split bacterium becomes independent, grows to a certain size and then splits into two to give four bacterial cells.

You should note and remember that bacteria can reproduce at a very rapid rate. Just one bacterium could give rise to millions of 'daughter' cells within just 24 hours.

Q What does a microbiologist usually mean by bacterial 'growth'? (HINT: think of a 'colony' of bacterial cells.)

A The term refers to the growth of the colony, i.e. to an increase in the total number of individual bacterial cells within the colony, rather than to an increase in the size of any particular individual bacterial cell. In fact, each individual cell does not grow very much at all before it splits into two.

---

5 Growth of bacteria (i.e. an increase in the total number of individual, single celled bacteria within a colony) can only occur under the right conditions. Ideal conditions for most bacteria important in food hygiene means plenty of food (especially meat dishes, dairy produce and fish), moisture (remember that water must be 'available'), and a near neutral pH (i.e. neither acidic nor alkaline).

REMEMBER — food, moisture, warmth and a neutral environment are necessary for bacterial growth.

Q How could water become 'unavailable' to bacteria?

A By being bound up within a concentrated solution (e.g. sugar in jam) and thus having a high osmotic pressure or by being frozen. (These concepts were discussed within an earlier programme. Revise them if you are unsure of them – see page 19.)

---

6 We have seen that bacteria of many different types are everywhere around us. It is virtually impossible to go anywhere without some type of bacterium being present. In the deepest oceans, highest mountains, edges of hot sulphur springs, polar ice-caps, some type(s) of bacterium will be found.

Q How do you think bacteria can get about from place to place?

A Some can 'swim' in liquids by means of hair-like filaments (called **flagella**) which are attached to their 'bodies' (which of course consist of a single cell). Only bacteria with flagella can 'swim' in this way. Some bacteria have only one flagellum; others have many. (The *Salmonella* organisms, of which we will hear a lot more in later programmes, are usually covered in flagella. They are bacilli, i.e. sausage shaped. The average *Salmonella* looks like a very hairy sausage!)

In other cases, bacteria are carried in water currents, on air currents or on or in the bodies of humans, insects, animals, or birds.

7 Bacteria need food for the same reasons as other living organisms. (See Programme 2, page 10, if you have forgotten why). They like a wide variety of foods but those of most concern to us in food hygiene prefer those which are perishable — notably meats (red and white, cooked and raw), eggs, milk and other dairy products, fish, and made-up foods containing any of these.

Q Why do you think bacteria prefer perishable foods?

A This question is really the wrong way round! Perishable foods ARE perishable just because they are of a type which bacteria prefer. They perish (i.e. spoil or rot) chiefly because bacteria are growing within them.

---

8 Bacteria must have water, which is in a form that they can absorb (i.e. they must have available water). They may die rapidly if dried. (Bacterial spores are an exception to this, but they will be described elsewhere.)

Q What requirements do bacteria have for air?

A If you recall our earlier programmes you should remember that bacteria may be aerobes or anaerobes; most of them are facultative anaerobes. (If you did not remember this, then re-read Programme 2, pages 10 to 17.)

---

9 Bacteria prefer an environment that is near to neutral pH (about pH 7 to 8 in most cases). They are tolerant of slight alkaline conditions but the majority are inhibited by acidic environments.

Q Do you think that bacteria can be killed if their environment is too acidic or too alkaline?

A If it is very acidic or very alkaline, they probably would be. Most species cease to grow if the pH falls below about 6 or above about 8 (neutral remember, is 7, at which the environment is neither acidic nor alkaline), but they would not necessarily be killed.

---

10 Bacteria may be psychrophilic, mesophilic or thermophilic (see page 21 if you cannot remember what these terms mean). Most of those which can produce food poisoning cease to grow below about 5 °C or above 65 °C.

Q Can bacteria be killed at low temperatures? Can they be killed at high temperatures?

A We will discuss this in more detail in the next programme. Generally, they will not be killed at low temperatures but they can be killed at high temperatures as long as the high temperature is maintained for long enough (about 65 °C for 30 minutes, 85 °C for a few minutes, BUT in the case of bacterial spores, you would have to boil them at 100 °C for 3–5 hours to kill them. Spores are dealt with in detail within the next programme).

KEY FACTS

1. Bacteria are single-celled organisms which can only be seen by means of a microscope capable of 1000 times magnification. (To see any detail, we need an electron microscope capable of 100 000 times magnification.) Many thousands of bacteria could fit on the head of a pin.

2. Some types of bacteria (pathogens) can cause disease in man, animals or plants. Other varieties can rot food, but in fact, many bacteria are entirely harmless; some are even useful to us.

3. Bacteria reproduce asexually, by a process called **binary fission**. In this process, the bacteria grow to a certain size and then split into two. We then have two bacteria where before there was only one.

4. Bacteria can reproduce at a tremendous rate. We could get millions of daughter cells from just one 'mother' in 24 hours.

5. When a bacteriologist refers to bacterial growth, this means an increase in the number of individual bacteria within a colony.

6. In order to grow, bacteria need an appropriate food supply (most grow well in perishable foods), water (which must be in a form in which it can enter the bacterial cell), warmth, and a suitable pH (neither too acid nor too alkaline).

7. Some bacteria must have oxygen (air) in order to grow (aerobes); others would not grow in the presence of air at all, and might be killed by it (anaerobes); whereas many bacteria can use air when available AND grow without it when it isn't available (facultative organisms).

8. Low temperatures do not kill bacteria but high temperatures can (if they are sustained for a long enough period of time).

PROGRESS PAPER 4

Try to answer the questions below. Having attempted them all, then, and only then, turn to the answers (page 32) and if you could not answer any questions, or got any question wrong, take special note of the model answer. Do not worry if you have to read any programme again, remember that it takes time for anyone to learn anything.

1 What are bacteria?

2 What are the most usual shapes of bacteria? How small are they?

3 What harm may bacteria do? Are they all harmful?

4 What would be indicated if a bacteriological (laboratory) analysis revealed *E. coli* type I in a food?

5 How do bacteria reproduce and how do they grow?

6 What types of food do bacteria prefer? (Give examples.)

7 What conditions are necessary for bacterial growth?

8 Are bacteria aerobes, anaerobes or facultative anaerobes?

9 Below what temperature and above what temperature, can food-poisoning bacteria not grow?

10 Can bacteria be killed by low temperatures?

ANSWERS

1 Bacteria are single celled microorganisms which can only be seen with the aid of a powerful microscope.

2 Spheres (chained together = streptococci, clumped together like a bunch of grapes = staphylococci); sausage shaped (bacilli); comma shaped (vibrios). They are extremely small; many thousands would fit on the head of a pin.

3 They may rot or spoil food. They may cause disease in humans, animals or plants. Not all bacteria are harmful, in fact many of them are useful to humans.

4 That a food handler had been careless in his or her personal hygiene. *E. coli* type I is virtually only found in human faeces. If found on food, it is likely that a food handler did not wash his or her hands properly after using the toilet.

5 Bacteria reproduce by a process called binary fission in which they grow to a certain size and then divide into two to form two separate cells where previously there was one. When we refer to 'bacterial growth' or the 'growth of bacteria', we usually mean a growth of a colony of bacteria, i.e. an increase in the number of individual bacterial cells within a colony.

6 Perishable foods, especially red or white meat (raw or cooked), milk and milk products, eggs, fish or made-up foods containing any of these.

7 Warmth, moisture, food and neutral environmental conditions.

8 They can be any of these. Most species of bacteria are facultative anaerobes (refer to page 14 if you cannot remember just what these terms mean).

9 Below 5 °C and above 65 °C. (Remember you start school at 5 and retire at 65.)

10 No, some of the individual bacterial cells would die, but many would survive. Growth would stop but resume when the environment became warm again.

PROGRAMME 5
Bacteria II

1 Bacteria are probably the most commonly encountered living things. They are everywhere. They can be expected to be present in and on raw foods, on the human skin, inside the human body (for example, in the gut, nose and mouth), on and in the bodies of insects, pests and pet animals. A copious variety of bacteria can be found in the soil.

Q Given all these possible sources of bacteria, can you think of the ways in which food, and food preparation areas, might be contaminated with them?

A The most common causes of bacterial contamination of food and the food environment are: raw foods contaminating ready-to-eat foods, utensils or surfaces, food handlers passing organisms from gut to hands to food, surfaces or utensils (poor personal hygiene following use of toilet or food handlers contaminating fingers from the nose, mouth etc., and the fingers then contaminating food). Human contamination of food or food environments, may arise directly from an infected cut or other lesion on the hands (these must always be covered with waterproof dressings), or as a result of sneezing or coughing. Pests (such as rodents, birds or insects), may contaminate food or the food environment directly, as may pet animals. Soil from raw vegetables will most usually contain bacterial spores which can become airborne and contaminate food or food environments.

---

2 Not all bacteria are harmful however. In fact, the vast majority of types are either neutral as far as humans are concerned, or they actually contribute some good to him. Bacteria on the human skin and in the human gut (being specific types of organism which live with us but usually do us no harm — commensals), will actually protect us to a great extent from the ravages of less friendly organisms.

Q What is the name given to organisms which may produce disease in humans or animals? What name is given to organisms which rot food?

A Organisms capable of producing disease are called **pathogens**; those which rot food are termed **spoilage organisms**. The division between the two types is not strict and some organisms may be both spoilage types on some occasions, and pathogens on others.

3 Bacteria differ greatly in their resistance to adverse conditions. Some can survive and grow (i.e. reproduce) under extremely hostile conditions. Others can tolerate adversity but can only grow in ideal, optimum conditions. Most are well able to 'switch off' as it were, (i.e. to shut down all life processes) when adverse conditions do arise, and to recommence active growth upon the return of more favourable conditions.

Q What types of adverse conditions do you think could disrupt the normal life of bacteria? (HINT: think about conditions bacteria like, e.g. warmth, moisture, food. Conditions they don't like must be the opposite of these.)

A Cold (below about 5 °C); high temperatures (above about 65 °C); dryness or absence of available water; lack of a suitable food source — all these will inhibit bacteria and some will die. In addition, anaerobes will be inhibited (perhaps even killed) in the presence of oxygen whereas aerobes will not be able to grow in its absence (though the vast majority will merely switch off until free oxygen becomes available again). Acidic or alkaline environments will inhibit the growth of bacteria.

---

4 Bacteria of two main genera (the *Clostridium* and *Bacillus* genera) are able to form themselves into very specialised structures called **spores**. Bacterial spores MUST NOT BE CONFUSED with fungal spores (which are like plant seeds) as they are entirely different.

Q What special properties do you think bacterial spores have? (Have a guess!)

A They are able to withstand adverse conditions and, therefore, they enable *Bacillus* and *Clostridium* to survive great adversity.

---

5 Bacterial spores can resist heat, chemicals and drying. Most **vegetative** bacteria (i.e. those which are actively growing and multiplying) will be killed if exposed to temperatures of about 85 °C for a few minutes. Bacterial spores, however, require to be boiled (at 100 °C) for 3–5 hours before they will succumb. Few chemical sanitisers will kill spores and they can survive drying for very considerable periods of time.

Q Why, do you think, can bacterial spores resist heat, chemicals and drying? (Have a guess.)

A Because the spore consists of a very thick and hard coat (almost like a coat of armour) which is formed around the bacterium. The spore is very dry inside and this increases its resistance to heat. Dry heat (when no moisture is present) takes many hours to kill bacteria. Normally there is a lot of water inside bacteria so heat will readily kill them. In the case of a spore the inside is dry and the hard outer coat (armour) prevents water entering it even when it is boiled. Eventually even a spore succumbs to such treatment, however, and 3–5 hours' boiling will kill them.

6 The fact that some bacteria can form spores is of great importance to us in food hygiene. Spores are common in soil and even in the human gut (where normally they do no harm). They are, as we have seen, very resistant to adversity and are very light so they can be carried into food areas on air currents.

Q How do spores contaminate food?

A They will often be present in the soil on vegetables etc., and may become airborne from storage or preparation areas (therefore 'veg-prep' areas must be totally separate from other food areas as must vegetable storage areas. Spores may be passed on to food from food handlers, pests, etc. and (because some are present normally in animal guts), they may already be present on raw meats brought into food handling areas.

---

7 We can expect that bacterial spores will get into the food environment on many occasions. This is serious because they will be very hard to kill. They will lie dormant until conditions arrive which are favourable to their germination and growth (warm, moist and plenty of food). Once they germinate they will turn back into vegetative bacteria. Both the *Clostridium* and *Bacillus* genera include species which are able to cause food poisoning. It can be seen if you think about it for a little while, that these bacteria could get into food as spores, be difficult to kill, and lie dormant until favourable conditions arise again.

Q Under what circumstances might such a possibility give rise to great danger?

A Take as an example, a made-up food such as stew, casserole, meat-pie, gravy, soup etc. These will be cooked, and the cooking process should kill the vegetative organisms very effectively. It will not however, kill any spores which are present. If these foods are allowed to cool slowly, the spores will germinate and vegetative bacteria will emerge. If these foods are then stored at warm temperatures or are reheated, the vegetative bacteria will multiply and food poisoning may result in any consumer. The reheating process will not be sufficient to kill the vegetative bacteria.

---

8 Once foods which are to be eaten hot are cooked, they should be held above 65 °C in order to prevent the growth of any organisms that survived the cooking process. If bacterial spores are present, they will almost certainly have survived cooking. If the food is allowed to fall below 65 °, the surviving spores will germinate.

Q What about a cooked food that is to be eaten cold — taking into account the special properties of spores. How do we ensure safety in their case?

A We must cool the food rapidly to below 5 °C and hold it below 5 °C so that any bacterial spores which are present cannot germinate. (They won't have time to germinate if we cool the food quickly and if it is kept below 5 °C, they won't germinate because it is too cold for them to do so.)

9 We know that bacteria are very common organisms; we know that some of them can produce food poisoning and we now know that a few genera can turn themselves into the extremely resistant forms called bacterial spores. We now need to consider how we can control bacteria in order to make our food supplies safe to eat.

Q How can we control bacteria? Must we always kill them in order to be safe?

A No, we do not always have to kill them in order to achieve safety. Different types of bacteria produce disease in different ways. Some need to invade the gut itself, others produce chemical **toxins** (poisons) which are excreted into the food in which they are growing. In the former case, it is necessary to eat a certain minimum number of bacteria (an **infectious dose**) before harm can result, and in the latter, a certain amount of growth is needed for the bacteria to produce enough toxin to produce disease.

Therefore, if we cannot kill all bacteria in a food (which in most cases we cannot), we can at least achieve a fair degree of safety if we deny them the possibility of growing.

---

10 Bacteria can be killed by heating, but there must be moisture present to kill them in reasonable time. Ordinarily moisture is present in the food itself. It must be remembered that it is the combination of temperature and time that matters. Most bacteria can be killed in 30 minutes at 65 °C, or in a few minutes at 85 °C. Notice that at lower temperatures a longer period of time is needed to ensure a 'kill'.

Extreme cold will kill a proportion of bacteria within a colony, but many WILL survive to recommence active growth upon the return to more favourable conditions.

Q What else do you think, could we use to kill bacteria?

A Chemicals — in the form of **sanitisers** (the term 'sanitiser' means a chemical substance which will kill some bacteria. If used on the skin, to kill bacteria in a wound for instance, the term **antiseptic** should be used). The term 'disinfectant' should NOT be used as it indicates strong-smelling chemicals which should NOT be used near food.

11 Chemical sanitisers are many, and we shall discuss them again in Programme 13 when we discuss cleaning techniques. We could remove a large number of bacteria from a food-preparation surface merely by washing it with hot water containing a detergent, but it must be well noted that we would only wash a number of the bacteria off the surface and we could not kill them this way. Bacteria are 'sticky' and they tend to adhere strongly to any surface.

Q As well as killing bacteria, we can obtain a degree of safety by controlling their growth (i.e. preventing their reproduction). How do you think we could do this?

A By controlling the temperature of their environment (keeping foods above 65 °C or below 5 °C if the food is of a type and in a condition which is liable to support bacterial growth). We could make sure that water was not available to them, e.g. by dehydrating foods (such as milk powder), by ensuring the osmotic pressure of a food is high (such as in jam), or by freezing (which also of course, ensures a low temperature). We could also deny them any food by ensuring that work surfaces, utensils, equipment, etc., are cleaned regularly.

---

12 Probably the very best bacterial-control method of all is to ensure as far as we can, that bacteria do not contaminate food or the food environment in the first place. This is the subject of Programme 9 which deals in detail with contamination control.

KEY FACTS

1 Bacteria are probably the most common of all living things. Bacteria can, and will, enter a food preparation area from raw food (in which they are always present); via food handlers (especially from cuts or from food handlers who do not wash their hands after using the toilet); from pests such as rats, mice or insects; or from pet animals.

2 Not all microbes do harm to humans. Those organisms which can produce disease in humans are called 'pathogenic organisms' or simply 'pathogens'.

3 Many bacteria can survive adverse conditions very well. Most pathogens are however, quite sensitive, and their growth can be stopped by cold (below 5 °C); heat (above 65 °C); lack of available water; lack of suitable food source; and acidic or alkaline conditions.

4 Aerobic bacteria must have air in order to grow but they are not killed if it is not available. Facultative organisms can grow with or without air, whereas anaerobes only grow in the absence of air.

5 Bacteria of the *Bacillus* and *Clostridium* genera can form a protective coat around themselves. (These structures are called 'spores'.) These bacterial spores are NOT the same as fungal spores. The bacterial spores can resist adversity very well. They can only be killed by being boiled (100 °C) for many hours; they resist drying and are very hard to kill by means of chemicals (such as sanitisers).

6 Only *Bacillus* and *Clostridium* can form spores — other types of bacteria cannot. If the spores of these organisms get into food, (soups, gravies, stews etc), they will NOT be killed by cooking. When the food cools down, the spores will germinate again and start to reproduce. Spores of both *Clostridium* and *Bacillus* are very dangerous because they can cause food poisoning.

7 In order to keep food safe, hot food must be kept hot or be eaten soon after cooking and cold food must be kept cold. Cooked food which is to be eaten cold must be cooled quickly, and kept cold.

8 Bacteria may be killed by heat if the temperature (above 85 °C) is maintained for long enough, but bacterial spores must be heated to 100 °C before they can be killed. Heat of the order of 85 °C–100 °C will only kill bacteria if moisture is present; dry heat at these temperatures would fail to kill the bacteria. (NOTE: in the case of most foods, moisture *is* present in the food itself).

9 Chemical sanitisers (sometimes incorrectly called 'disinfectants') can also be used to kill bacteria, but bacterial spores are very resistant to chemicals.

10 The control of bacterial growth (by means of low and high temperatures) can provide a degree of protection from food poisoning. A small number of bacteria can be tolerated by our bodies without harm.

PROGRESS PAPER 5

Try and answer the questions below. Answer them fairly, and if you get any wrong or cannot answer any (even after you have 'had a guess'), take special note of the model answers which follow. If you still don't understand, read the whole programme again. This may seem like a lot of work, but it really is the only way to make sure that you learn the topics in this book. Be patient and you will make progress.

1 What are pathogens?

2 What adverse conditions may prevent bacteria from growing (multiplying)?

3 What are bacterial spores?

4 What special properties do bacterial spores have?

5 Why do these special properties make bacterial spores especially dangerous as far as good hygiene is concerned?

6 What must we do to a cooked food (which is to be eaten hot) in order to ensure safety?

7 How can we kill bacteria? (NOTE: make special mention of spores).

8 How can we control bacterial growth?

9 What is a sanitiser?

10 Can detergent kill bacteria?

ANSWERS

1 Organisms which are capable of (but do not always) producing disease in humans, animals or plants.

2 High temperature (above 65 °C); low temperature (below 5 °C); making water unavailable (by freezing, high sugar content, drying, etc.); making food unavailable.

3 They are hard, shell-like structures (like armour), produced by a species of *Clostridium* and *Bacillus* bacteria.

4 They are very resistant to heat, drying and chemicals, and they don't need food at all.

5 They will often be present in the environment. They come from raw food, soil, food handlers, and even air currents. They may contaminate food but will not usually be killed by normal cooking. They can germinate back into vegetative cells when conditions favour them. If, for example, spores get into a stew, the cooking process won't kill them. If the stew is then kept warm (between 5 °C and 65 °C) the spores will germinate and the emerging vegetative bacteria will grow to numbers which make food poisoning possible. (Remember that a very small number of food-poisoning bacteria can be tolerated, but, once an 'infectious dose' is reached, disease is liable to result in anyone eating the food. By keeping bacterial numbers down to a minimum, we can make food safer to eat.)

6 We must keep it above 65 °C in order to prevent bacterial growth. Bacteria (especially spores) may well have survived the cooking process or of course, some may gain entry to the food after cooking. If the food is kept between 5 °C and 65 °C for any length of time, any bacteria present will start to grow, the total number of bacteria present will increase and a dangerous situation will result.

7 By heating them to a high enough temperature for long enough (if moisture is present, about 65 °C will kill most bacteria in about 30 minutes, 85 °C will do so in a few minutes). If moisture is not present — which would be very unusual in food-processing conditions — or in the case of a spore, 100 °C is needed for 3–5 hours. As well as using heat, we could use an appropriate sanitiser (discussed in more detail in Programme 13).

8 By maintaining the temperature of their environment below 5 °C or above 65 °C, by drying (as in milk powder), by making water unavailable (as in the high osmotic pressure — concentrated fluid — of jams, etc.) or by ensuring that food is not available (by cleaning properly).

9 It is a chemical substance which is capable of killing some types of bacteria.

10 No, it cannot. The purpose of a detergent is to help water to clean a dirty or greasy surface. Bacteria may be washed away by a mixture of detergent and water, but they are sticky and many will remain adhering to the surface.

PROGRAMME 6
Fungi

1 We now turn our attention to the fungi. We will consider their characteristics, and how to control their undesirable activities, in general terms.

Q How do multi-celled fungi grow?

A By adding new cells on to their filaments (hyphae).

---

2 Fungi can be considered to be quite 'advanced' microbes. They range in complexity, however, from simple, single-celled yeasts, to the highly complex fungi familiar to us all as mushrooms and toadstools.

Q What are moulds?

A They are multi-celled fungi which possess hyphae of two types. The inter-meshing hyphae of moulds form the mycelium or main body of the organism. These hyphae ramify (branch) throughout the whole food substance upon which they are growing. Other hyphae stick up into the air above the food substance (aerial hyphae) and it is these which produce the spore 'seeds' of the mould. All moulds are aerobes and all need oxygen in order to grow.

---

3 Yeasts are single-celled fungi which obtain most of their energy by means of fermentation processes. They are familiar to us in bread and beer making especially, but some are well capable of rotting a wide variety of foods. No yeast produces any form of food-borne disease — they can be considered to be 'spoilage' organisms and nothing more. Because they perform fermentation (which is an energy-yielding process where electrons are merely passed around from food molecules of large size to molecules which have been made smaller in the process), they do not need oxygen in order to grow.

Q How do yeasts reproduce?

A They grow to a certain size and then produce a 'bud', which bulges out from the yeast cell to eventually break away and grow into a new (daughter) organism.

---

4 As far as food is concerned, fungi do not produce any infectious disease in humans. Some are capable of producing toxins (called **mycotoxins**) which are capable of producing some ill effects. A lot of evidence, coming from much research into this topic, indicates that some of these toxins could produce tumours in humans. Because of the seriousness of this possibility, research into mycotoxins is continuing.

Q What other kind of harm (or damage) can fungi produce?

A They are spoilage organisms which rot food. They tend to prefer slightly acidic foods which are moist but some types (notably some yeasts) are well able to rot foods which have a high osmotic pressure (i.e. foods which are concentrated such as jam, and in which water would not normally be 'available' to microbes).

---

5 It used to be almost universally agreed that food which was mouldy was safe to eat. It is still considered to be acceptable practice to cut off a mouldy area of cheese and sell the rest, as long as the mould has not penetrated the food so much as to change its character entirely. Of course moulds and yeast are actually used in cheese making. With the rapidly growing evidence that many fungi produce potentially harmful mycotoxins, it may be that in the future, all mouldy food is considered unfit to eat.

Q What about the case where the food is very mouldy — do you think it would be unfit to eat?

A Yes, it would be unfit. The only time it is permissible to cut off mould is in the case of cheese, which frequently can have a layer of slight mould growth on the surface, but will usually be unaffected elsewhere if mould hyhae have not penetrated further.

---

6 Moulds can also be seen on raw meats on occasions. These take the form of white or black spots. A particularly striking mould can sometimes be found in bread, (this is called *Monilia*) which makes the bread bright pink (it looks as though pink talcum powder has been spread on it). Such bread is unfit to eat and this mould can be especially difficult to get rid of if it gets hold within a bakery.

Q What harm (or damage) do you think yeasts can cause?

A They can spoil and rot foodstuffs by growing within them (usually by means of fermentation processes). Some varieties are very resistant to concentrated foods. Both yeasts and moulds are capable of growing in jams (for instance).

---

7 Moulds and yeasts are the two types of fungus of most interest to us in connection with food. Their spoilage activities can prove expensive and some are capable of changing the flavour of certain foods (e.g. yoghurt, cheese, fruit drinks, etc.) and making them offensive to eat.

Q In addition to some fungi being able to grow within concentrated foods, what other special 'resistances' do you think they have?

A Many can grow at lower temperatures than most bacteria can, making it especially likely that they are responsible for spoilage of refrigerated foods. They are, however, killed at even lower temperatures also, and are not very heat resistant (except possibly their spores — see below). Fungi are slightly harder to kill by means of sanitisers than are bacteria. Fungi are more resistant to acidic environments than are bacteria; in fact, they prefer to grow in a slightly acidic medium.

8 Mould spores constitute a kind of 'seed'. They are produced on aerial hyphae put up into the air (usually) by the mould mycelium ('body'). Fungal spores are very small and very light, and consequently they can be carried vast distances by air currents. They are resistant to drying (the growing mycelium would soon die if it became dry) and are slightly more resistant to heat than their parent 'mycelium'. If they land on a suitable food supply, they will germinate and grow into a new mould mycelium.

Yeasts are not especially resistant to anything. They can be killed at lower temperatures than can bacteria but are slightly more resistant to sanitisers.

Q Why do you think a piece of bread soon gets 'mouldy' if left out?

A Many thousands of mould spores will be present in the air at any time. Inevitably some will fall on to the bread which, if not too dry, will well support their germination and subsequent growth. Spore-formation is a kind of reproduction. In addition, moulds can 'reproduce' if some of the hyphae break off. They then start to grow into a 'new' mycelium.

---

9 If mouldy food is allowed to stay in a store, fridge, etc., it is inevitable that some spores will go directly on to other foods stored there. It is therefore ESSENTIAL to clear out all mouldy food and to remove mould deposits from surfaces, etc.

Q Can you think of anywhere where you have seen mould growing near food? (HINT: think of a black-spot mould growing on a surface.)

A The walls of large (walk-in) storage refrigerators frequently have black spot moulds growing on them. The walls are especially liable to condensation and the black spot (mucortype) moulds find these conditions ideal. They can grow even at the very low temperatures of such fridges.

---

10 Fruit (and even vegetables) can also be spoiled by fungi. Yeasts can ferment in rotting fruits, fruit juices, etc. In the case of soft, whole fruits, it is usually a mould that grows first. This ordinarily grows as a result of damage to the fruit skin. The mould gains access to the soft and moist inside, and starts to grow very quickly.

KEY FACTS

1. Multi-celled fungi grow by adding new cells to their hyphae.
2. Moulds are multi-celled fungi that have two types of hyphae; one type buried in the medium (e.g. food) in which they grow; and the other type (which form spores which can be released like plant seeds to germinate when they find a suitable food), stuck up into the air.
3. Yeasts are single-celled fungi that reproduce by a process of 'budding'.
4. Fungi spoil food — they do not produce 'food poisoning' as such, but some types can produce poisons (mycotoxins) which may produce tumours in humans.
5. Very mouldy food is unfit to eat. (Primarily because it is unpleasant to eat but there is also a possibility that it could be harmful.)
6. Yeasts can cause some types of food spoilage, especially of highly concentrated foods such as fruit juices.
7. Most fungi can grow at lower temperatures than most bacteria and they are better able to tolerate slightly acidic conditions, but they are easier to kill by means of heat.
8. If mouldy food is left in a store or a fridge, the spores produced by the mould could be carried to other foods in the same store and cause them to go mouldy too.

PROGRESS PAPER 6

Now, try and answer the questions below. Do not 'cheat' otherwise this book will not be able to help you to learn. Answer all the questions before looking at the model answers. If you cannot answer a question or if you get any wrong, read the programme again and then re-test yourself. (NOTE: some of the questions below may relate to previous programmes. These questions help you to revise what you have learned before.)

1 How do single-celled fungi grow?

2 How do multi-celled fungi grow?

3 How do yeasts reproduce?

4 How do moulds reproduce?

5 What are moulds?

6 What kind of harm may fungi produce?

7 On what types of food might moulds be found?

8 What special resistances do fungi possess? (For example, can they grow in concentrated food?)

9 Is mouldy food unfit food?

10 How could mould spores be killed in a food that was to be cooked?

ANSWERS

1 Single-celled fungi are yeasts. They grow to a certain size and then a bud forms which eventually breaks away to become an independent 'daughter' yeast cell.

2 The multi-celled fungi of interest to us in food hygiene are the moulds. They grow by adding new cells to their hyphae.

3 Yeasts, which are single-celled fungi, reproduce by means of forming a bud which breaks off and becomes an independent 'daughter' cell.

4 Moulds reproduce by forming spores on aerial hyphae. These are very like 'seeds', are carried about on air currents and will germinate when they reach a suitable, moist, food if temperature and other conditions are suitable.

5 Moulds are aerobic, multi-celled fungi which are made up of filaments (hyphae) and which produce spore 'seeds'.

6 Some may produce toxins (mycotoxins) which may be responsible for producing some human tumours. They are generally considered to be spoilage organisms which reduce the shelf-life of food by causing it to rot.

7 Bread, cheese, fruits (especially if skins are damaged), jam, meat (black or white spot on raw meat especially), confectionery, milk and milk products, and vegetables.

8 Many can grow on concentrated foods. Many can grow at low temperatures. They are tolerant of acid and, indeed, most prefer to grow in a slightly acidic environment.

9 On the whole, yes. Although superficial mould growth on the surface of cheeses can be cut off and the rest of the cheese eaten, as long as the cheese substance has not been changed by the fact that mould has been growing on it.

NOTE: Moulds prefer very damp conditions. Mould growth is encouraged if food is wrapped in polythene which seals in moisture. If bread is wrapped in polythene, or other impervious material, when still warm, it is almost certain to 'turn mouldy' very quickly.

---

10 By being heated to a high enough temperature for a long enough time. Mould hyphae can be killed at quite low temperatures but mould spores are more resistant. Heating at 85 °C will, however, usually kill them with certainty if maintained for the average cooking time of most foods.

NOTE: It is very important that you do NOT confuse mould spores and bacterial spores. Bacterial spores are extremely resistant to heat and would have to be boiled at 100 °C for 3–5 hours to be killed. Bacterial spores are entirely different to mould spores.

PROGRAMME 7
Viruses

1 So far, throughout our discussions of the preceding programmes, we have avoided any detailed references to the viruses. You were promised that these creatures would be discussed in a later programme — this is that programme.

The reason why we have left a discussion of viruses to this point is simply that these creatures break every rule so far as biology is concerned. They are unique and demonstrate totally different life characteristics from all other living things.

Q Can you remember what the primary characteristics of living things are? (HINT: living things 'do' certain things.)

A Living things usually move and/or grow. They breathe, drink, eat and reproduce. It is these main characteristics which distinguish a living creature from a lump of rock.

---

2 Viruses do not drink; they can go without water altogether. Although many types will die quickly if they are dried, others can survive quite well in such a state. They don't eat either, they don't breathe at all (either with or without oxygen) and for them, 'growth' means reproduction (i.e. increase in numbers of virus particles) alone. No variety is capable of independent movement, each needs to be carried around by air currents, water currents and so on.

Q If viruses do not perform the normal activities of living things, do you think they should be considered 'alive' at all?

A There are two prevailing views of how we look upon viruses. One states that they are very simple forms of life; the other view considers them to be very complex chemicals. Biologically speaking, they should be considered to be living things because of their capacity to reproduce.

---

3 Viruses actually are very like complex chemical crystals. They may be arranged in a spiral shape, or like a lunar landing module, a bullet, a satellite and so on. Each one has a crystal-like structure which is made up of a gene-core (carrying the reproductive information for the virus) surrounded by some form of protective coat. The protective coat may be simple or complex depending upon the type of virus concerned.

Q How do you think viruses obtain energy? (HINT: all viruses are pathogenic to some type of host or other.)

A All viruses are pathogens for something — be they human, animal or plant pathogens, they will be parasites on some form of living thing (even bacteria suffer a type of virus infection!). It is conceivable, therefore, that viruses obtain energy from their host. In practice, this is very close to the truth.

---

4 It is not strictly compatible, however, with what we know of how other forms of life obtain their energy. Viruses actually do nothing except reproduce. This they can only do when they are INSIDE a host cell. They reproduce by enslaving the host cell, taking over its chemical processes and making it produce new viruses. Eventually the new viruses rupture the cell membrane and are released to invade new host cells or even entirely new hosts.

Q If the viruses are always parasitic on other living things, do you think they can cause food to spoil also?

A No, they cannot. Outside host cells viruses are capable of remaining potentially active — but only ever reproduce inside host cells. Viruses show no sign of life at all until they get into a host cell. Once inside the host cell, they cause it to make new virus particles. This the host cell can only do if it is alive itself. Food that we eat is not alive (with rare exceptions, such as raw oysters). The cells within have died and therefore a virus cannot cause any changes to take place in our foods because the cells of that food are themselves dead.

---

5 Viruses are extremely small — from about 100 to 10 000 times smaller than the average bacteria. They cannot spoil food, they can only invade the living cells of an appropriate host (each virus has one or, at most, only a few types of host it can infect), and may produce disease within the host because of such invasion and enslavement of the host cells.

Q Why do you think we are interested in viruses as far as food hygiene is concerned?

A Because certain types of virus are capable of producing **gastro-enteric** (stomach and gut) illness usually characterised by vomiting and diarrhoea.

---

6 It is possible to become infected with the enteric viruses via food and water. It is therefore, possible for faults in food hygiene techniques to spread these unpleasant (and sometimes very dangerous) infections. We want to be aware of enteric viruses and of how they may be spread, so that we can control them and prevent disease.

Q How do you think poor food hygiene practices might give rise to the spread of enteric viruses? (i.e. viruses which affect the gut).

A Remember that the term 'enteric' refers to the gut. If a food handler is infected with viral enteric disease, the viruses will be excreted in the faeces. Inadequate personal hygiene after using the toilet can soon lead to such food handlers contaminating food with enteric virus which will then be eaten by a consumer of the food.

7 Enteric viruses are of several different types. Comparatively little is known about some of them whereas other types are well known. Some varieties are airborne (causing a kind of gastric flu) and are caught by being breathed in. Others may be air- or food-borne, whilst still others are usually spread via food.

Q Can you think of any other ways, (besides 'faeces-to-hand-to-food'), in which viruses might contaminate foods?

A We said that these viruses require to be moved about in air or water currents. This should have given you a clue. Water supplies may be contaminated with these viruses and of course, any contamination of water supply is liable to lead to contamination of food. Although water supplies are usually (in the UK always) treated to kill any pathogens which are present, some enteric viruses are capable of surviving such treatments. Enteric viruses of the airborne type could contaminate foods by means of infected persons sneezing on to exposed, unprotected foodstuffs.

---

8 Viruses are normally very susceptible to heat so we will usually kill them quite easily by normal cooking methods.

Q This being the case, what kinds of food do you think are most likely to be potential spreaders of enteric viral infections?

A Ready-to-eat foods which will not be subject to any form of heat treatment before being consumed, e.g. cooked meats, cream cakes, etc.

---

9 Quite a large number of virus particles need to be eaten (or inhaled in some cases) before disease will result, but far fewer than is normally the case with most bacteria. Enteric viruses therefore, can be considered to be quite highly infectious. The only sources of contamination of food by enteric viruses is a human sufferer or water supply. The human carrier (sufferer OR someone who is infected but is showing no symptoms) is by far the most likely source of contamination of foodstuffs.

Q How can we prevent the contamination of foods by enteric viruses?

A As the most common source of these viruses is human beings, it is essential to exclude any food handler from a food establishment who shows signs of disease. Even a cold or 'flu means that a food handler must be laid off work until fully recovered. In this case, 'food handler' includes ANYONE who works in the food establishment, e.g. cook, porter, cashier, cleaner, etc.

We can do little to prevent the spread of viruses via water; fortunately, modern water treatments (from the water authority treatment plants) usually ensure the absence of enteric virus from water supplies. Sometimes a few may survive but they should be killed during food processing in which the water is used as an ingredient.

10 Viruses may contaminate the food environment, such as preparation surfaces, as well as the food itself. For this reason, any food handler (including cleaners, cashiers, etc. — they are 'food handlers' as far as food hygiene is concerned as they all come into contact with the food environment whether or not they handle the food directly) who is suffering any 'tummy bug' or cold, 'flu etc., MUST be sent home until fully recovered. All foods displayed for sale must be covered and protected, or wrapped, so that customers sneezing on them will not give rise to possible contamination.

Q Even so, it is still possible that someone will sneeze on to a food preparation surface — what should we do then?

A Wash and sanitise the surface that has been contaminated.

---

11 Viruses can be killed if treated with appropriate sanitisers (discussed in Programme 13 — page 112, which relates to cleaning). But some may survive even this treatment. Our main defence against enteric viruses is to ensure that those who are infected with them do not come into a food room (i.e. place where food is handled, stored, processed etc.).

Q Is it possible do you think to always know if we are infected with an enteric virus?

A No, it is not. We can tell quite easily if we have symptoms (sneezes, diarrhoea, etc.), but, like all other infectious diseases, it is possible to be infected with an enteric virus and not to have any symptoms. We can do nothing in such cases.

---

12 Similar problems arise with any symptomless carriers of a disease. Because they have no symptoms at all, they cannot inform anyone they are ill, so they continue working within food rooms in all innocence. This is one reason why strict personal hygiene is essential (ALWAYS wash carefully after using the toilet — see page 126 for more details of hand washing). It is obviously essential of course, to report to your manager or manageress any illness you are suffering. It will then be possible to decide (after consultation with the Health Inspectors i.e. Environmental Health Officers), whether or not it is safe for you to be at work.

All too often when people are 'sick' or have a 'tummy upset', they blame over-eating, over-drinking (or a 'bad pint'). Those who come into contact with food rooms and the food environment must NEVER do this — if in any doubt, if you have had ANY symptoms (especially after returning to work from a holiday), inform your manager or manageress who MUST then seek advice from the Health Authorities (Environmental Health Officers in the UK).

KEY FACTS

1 Of all the processes which go to make up 'life', viruses perform only one of them — they reproduce.

2 Viruses reproduce inside a 'host' cell of another creature. They are parasites inside those cells. Outside the cells of a host, they are just like chemical crystals and do not show any signs of life at all.

3 Some viruses produce viral food poisoning, but they cannot spoil food. We can become infected by some enteric viruses (those which affect the gut), by eating food which is contaminated by them. Some enteric viruses can infect us by being breathed in through the lungs (to cause gastric 'flu). Some such viruses can also be present in our water supplies or could get into food if a food handler is infected with them.

4 If someone is suffering from viral enteritis (gastric 'flu), they could easily contaminate food if they were a food handler (especially if they are not VERY careful about washing their hands after using the toilet).

5 Viruses are very susceptible to heat and normal cooking should kill them easily.

6 If someone sneezes on to a food-preparation surface, the surface should be sanitised carefully. Ready-to-eat foods that are sneezed on must be discarded.

7 Some people can be infected with pathogenic organisms and not know about it (symptomless carriers).

8 Any food handler who has a 'tummy upset' of any kind should NOT prepare food because it could well be that they are infected with a pathogen that could be spread to someone else via food.

PROGRESS PAPER 7

Try and answer these questions, then look at the model answers. If you get any wrong, read the programme again. Keep your answers brief and write them on a separate sheet of paper.

1 Describe viruses in general terms (include, for example, that they are very small and describe their shape etc.).

2 What characteristics do viruses share with other living things?

3 What harm can viruses do (so far as good hygiene is concerned)?

4 Can viruses spoil (rot) food?

5 How can anyone become infected with an enteric virus?

6 How can we kill viruses?

7 How can we protect food from contamination by enteric viruses?

8 What should food handlers do if they have suffered symptoms of illness? (Especially vomiting and/or diarrhoea)?

9 Who are food handlers? (e.g. is a kitchen porter a food handler? Who else is a food handler as far as we are concerned?)

10 How do viruses reproduce themselves?

ANSWERS

1 They are extremely small, crystal-like creatures. They may be spiral, globular, satellite shaped, 'lunar landing-module' shaped or bullet shaped. They consist of a gene core surrounded by protective material. They can be thought of as being very simple creatures or very complex chemicals. Viruses are considered to be living things because they reproduce. They are all parasites of some type of living cell.

2 Only one — they reproduce.

3 Some types can cause enteric illness and some of these may be transmitted via food.

4 No, they cannot do so because food cells are dead and viruses are only active within living host cells.

5 By breathing it in or by consuming contaminated food or water. (It all depends upon the type of virus concerned; poliomyelitis — causing infantile paralysis for example — is in fact an enteric virus-type disease which is transmitted via untreated water, untreated, contaminated milk and other foods in most instances.)

6 By heat (normal cooking should readily kill them) or by means of sanitisers (when surfaces are contaminated etc.).

7 By excluding all sick food handlers from food premises and by keeping foods wrapped, covered or screened so that infected customers do not contaminate the food by sneezing etc.

8 Report to their manager or manageress BEFORE starting work. (The manager or manageress may then seek advice from the Environmental Health Officer.)

9 For our purposes, a food handler is anyone who comes into a food environment whether or not they handle food directly. Examples include cooks, chefs, waiters and waitresses, porters, cashiers, cleaners, bar staff, etc.

10 They take over control of the host cells they infect and cause the host cell to make new virus particles. They never 'grow' in size as such, they only reproduce by this rather bizarre method.

PROGRAMME 8

Protozoan and Metazoan Parasites

1 In this short programme, we shall look at a group of organisms, most of which are not microscopic but which can be transmitted to humans via food.

The **protozoa** are single-celled and the **metazoa**, multi-celled. The varieties in which we are interested are known commonly as **intestinal worms**. They infect humans if they are eaten in food and most of them grow within the intestinal tract (the gut) and reproduce there. Usually the parasites' eggs are excreted with a victim's faeces.

Q If eggs are excreted in the faeces of a host, how do you think food might be contaminated with these eggs?

A By the so called 'anal–oral' route. The hands of a host will become contaminated with eggs following toilet use unless very strict personal hygiene is observed.

---

2 Some intestinal parasitic worms can infect a human who eats meat that has been contaminated by an infestation in the meat animal. Meat animals are susceptible to many types of parasite. Most common are the beef and pork **tapeworms.** Of these, pork tapeworm is potentially more dangerous.

In both cases, the cow or pig eats eggs deposited in animal faeces, on grass, in foodstuffs etc. The eggs hatch in the animal gut and a **larva** (little grub) emerges to pass to the animal's muscles where it **encysts** (forms a cyst). If the meat is then eaten, the cyst emerges in the human gut and a tapeworm starts to grow. The tapeworm is attached to the gut wall of the host by suckers and/or hooks.

Q What harm do you think these tapeworms can do to a human host? (HINT: some can grow to over 9 metres — 30 feet — in length!)

A They are very thin worms, like a tape measure (hence their name), but their potential for growing to great lengths can result in the gut (bowels) being blocked. If not treated, this can result in the gut being torn apart.

---

3 This would be an extreme case and the most usual effects consist of a degree of malnutrition as the worm absorbs food directly from the host. They therefore 'steal' food from the host. Contrary to popular belief however, a host will NOT feel perpetually hungry, but may well have diarrhoea and miscellaneous other symptoms.

Pork tapeworms are more dangerous than beef tapeworms because their cysts can multiply in humans and cause infection. The cysts are more dangerous than the adult worm because they have a liking for soft tissues in humans such as the brain, and for powerful muscles such as the heart.

Tapeworms are segmented; to reproduce they form eggs in the last segment along their length and it is the whole segment which is voided in the faeces.

Eggs are formed in the last few segments, and a few segments are voided in the faeces every day. Eggs are resistant to sewage treatment and therefore can be spread back onto pasture in sewage sludge.

Q How do you think we could treat raw meat to kill any tapeworm cysts which might be present?

A Fortunately, the cysts are very susceptible to heat and proper cooking will kill them easily. The cooking must be THOROUGH to ensure their death.

---

4 Cows and pigs are inspected in the UK (and the vast majority of other countries) after slaughter, and this usually detects any cysts which might be present. The animals themselves can be protected from initial infestation by careful farming. The incidence of tapeworm infestation in humans within the UK is very small indeed, but nonetheless, the possibility should be remembered.

By this stage in the book you should be starting to realise that bacteria are not the only hazard to our food.

Q Beside bacteria and worms, what other organisms might present problems to our food?

A Fungi (yeasts, moulds) and viruses.

---

5 Pork may contain another type of worm — a **roundworm** — this time called *Trichinella* (pronounced *'trick-in-nella'*). These worms can exist as cysts in raw pork and will be passed on to a food consumer if the pork is not thoroughly cooked. They tend to migrate to the body's main muscles. It is thought that some cases of 'rheumatism' in humans might be produced by the presence of these worms. Fortunately, the incidence of *Trichinella* infestation in the UK is very low. Again, however, it is a possible food contaminant which should be borne in mind.

Q How do you think we can make sure that *Trichinella* in pork does not infect a consumer?

A Once again, heat comes to our aid. If the pork (which remember includes bacon), is properly cooked, no problems should arise. It is unlikely that pork on sale in the UK will be infested with *Trichinella* in the first place, but it is always better to be safe than sorry.

6 The only other intestinal parasites of interest to us are a group of protozoa (single-celled organisms which, although not visible to the naked eye, are much larger than bacteria), of the **amoeba** group of organisms (pronounced *'am-me-baa'*). These usually infest food as a result of contamination from food handlers. Some varieties can be 'caught' from contaminated water supplies and some produce a very severe intestinal disease called **amoebic dysentery**. Generally they are confined to tropical lands (although some are found in the UK). The incidence of human infestation with these organisms in the UK is minor. Correct personal hygiene and proper cooking of food can effectively eliminate any risks to food consumers.

KEY FACTS

1. In addition to bacteria, fungi and viruses, certain single-celled and multi-celled parasites can also infect us via food.
2. Protozoan parasites are single-celled whereas metazoan parasites are multi-celled. The metazoan parasites are commonly called 'worms'.
3. The intestinal worms grow in a host's gut and produce eggs which are then excreted in the faeces. If these eggs get on to food and are eaten by a new host, they may grow in the new host's gut and a new 'worm' grows within the victim.
4. Some types of worm (tapeworms) may be present as cysts in raw pork or raw beef. If the meat is not properly cooked, the cysts survive and a new tapeworm can then grow in the gut of the food consumer. (The cysts hatch inside the gut of the host and the worm then grows within the host.)
5. Some intestinal worms can grow to about 9 metres (30 feet) in length and can therefore block the host's gut.
6. The most usual harmful effect of worms is they cause a certain amount of malnutrition because they 'steal' food from the host. Contrary to popular belief, someone with 'worms' will not however, be constantly hungry.
7. Certain types of roundworm (*Trichinella*), can sometimes be found in pork. They are present as cysts in the raw meat and they will infect a new host if the meat is not properly cooked. These worms can produce serious effects in the host.
8. Parasitic worm cysts can often be detected during meat inspection. All meat is inspected by officials in the UK, after slaughter and before it can be sold.
9. Fortunately, parasitic cysts and eggs are susceptible to heat and proper, thorough cooking will kill them.

PROGRESS PAPER 8

We have now completed several progress papers. In order to help you revise the topics concerning microbiology which we have studied so far, this progress paper will be longer than normal. Work through each question carefully; don't cheat, otherwise the test will not help you. Try to answer each question and remember that even a guess may turn out to be correct.

Compare your answers with the model answers only after you have attempted all the questions. Don't worry if your answers do not exactly match the model ones. The model answers have been written to help you so, if your answers are essentially the same in meaning, it does not matter that the models are worded differently. In some cases you will find that the model answer is longer than yours. Don't be concerned — the models are meant to provide you with more information. Now, have a go at the questions below. Write your answers on a separate sheet of paper.

1 What harm may bacteria do to us and our food?

2 What harm may fungi do to us and our food?

3 What conditions do bacteria need in order to grow?

4 How do bacteria, fungi and viruses reproduce (grow)?

5 How can bacteria be killed?

6 At what temperatures will bacteria NOT grow?

7 At what temperature should soup be held in a ***bain-marie*** awaiting service?

8 Why is it important for food handlers to wash their hands after using the toilet?

9 Why must a cut on a finger be covered with a waterproof dressing?

10 What kind of waterproof dressing should be used — ventilated (with holes in) or unventilated?

11 Besides fungi, bacteria and viruses, what other kinds of organism could present danger to a food consumer?

12 What are bacterial spores?

13 Why are bacterial spores especially dangerous?

14 Can a detergent and water solution kill microbes on a work surface?

15 What must food handlers do if they have symptoms of illness?

16 Can moulds harm a food consumer?

17 Can microbes be killed by being frozen in food?

18 For how long and at what temperature must bacterial spores be heated in order to kill them?

19 Why do bacteria need a food supply of their own?

20 Why do bacteria NOT grow in jam?

ANSWERS

1 Some varieties may produce food poisoning and some can spoil (rot) food.

2 Some may cause food spoilage. This is considered to be the major harm fungi do to food, but some are thought to be able to produce toxins which, if eaten in food, could produce severe disease. So far, this has been proved to occur only in the case of particular fungi growing in special circumstances. (These toxins are called mycotoxins.)

3 Warmth, food supply, 'available' water, a neutral or near neutral chemical environment, air or absence of air if an anaerobe. Remember aerobes need oxygen, anaerobes don't and some may be killed in its presence but NO anaerobes will grow in its presence. Facultative organisms can grow with or without oxygen.

4 Bacteria reproduce (which is the same as 'grow' in their case), by a process called 'binary fission' in which they enlarge to a certain size and then split into two.

Fungi grow either by means of adding more cells on to their hyphae or, occasionally, by pieces of hyphae breaking off. Some produce spores which are like plant seeds. Yeasts, which are single-celled fungi, reproduce by forming a bud which eventually breaks off.

Viruses reproduce (they don't 'grow' at all in the ordinary sense of the word) by entering an appropriate host cell, enslaving that cell, and making it produce more virus particles. These are eventually evacuated from the cell to infect other cells.

5 By heat (about 65 °C for about 30 minutes, or about 85 °C for a few minutes, but, note the extreme heat resistance of spores — see answer 18 below) or by means of appropriate chemical sanitisers.

6 Generally pathogenic (disease-producing) bacteria of interest to us in food hygiene will not grow below 5 °C or above 65 °C. (NOTE: some spoilage organisms are capable of growth down to at least −7 °C i.e. minus 7 °C.)

7 Above 65 °C so as to stop growth of any pathogenic bacteria which might have gained access to it. Remember that it is usually safe to eat a small number of bacteria but, if we can keep their numbers down we can add to food safety. (It is better, of course, to stop them entering the food in the first place, but proper temperature controls add to food safety. This is discussed in Programme 10, page 84.)

8 Because their hands may have become contaminated with pathogens from their faeces or genitals.

9 Because pathogenic bacteria (staphylococci) may be present in the cut. By keeping the cut covered with a waterproof dressing, they are prevented from gaining access to food.

10 Unventilated (ventilated ones do not stop bacteria entering the food). Note that BLUE waterproof plasters should be used so that they can be seen if they fall off into food. More serious cuts or skin lesions must be covered with a plastic finger-stall.

11 Protozoan and metazoan intestinal parasites (worms and amoeba).

12 They are a special form of resistant armour used by some bacteria (*Clostridium* and *Bacillus* species) to enable them to withstand adverse conditions. (They are very resistant to heat, drying and chemicals.)

13 Because they are resistant to heat, drying and chemicals. They could get into food and survive cooking processes and germinate later when conditions become favourable again.

14 No. Detergent and water mixtures will only 'clean' a surface and remove grease. Some microbes will be washed away, but many will remain sticking to the surface.

15 They must report to their manager who can ask advice from the Environmental Health Officer. (In some cases, e.g. in cases of vomiting, diarrhoea, sore throats, colds, etc., food handlers must stay at home until fully recovered, otherwise they might pass infection on to others via food.)

16 The current opinion is no, but doubt does exist as it has been suggested that some moulds may produce toxins. More research into this point will be needed before anyone can be certain.

17 No, some will certainly die, but many will survive to become active again when the food is defrosted.

18 At 100 °C (boiling-point of water) for three to five hours.

19 Like most other living things (except, notably, the viruses) as a fuel for energy and as building blocks for their own life chemicals.

20 Because the osmotic pressure is too high. (The water is too concentrated for the bacteria to take up water from the jam — the water in the jam is not 'available' to them. Some fungi, notably some moulds, can grow in jam because the osmotic pressure (concentration) of their cell contents is higher than the concentration of the jam, therefore they can take up moisture from the jam itself).

NOTE: If you could not answer the majority of the questions, or if you got more than a few wrong, or if you could not understand the model answers — **go back and re-read Programmes 1–8. There is no point in you continuing to read on until you have learned these programmes.**

Don't worry, however, if you have to go back in the book. Different people learn at different rates. Revise the programmes again and all will start to become clear. You must expect to have to put in a lot of effort to learn the contents of this book, but the effort will be very worthwhile in the end.

Food Hygiene Practices

Introduction

In this section of the book we will be concerned with the three major practices of food hygiene which together provide by far the greatest protection for consumers.

The three practices referred to are:-

(i) Contamination control
(ii) Temperature control
(iii) Cleaning (decontamination)

These three areas of study are so very important that they must be carefully learned and practised if those who consume the food we prepare are to be adequately protected.

All the technical details of food-room design, layout, finishes and equipment are secondary to these three major areas of food hygiene practice. Everything else which goes to make up the subject of food hygiene will come to nothing if food hygiene practice is not correct.

It is even theoretically possible to produce safe food in premises which are far below the ideal, and with equipment that is ill-designed, if the food hygiene practices of contamination control, temperature control and decontamination are excellent. The opposite is NEVER the case.

You could have the best designed, built and equipped food premises imaginable, but if these three practice areas are not perfect, you would produce potentially lethal foodstuffs for the consumers.

Good design, proper surface finishes, good equipment, are necessary, but they are needed to aid and assist the attainment and maintenance of good food hygiene practice; by themselves, they are useless.

With these preliminary remarks clearly in mind, we will now look at food hygiene practices in detail. Remember just how vitally important they are.

You must also remember that everything we have learned before (in previous programmes) is also important. Just because food hygiene practices are the most important aspect of food hygiene, this does NOT mean that everything else connected with the subject is unimportant.

You should ensure, especially, that you fully understand the principles of microbiology contained in the previous programmes. Food hygiene is very much an exercise in applied microbiology. If we bear in mind what microbes can do, what they are resistant to, what they are sensitive to (such as heat, cold and chemical sanitisers), we can control them. Food hygiene has two main aims — to prevent food consumers from becoming ill and to delay food spoilage. Both food-consumer illness and food spoilage are caused by microbes; it is by controlling their activities that we can stop illness and delay spoilage. The three main areas of food hygiene practice — contamination control, temperature control and decontamination — can help us to control the activities of those microbes which could do us, and our consumers, harm.

PROGRAMME 9
Contamination Control

1 By far the largest, and most common, danger which threatens food is contamination by pathogenic (disease-producing) or spoilage (food-rotting) microbes. You should remember that these are not the only risks to food but they are the most frequently encountered.

Q What other 'risks' might we meet so far as food is concerned? (HINT: what else could be in food which would present a risk to a consumer of that food?)

A Chemical (especially metal) contaminants (to be discussed in a later programme); viruses (which could produce disease in a consumer but which do not spoil food); protozoan or metazoan parasites (especially worms); additives (of the wrong type or in the wrong quantity); fungi.

---

2 We know that microbes are the most common of all living things. We can find them in soil, in the air (in small numbers), in water, in humans (on and in our bodies), on and in animals and insects. Although the vast majority of microbes we are ever liable to come into contact with are harmless, some are well capable of causing harm — either by producing disease in humans, or by spoiling food. It is these organisms we must deal with and control.

Q What is the very best method of controlling pathogens and spoilage organisms?

A By stopping them from contaminating foodstuffs in the first place. You can remember this principle quite easily if you remember the maxim that 'prevention is better than cure'. It will not always be possible to prevent food contamination, but we must always do so wherever it is possible.

---

3 So our first line of defence in the protection of the consumer from illness, and the protection of foodstuffs from spoilage, is to prevent (so far as we are able so to do) foods becoming contaminated in the first place. In order to do this, we must first know what the likely sources of microbe contamination are (i.e. where contamination is likely to come from).

Q What are the main sources of food contamination by microbes (e.g. rodents).

A Microbes that contaminate foodstuffs can come from food handlers, soil, the air, pests (rodents, insects), pet animals, birds, raw foods and water supply.

---

4 We must now consider each of these possible sources of contamination in turn to decide how we might prevent contamination of food by each one of them.

Food handlers themselves can be a potent source of contamination for foodstuffs. Most often this is due to their own errors — but leaving that point aside for a minute, we should remember that the human body can be the home of several different types of microbe. If these get into food, they will be likely to cause food poisoning in a consumer.

Q Where, in or on a human being, are we likely to find such microbes?

A In the gut (intestinal tract), nose, mouth, on the genitals and in cuts and other skin lesions.

---

5 It is especially important that any food handler (which, remember, includes cashiers, porters, cleaners, etc.) who has any symptoms of illness, reports the fact to a member of the management (even if they were ill on holiday or during an off-duty day). It is especially important to report illness which includes sickness (vomiting or nausea), diarrhoea (even if just a little looseness of the bowels), sore throat, fever or a 'cold'. These symptoms may well mean that the person concerned is suffering from an infection of a type that could be easily passed on to a food consumer.

Q What should managers do if they receive such a report?

A Lay the individual off work, seek immediate advice from the Environmental Health Officer, and don't allow the person back to work until the officer says it is OK to do so. (In some cases it may be all right to let the person stay at work, but let the Environmental Health Officer decide if this is so or not.)

---

6 You should always remember that, with some forms of food poisoning, it is possible to have recovered from the symptoms totally and yet still excrete the organism from the faeces. Therefore, if you are ill at the weekend (when off-duty, for example), but feel fine upon returning to work, you must still report the illness. Also, NEVER presume that your symptoms were due to over-drinking or a 'bad pint'. This might be so but it simply isn't worth taking the risk — report the symptoms in all cases.

Q We have said that skin cuts, other skin lesions, the mouth and nose, may be sources of microbes. How could they get into food?

A Cuts and other skin lesions must be covered with waterproof (unventilated) dressings, as otherwise any organisms in them may get into any food you touch. Sneezing, scratching the inside of the nose, licking the fingers — may all pass organisms to the hands and the hands will then pass them on to food. In fact, you must always wash your hands carefully after touching any part of the body (but especially after visiting the toilet for whatever reason) and before touching any food.

7 Food handlers are an especially hazardous source of infection if they happen to become symptomless carriers of food poisoning organisms as in this case they do not suffer any symptoms to warn of their infection. (We shall discuss the whole question of carriers in detail within a later programme; here you need merely remember that they can present problems to our food hygiene control efforts.)

Q Can you think of how a food handler's clothing might become a source of contamination to food?

A Clothing worn outside the food rooms can become contaminated with microbes from the air, soil etc. This is especially true of shoes (we all walk in dog excreta at some time or another, for example).

A food handler must change into clean overclothing (whites, uniform, etc.) before entering the food rooms; should always wear head covering (that completely encloses the hair which must be tied back if necessary) when in a food room; and should have one pair of shoes for use in food rooms only. If you go outside (even just a quick trip to a shop), you must change out of overalls, headgear, shoes, etc., so that they do not become contaminated from outside; otherwise, they will carry contamination into the food rooms.

---

8 Customers as well as food handlers, may contaminate food, especially if they cough or sneeze on to open (uncovered or unwrapped) food. The greatest danger in these cases is that they will contaminate food with viruses, but they may well contaminate food with their fingers also. To protect food from such dangers, it should always be covered, screened or wrapped when displayed at a servery, on a trolley, etc.

Q Animals are the next possible source of contamination we must consider. Which animals do you think can cause us most problems?

A Rodents (rats, mice), insects, (remember that insects are animals), birds and pet animals.

---

9 We must ensure that animals do not contaminate food or the food environment (such as work surfaces etc.). We must make the food premises rodent- and insect-proof, and ensure that neither birds nor pet animals can get in. No matter how carefully we do these things, it is still possible that some rodent, some insects etc., will enter. Insects are often introduced into food premises along with stores such as bags of flour, vegetables, etc. We must, therefore, be able to kill the pests if they do get into the food rooms, and to protect food from them.

Q How do you think we can protect food from pests?

A We must ensure that all food is wrapped properly or put away in pest-proof (and pest-free) stores. Leaving food lying around is bound to attract pests. Of course, some pests (especially rats and mice) can chew through wrappers. Some simple precautions can be taken to overcome this, such as keeping flour in plastic bins with closed, tight-fitting lids. In most cases, however, you will have to check stores frequently for signs of infestation and deal with them if found. (Pest control, killing pests, proofing against pests and detecting infestations are all dealt with specifically in Programme 20.)

10 Raw foods may themselves become a source of contamination to other foods. We know that raw foods will often be contaminated with microbes from source. For example, food animals may be contaminated on the farm (especially from contaminated animal feedstuffs), or the meat may become contaminated at the slaughter house. The most important thing to remember is that raw meats are likely to contain pathogenic microbes most of the time. Poultry, veal, pork are the most likely to be affected. Beef and lamb are less likely to contain pathogenic microbes, but as we cannot see the contamination, we must presume it is present on all raw meat, and act accordingly.

Q Besides raw meat, what other types of raw food are liable to be already contaminated with pathogenic organisms before they are even brought into the food premises?

A Raw vegetables, (because of bacterial spores in soil), raw fish, raw shellfish, duck eggs.

---

11 Raw foods can cause the special type of contamination known as **cross-contamination**; you should take special note of this term, remember it and remember what it means.

Cross-contamination is exactly what it sounds like. It is the process whereby organisms already on raw foods contaminate other foods by crossing over from one to the other. This cross over can occur in several ways. It may be either direct or indirect.

Q Can you name some of the ways in which cross-contamination could occur?

A Raw foods (such as raw meat) could touch other foods directly — this could occur during transport, handling or storage of the food. The raw food could contaminate other foods indirectly if the raw food is placed on a work surface (some of the microbes are then deposited on to the surface to be picked up by other foods if they are placed or handled on the same surface before that surface is properly sanitised). A similar effect can arise if the same utensils, slicer etc., are used for raw food and then for ready-to-eat food. (Organisms pass from raw food to slicer blade, for example, and from slicer blade to cooked meat sliced afterwards.) A food handler could touch raw food and pick up contamination which would be passed to ready-to-eat food if the hands are not properly washed. Raw meat stored above ready-to-eat food in a fridge presents a special hazard as contaminated blood may drip onto the ready-to-eat food below.

---

12 It can be seen that many opportunities exist for raw foods to contaminate ready-to-eat foods. In addition to the examples just discussed, raw vegetables can also present hazards. Vegetables are frequently contaminated with soil; soil is the natural habitat of spore-forming bacteria (which can also cause food poisoning), and these spores may soon become airborne and fall onto surfaces, onto food, etc.

Q How can we prevent this type of contamination from occurring?

A We could use only prepared (peeled and washed, fully prepared, frozen or canned) vegetables. This can often be inconvenient and many people prefer fresh vegetables. An alternative is to have vegetable storage and preparation rooms completely separate from other food rooms. Once the vegetables have been peeled, washed (thoroughly, in RUNNING water) and so on, they can safely be taken into other food rooms.

13 It is undesirable to have any pathogenic organisms on any food. We know, however, that pathogens will often be present on foods such as raw meats. (The food animals might have been infected on the farms or the carcasses being contaminated after slaughter.) Undesirable though this state of affairs is, it is beyond our control. Quite obviously it is not possible to eliminate soil organisms from most vegetables and soil is always a rich source of pathogenic organisms.

It is, however, a much more serious matter for pathogens to be present on ready-to-eat foods such as cooked meats, confectionery, prepared made-up foods (like stews, casseroles, soups and gravies, etc).

Q Why is it dangerous to have pathogens on or in ready-to-eat foods but far less dangerous for them to be on or in raw food?

A Most raw foods will eventually be subjected to processes of cooking which, if carried out properly, will kill any pathogens on the raw food. Bacterial spores will survive, and so may a few vegetative bacterial cells, but so long as proper temperature controls are carried out (see Programme 10), these will not be able to multiply to dangerous levels. Ready-to-eat foods will not be subjected to any process liable to kill any pathogens which contaminate them and, therefore, the pathogens are bound to survive to infect the consumer. Note, however, that the presence of pathogens on raw foods is still highly undesirable as they may cross-contaminate other foods, utensils, equipment or work surfaces, as discussed previously.

14 Cross-contamination control is really a question of being aware of the risks. So long as you always remember that all raw foods are liable to be contaminated most of the time, and treat them accordingly, cross-contamination need never arise.

The obvious precautions which must always be taken against the risk of cross-contamination include: having separate vegetable storage and preparation areas; using different surfaces (e.g. preparation tables), utensils, equipment (especially slicing machines), for raw and ready-to-eat foods; being careful not to carry contamination from raw to ready-to-eat foods on your fingers; and correct storage. (Raw and ready-to-eat foods should be stored separately and displayed separately, but if you must store raw meat and ready-to-eat food in the same fridge, store the raw meat on the BOTTOM shelf).

Q How could we design food premises so that the risk of cross-contamination was reduced? (HINT: remember that raw and ready-to-eat foods must always be kept separate.)

A We should have separate rooms, where possible, for handling raw and ready-to-eat food. If this is not practicable in any particular case, we must, at least, have separate areas set aside for each. Separate work surfaces should be used (and each one marked 'raw food only' and 'ready-to-eat food only'). The workflow must always be from raw food passing to ready-to-eat food (finished product) and no back-flow should occur. Separate storage and display facilities (including refrigerators) should be available for raw and ready-to-eat foods wherever possible.

15 Some microbes are present in the air at all times. No organisms actually live in the air; they are merely swept up and carried about in air currents. Some will undoubtedly die in the air, as they will often become dehydrated. Spores of bacteria will usually survive, and fungal (mould) spores will be present in large numbers. Although far less resistant than bacterial spores, mould spores are well able to survive in air for long periods.

Q Why does the presence of microbes (especially bacterial and fungal spores) in the air cause us concern?

A Because they can fall on to food and contaminate it. There is little we can do to prevent this. Wrapping food and keeping open (unwrapped) food covered can certainly help, but sooner or later some food will be found to become contaminated with airborne organisms. This is the usual way for mould spores to be spread. Our only practical defence is to ensure that hot foods are kept above 65 °C and that cold foods are kept below 5 °C (if they are of a highly perishable type — obviously it is not practicable to store vegetables at this low temperature). These measures will prevent any contaminating organisms from growing (multiplying or reproducing) in the food if they do contaminate it.

---

16 Water supplies can sometimes be contaminated with pathogens. Within the UK, all mains water is treated to kill any pathogens, but such treatment cannot be guaranteed to be successful at all times. Although it is very effective, a few organisms may still slip through the net, especially some viruses.

There is nothing we can do about this in food hygiene, but we might be able to stop any contaminants surviving to be passed on to our finished food products.

Q How could we do this?

A Normal cooking processes should kill any contaminants which might be present. Most water used in food preparation is used mainly as a food ingredient in foods that will be cooked or heated to high temperatures. It is always essential to use only COLD water from the mains as a food ingredient. Stored water (from the hot tap) can easily be contaminated (dead rats, birds or insects, may be in the tank — this is NOT unusual). So, when using water as a food ingredient, always draw it off from the cold (mains supply) tap.

---

17 You must remember that not only food may become contaminated. We must do all we can to prevent contamination of work surfaces, utensils, equipment and of ourselves (we could pass it on to food).

Because so much contamination WILL be brought into our food rooms (on raw foods especially) it is not possible to prevent all contamination. This is why we should have separate work surfaces, utensils and equipment for raw foods. We know that raw foods will contaminate them but we can sanitise the surfaces, equipment, etc. What we MUST do is to prevent contamination of work surfaces, utensils and equipment that will be used for ready-to-eat foods.

Q What can we do to prevent ourselves from contaminating ready-to-eat foods, surfaces etc., once we have become contaminated from raw foods?

A Hand washing and general personal hygiene are the safeguards we should use.

18 In this programme we have learned that the first line of defence against food poisoning and food spoilage is to prevent microbial contamination of food in the first place. We now know that this is an ideal that cannot be attained in all cases. We know that many sources of contamination exist. Personal hygiene is vital. Rodents and other pests must be controlled, and food must be protected from them (we shall discuss just how in Programme 20). We also know that, no matter what we do, at least some contamination is bound to come into our food rooms on raw foods. Control of cross-contamination can help us here. It is important to remember that ALL food hygiene practices are important. Contamination control is only one of these practices: we shall consider some more in the programmes which follow.

KEY FACTS

1 One of the main, and most effective, ways of protecting food consumers is to prevent food from becoming contaminated by pathogens.

2 Food may become contaminated by food handlers, raw food, contaminated surfaces and utensils, pests, or the air, or if contaminated water is used in food preparation.

3 Pathogens can be found on the skin of food handlers (especially in skin cuts and boils), in their gut or in their lungs.

4 If a food handler has illness symptoms, it is most important that they report the facts to their superior. They should be excluded from the food premises until they are fully recovered (AND are cleared to return to work by the Environmental Health Officer).

5 Clothing, including shoes, worn inside a food room should not be worn outside. Outside clothing, including shoes, should not be worn inside a food room (i.e. a room in which food is handled, prepared, served or stored).

6 Raw foods (notably raw meat) are often contaminated with pathogens, but if the cooking process is correct, the pathogens will be killed. The raw foods to watch out for are ALL raw meats and root vegetables (potatoes, etc.).

7 Pathogens will, therefore, be repeatedly introduced into food premises. The raw food must not be allowed to contaminate ready-to-eat foods. Separate storage and preparation areas and separate utensils should always be used for raw foods.

8 Cross-contamination is a process whereby the pathogens (which will often be present) on raw food are transferred to ready-to-eat foods. The ready-to-eat foods will not be cooked again, so any pathogens that are transferred to them will survive to infect a food consumer.

9 Cross-contamination may arise most often:

— if same utensils are used for raw, then for ready-to-eat foods.
— if same slicers/mincers/mixers are used for raw, then for ready-to-eat foods.
— if same surfaces are used for raw, then for ready-to-eat foods.
— via food handlers who handle raw food then handle ready-to-eat without properly washing their hands.
— via the air (from soil on potatoes, etc).

10 Raw and ready-to-eat foods should be kept separate. Separate preparation areas, work surfaces, storage (including fridges), utensils and equipment, should be used for raw and ready-to-eat foods. Food handlers must always wash their hands thoroughly after handling raw foods (raw meat and root vegetables especially).

PROGRESS PAPER 9

This progress paper is exactly like those we have done before. It is intended to help you, so please complete it fairly. Have a go at each question and then check your answers with the model answers that follow.

Don't worry if your answers are not exactly like the models, my answers are sometimes intended to expand on certain points. So long as the main gist of your answer is the same, you are correct. If you get any answers wrong or cannot answer any, take special note of the model answers and revise the whole programme again if you think you have not learned it thoroughly. Take your time, learning is a slow process, but if you work at it, you will get there in the end.

1 What are the three MAIN topics of food hygiene practices?

2 Why is it important to have good food room design, equipment and work surfaces?

3 Pathogenic organisms produce hazards to a food consumer. What is the name of those which rot food?

4 Besides bacteria, what else might food be contaminated with?

5 What are the main sources of contamination of food?

6 Where are microbes most likely to be found, on or in a food handler?

7 Which animals might contaminate food?

8 Which raw foods are the main sources of contamination to a food room or other foods?

9 What is cross-contamination?

10 What are the main methods of preventing cross-contamination?

11 With respect to the design and layout of food premises, what should we do to help prevent cross-contamination?

12 Contamination of ready-to-eat food is a far more serious matter than contamination of raw food — why?

13 How does raw meat most often become contaminated with microbes?

14 What should a food handler with a cut or other skin lesion on the finger do?

15 Who else besides food handlers might contaminate food?

16 Where should vegetables be stored and prepared?

17 Explain your answer to question 16.

18 Why is it necessary to stop insects entering food premises (and to destroy them if they do get into such premises)?

19 If raw meat and cooked meat are stored in the same fridge, which should be on the bottom shelf? Explain your answer.

20 A chef goes to a shop during working hours still dressed in his 'whites'. Is this OK? If not, why not?

ANSWERS

1 Contamination control, temperature control and cleaning (decontamination).

2 Because these things help us to attain and maintain good standards of food hygiene practice.

3 Spoilage organisms.

4 Chemicals, protozoan or metazoan parasites, fungi and viruses.

5 Food handlers, customers, soil, air, pests, pet animals, birds, raw foods and water.

6 In the gut (intestinal tract), nose, mouth, on the skin (especially genitals), and within cuts and other skin lesions.

7 Rats, mice, birds, inseets and pet animals.

8 Raw meats and raw vegetables.

9 It is the process whereby microbes from raw foods are directly or indirectly passed on to ready-to-eat foods.

10 Have separate vegetable storage and preparation areas; use different surfaces, utensils, equipment, for raw and ready-to-eat foods; be careful not to carry contamination yourself (hand washing after handling raw foods and always before handling any other foods at all) and have correct storage and display (raw and ready-to-eat foods separated).

11 Ideally we should have separate rooms for handling raw and ready-to-eat foods, or at the very least we must have separate areas set aside, separate work surfaces etc. Vegetable preparation and storage areas should always be entirely separated. Work flow should be from raw foods to finished product; no back-flow should arise.

12 The raw food will be cooked which should kill any pathogens present. Spores will survive, but proper temperature controls can help us here (discussed in Programme 10). Ready-to-eat foods will not be subjected to any processes which could kill any microbes present — therefore the microbes are bound to survive to be passed on to the food consumer.

13 The meat animal may become infected at the farm (especially by contaminated foodstuffs), or the carcass may become contaminated after slaughter (usually from the carcass of an animal that was infected before slaughter).

14 Cover it with a waterproof (unventilated) dressing.

15 Customers. People who visit the food premises must NOT be allowed to enter any food room except public areas.

16 In an area which is entirely separated from other food rooms.

17 Raw vegetables are often contaminated with soil which is a rich source of pathogens — especially those which can produce spores (*Clostridium* and *Bacillus* species). Spores may be swept up in air currents and be carried to other food. Complete separation of the vegetable storage and preparation areas prevents spores (or even soil particles containing vegetative cells) gaining access to other food areas. Once the vegetables are peeled, washed, etc., they can safely be taken into the other food rooms. (NOTE: vegetables must always be washed in running water.)

18 Because insects frequently carry pathogens in or on their bodies. They may gain access to foods and contaminate them.

19 The raw meat. The blood might drip from the raw meat and fall onto the cooked meat if it is stored below it.

20 No, it is not. The over-clothing worn by a food handler is intended to protect food from microbes which may get on to outdoor clothing from outside the food areas. A food handler MUST wear over-clothing, headgear and a particular pair of shoes kept for the purpose, within the food areas ONLY. Change out of these whenever you leave the food areas and change into them again before re-entering the food areas (ANY food areas).

PROGRAMME 10
Temperature Control I

1 We know that the very best way to protect a food consumer is to prevent microbial contamination of food. We also know that raw foods (especially white and red meat and root vegetables) will be contaminated with microbes from source. Even uncontaminated foods may become so if mishandled. Foods of a type that will readily support the growth of moulds are virtually bound to become contaminated with mould spores from the air on many occasions.

We MUST stop food from becoming contaminated with microbes as far as we are able to do so, but some contamination (such as on raw food) is beyond our control.

Q If we cannot prevent contamination of raw food (because it is contaminated at source before it reaches our premises), how can we make it safe to eat?

A By killing the microbes which are present by means of proper cooking.

---

2 Once we have done this we can be reasonably sure that the food will be safe to eat, but how can we be certain that we have, in fact, killed all the microbes that could be present?

Q What form or type of microbe would we not be able to kill with certainty during cooking?

A Bacterial spores. To kill them requires heating at 100 °C (boiling point of water) for 3–5 hours. We cannot ensure that we will cook at a high enough temperature (even in an oven which operates way above 100 °C) for long enough to ensure that all spores are killed. Some bacterial spores will undoubtedly be killed, but by no means all.

---

3 Much depends upon the efficiency of heat penetration (a topic we will discuss shortly) and it is even possible for vegetative cells of bacteria (i.e. not spores) to survive cooking processes. For this reason the cooking process must be correctly carried out to ensure that we do kill as many microbes as possible.

Q Do ALL raw foods need to be cooked to make them safe to eat?

A No. Obviously fresh fruit is not usually cooked and neither are tomatoes, lettuce, cucumber etc., used in salads. These foods will not, however, usually support the growth of those microbes which are most likely to produce food poisoning (the bacteria) and may, therefore, be eaten safely so long as they are obtained from a reliable, hygienic, source.

---

4 We can help to ensure that raw foods will be safe to eat by killing microbes within them (if the foods are of a type that will support food-poisoning organisms, e.g. meats, gravies, foods made up of meats, milk, cream and egg dishes). Milk and cream are usually heated during processing, but raw meats, etc., are not. If we cannot be sure that our cooking methods will kill all the potentially dangerous microbes that could be present, we must be able to use other safeguards in addition to cooking.

Q What else could we do, in addition to cooking hazardous raw foods (such as raw meat), in order to make them safe?

A We can prevent any organisms that do survive cooking from multiplying. You must always remember that we can tolerate a small number of microbes in our food: it is when the numbers get high that trouble begins. If we can stop any bacteria in food from growing, we can increase the safety of the food. Likewise, bacterial spores can be prevented from germinating if we control the food's temperature.

---

5 So, we now have two possible ways of increasing the safety of food by means of temperature. We can cook certain foods in an attempt to kill all the potentially dangerous microbes that could be present in the foods, and we can prevent the growth (multiplication) of any that survive the cooking process (as well as stopping any bacterial spores from germinating).

In Programmes 1–8, we discussed some of the main properties of bacteria and other microbes. By applying the knowledge we obtained there we can decide just what temperature we need to use to help increase the safety of food. We need to consider two things: at what temperature/time combinations (remember that time is important) will bacteria, fungi, viruses and parasitic worms be killed, and at what temperatures will they be prevented from growing (multiplying)?

Problems concerning the multiplication of microbes are caused mainly by bacteria and fungi — viruses don't multiply in dead cells and neither do parasitic worms. We MUST kill parasitic worms and viruses if we are to be safe as a very small number of them can produce disease. We cannot tolerate them in food at all.

Q At what temperature/time combinations will microbes (of all types) be killed, and at what temperatures will bacteria and fungi be stopped from growing?

A Viruses, fungi and parasitic worms are all more sensitive to heat than are bacteria. Therefore, if we choose a temperature/time combination that will kill vegetative bacteria (i.e. not spores) we will achieve a high level of safety. The temperature/time combinations are 65 °C for about 30 minutes or 85 °C for a few minutes. Those bacteria which may produce food poisoning cease to grow at 5 °C. Some spoilage bacteria and some fungi can grow at lower temperatures but, although they will spoil food, they will not cause direct harm to a food consumer. Neither pathogenic bacteria nor fungi will grow above 65 °C.

6 The use of temperature control to increase food safety consists of FOUR separate considerations, all of which are important. These are:

(i) Cooking appropriate raw foods thoroughly so as to kill as many microbes as possible.
(ii) Holding the temperature of cooked food above 65 °C until eaten. This prevents bacterial growth and the germination and growth of bacterial spores.
(iii) If the cooked food is to be eaten cold, cooling it as rapidly as you can and holding it below 5 °C until eaten. This stops any surviving bacteria or bacterial spores from growing.
(iv) Holding all cold foods, of a type that will support bacteria of the food-poisoning type, below 5 °C until eaten. (Once again this stops bacterial and bacterial spore growth.)

Q Why should we keep cold foods below 5 °C if they have been properly cooked?

A Because firstly, we cannot be sure that the cooking process has killed all bacteria and bacterial spores. Even if it has done so, we cannot be sure that the food has not become contaminated since cooking (or since the manufacturer applied heat processing in the case of milk, cream, etc). By holding these foods below 5 °C, we can ensure that any bacteria present will not multiply and that any bacterial spores present will not germinate.

7 We have hinted at the fact that these four aspects of temperature control apply only to certain types of food. They apply to those types of food which are most likely to support the growth of food-poisoning bacteria. These foods are meats, (raw and ready-to-eat); foods containing meat (e.g. meat products, casseroles, stews, etc.), or meat extracts (such as gravies); milk and milk products (cream, custards, etc); egg products; fish and fish products. Fruit and vegetables that are to be eaten raw are reasonably safe.

You should note that we are now considering dangers from food poisoning. We will need to use temperatures lower than 5 °C to prevent most food spoilage but this topic will be dealt with in Programme 18. For now, let us consider the prevention of food poisoning by means of temperature controls.

Q What do the foods listed above (the ones that must have careful temperature control applied to them) all have in common? (HINT: what is the property common to each of them?)

A They are all highly perishable foods. These types of food require the greatest care. They are highly perishable simply because they support the growth of bacteria very well. They will, therefore, support the growth of our arch-enemies (the food poisoning bacteria) very well also. Such bacteria are unlikely to grow readily on fruits, lettuces or similar foods.

8 Let us recap what we have learned so far. We now know that in order to use temperature controls to make highly perishable foods safer to eat, we must consider:

(i) Cooking methods.
(ii) Holding hot food above 65 °C.
(iii) Cooling hot food below 5 °C.
(v) Holding cold food below 5 °C.

In all these cases, we are trying to kill food-poisoning bacteria (if we can do this we will also kill viruses and intestinal worms that could harm food consumers) and/or prevent the growth of such bacteria, and/or prevent bacterial spores from germinating. We will now consider just how we can carry out these four aspects of temperature control in practice.

Q Between what temperatures will most pathogenic bacteria not grow, i.e. not multiply? (HINT: to answer this you need to think about both a low and a high temperature).

A BELOW 5 °C and ABOVE 65 °C. These are the 'magic' temperatures. Between 5 °C and 65 °C (5 °C–65 °C, i.e. 5 °C, 6 °C, 7 °C . . . 63 °C, 64 °C, 65 °C) is the DANGER ZONE. If any food of a type that will support the growth of these pathogens is held between 5 °C and 65 °C any such pathogens present in or on the food will multiply, and any bacterial spores will germinate and then start to multiply. Our safety margin lies in keeping foods of the appropriate type BELOW 5 °C and ABOVE 65 °C as may be most appropriate.

9 Let us look therefore, at the first of our four major aspects of temperature control — cooking methods. The problem that we face here is to ensure that ALL bacteria, viruses, worms etc., present will be heated above 65 °C for at least 30 minutes. When we think about just how hot an oven can get, how hot the fat in a deep fat fryer is, or how hot boiling water is, it doesn't seem very difficult to reach 65 °C and maintain it for 30 minutes. You must remember, however, that we must get ALL the organisms that may be in the food to this temperature. This means that we must ensure that the heat PENETRATES right through to the very centre of the food mass. This is our problem. The outside of the food will get hot quickly but it takes time for the centre to get hot and, if we use too high a temperature to start off with, the outside of the food may burn before heat penetrates to the centre.

We will generally be cooking food in one of two forms: either as a chunk of solid food (like a chicken, meat joint, etc); or as a semi-liquid or liquid (stews, soups, gravies, etc.). In both cases, we must get heat to penetrate to the inside (centre) of the chicken, joint of meat etc., or to spread throughout the whole of the soup, stew or similar foodstuff.

Q If we had a football-shaped chunk of meat and a long sausage, in which of these would heat penetrate most easily to the centre?

A In the sausage. The distance from the outside of a 'sausage-shaped' food and its inside (the centre) is less than in the case of a globular (football-shaped) mass of food such as a joint of meat.

10 We can say straight away therefore, that if we try to cook very large chickens, turkeys, meat joints, or very large quantities of fluid-type foods (stews, etc.), it will be harder to get heat to penetrate right through to the centre. Although the shape of the food (for instance a football-like joint or a sausage) makes a difference we can generalise and say that, on average, we will only get good heat penetration in joints, chickens etc., of about 3–5.5 kg (7–12 lb) or less in weight. In the case of stews, soups, etc., we can safely cook far larger quantities than this — so long as we keep them well stirred so that the heat gets right through. (In effect we are 'stirring the heat into them'.)

We must therefore be very careful about the quantities of food we try to cook at one go. A turkey weighing 9 kg (20 lb), for instance, should be cut in half before cooking. Otherwise, the outside is likely to burn before we get enough heat to penetrate to the inside. Heat penetration depends not only upon the quantity, type and shape of food we are cooking, but also upon the method of cooking we employ.

Q Try and rearrange the following cooking methods in order of efficiency of heat penetration: grilling; boiling; steaming (pressure-cooking); deep-fat frying; shallow-fat frying; oven (normal); oven (fan-assisted); microwave oven.

A The 'best' method from the point of view of heat penetration is cooking in a microwave oven. Then the order is cooking in a pressure cooker; a fan-assisted oven; a normal oven; boiling; grilling; deep-fat frying. Shallow-fat frying is the worst so far as heat penetration is concerned.

---

11 This answer does NOT mean that a microwave oven should be used for all food preparation, nor that shallow-fat frying cannot be used. Much depends upon how each method of cooking is employed. It is far safer to grill sausages carefully for the correct time than to put a large turkey in an oven and cook it for an hour. What the list does tell us is that we should be careful how we use each cooking method.

For instance, we should be very careful if we are deep-fat frying chicken 'drumsticks' as the outside is liable to burn before the inside is heated to a sufficiently high temperature for long enough. It would be far safer to pre-cook the drumsticks carefully in an oven, and then fry them.

We can help to ensure that we attain the heat penetration necessary by carefully choosing small joints of meat, small chickens, etc. (or by cutting up large ones before cooking); by cooking fluid foods either in small lots (2 to 2.5 litres or about 5 pints), or by cooking in larger lots AND keeping them well stirred; and by choosing an appropriate cooking method.

Q How can we ensure that we get sufficient heat penetration when grilling or shallow-frying sausages, bacon and similar foods?

A The sausage or bacon should be cooked for longer at lower temperatures, and should be frequently turned. In this way, we can ensure that we get good heat penetration without burning the outside. If you put sausages under a high grill, the outside is liable to get burned before heat has time to get through to the centre. Remember that it takes a short time to heat up the outside of a food, but it takes a lot longer for the inside to reach the same temperature. In the case of oven cooking for instance, it is better to use a lower temperature for longer and therefore to ensure good heat penetration without burning the food outside than it is to use a very high temperature for a short time. Fan-assisted ovens cook faster and are better at achieving good heat penetration, because the fan helps to ensure better heat distribution within the oven itself.

If you really must cook very fast, cook small quantities and use a microwave oven. These work by bombarding the food with microwaves, which cause the food molecules to rub together. Very great friction is produced which causes the food to be evenly heated throughout. (NOTE: always use microwave ovens in accordance with the manufacturers' instructions.)

---

12 Having once cooked our food it must be either eaten within a few minutes (less than 30 minutes) or held above 65 °C until it is eaten, OR be cooled below 5 °C. Let us now consider how food can be held above 65 °C until eaten.

By far the best method of keeping hot food above 65 °C is to employ the equipment already available in the kitchen. Ovens will keep food hot far more efficiently than will warm holding cabinets (the majority of which will not maintain food above 65 °C for any length of time at all). Boiling-pans, and similar large-scale cooking appliances, will maintain fluid foods (soups, stews, etc.) at above 65 °C with ease. Small quantities of fluid foods can be maintained above 65 °C by being held in pans, etc., on a cooking-range ('on a low light') but, in all cases, the fluid foods should be stirred regularly to ensure even temperature maintenance throughout.

Q What are the main disadvantages of holding food above 65 °C by means of the methods suggested above?

A Firstly, we usually need the food to be in a servery area (we cannot conveniently be travelling back and forth to the kitchen each time we are to serve a customer). Secondly, and this is a problem that is common to any method of holding food above 65 °C, the food may dry out to some extent and become less palatable.

---

13 The answer to the problem of food 'drying out' is that it must be served reasonably soon after preparation. This is, in any case, a good hygiene principle as it only requires the comparatively high temperature of 65 °C to be maintained for a short time.

Food will have to be held within servery areas for a certain period of time. Safety lies in holding only small quantities. Stock can then be replenished from the kitchen as needed. The warming cabinets and *bains-marie* normally used for holding food, cannot usually maintain temperatures above 65 °C (throughout the food, remember) for long. So long as the food is eaten within about 30 minutes, no great danger should arise.

Q What special precautions should be taken when holding food within hot cabinets or *bains-marie*, etc?

A When using hot cabinets keep the door closed unless actually extracting food from them. Hold as small a quantity of food as possible (whether in a cabinet, *bain-marie* or whatever) for as short a time as possible; keep lids on *bains-marie* and stir fluid foods at regular intervals to ensure good heat distribution. (Use a CLEAN spoon each time you stir the fluid.)

---

14 Special reference should be made to stock-pots as these represent a grave risk. It is the practice in some catering establishments to keep a stock-pot in which food scraps are heated up to form a base for gravy. Such a practice is totally wrong. The stock-pot will not be able to maintain temperatures sufficiently high for long enough to kill all the microbes that will undoubtedly gain access to it via the left-over foods. Certainly bacterial spores may well be able to germinate within it. Stock-pots should NEVER be used.

Q Having considered holding the food at high temperatures, we must now look at two other aspects of temperature control — what are they?

A Cooling food which is to be eaten cold and holding cold food at low temperatures. We will look at these points in the next programme, but first let us do another test paper.

KEY FACTS

1 Raw meat will nearly always be contaminated with pathogens when it is delivered to food premises. Proper cooking processes kill these pathogens and make the meat safe to eat.

2 Cooking will not normally kill bacterial spores (produced by *Clostridium* and *Bacillus* but not by other types of bacteria). Our only defence here is to ensure that cooked food is kept hot (above 65 °C) until eaten or is cooled quickly and held below 5 °C.

3 A considerable danger exists if food (especially stews, soups, casseroles, etc.) is cooked, cooled and then re-heated. Any spores in the food will not have been killed by cooking and will germinate as the food cools. Some non-spore-forming pathogens might survive too, and the storage of the food may allow pathogens to multiply. Re-heating would not be enough to kill these pathogens. The use of reheated food or of stock-pots therefore constitutes a very dangerous practice.

4 Raw meat must be cooked thoroughly to kill any pathogens which are likely to be present (which will usually be the case). The problem is to get the centre of the food mass hot enough for long enough. It is always the temperature/time combination that matters.

5 Hot food must be kept at above 65 °C until eaten, or cooled and held below 5 °C. Hold all cold perishable foods below 5 °C until eaten.

6 Large meat joints should not be cooked because heat cannot readily penetrate to the centre. It is the shape of meat that matters most. 'Sausage-shaped' foods will allow better heat penetration than 'football-shaped' masses of food.

7 Large volumes of soup, stews, gravies and so on, present similar problems to large masses of meat, in that it is hard to obtain heat penetration right through to the centre of the fluid. Avoid using very large volumes, and all 'fluid' foods should be stirred regularly (if possible) to help ensure proper heat distribution throughout the whole fluid volume.

8 Remember that raw food must be heated thoroughly, throughout the whole food mass or food volume.

PROGRESS PAPER 10

Try and answer the questions below. As before you should compare your answers with the model answers which follow. If you get any questions wrong or cannot answer a question, take special note of the model answers and re-read the programme if you are still unsure. Write all your answers before looking at the model answers.

1 We have two main methods of controlling microbes in food; one is to kill them, what is the other?

2 What type, or form, of microbe cannot be easily killed by cooking?

3 What types of food are most likely to require temperature controls? Give examples.

4 Can we be sure that proper cooking will kill all the microbes that are liable to be present in raw foods?

5 What is the 'danger zone' so far as temperature is concerned? Quote the temperatures and explain why the term 'danger zone' is used.

6 What must we do to raw food after cooking it, if it is to be eaten cold?

7 What must we do to cold food that is to be eaten cold?

8 What must we do to hot food that is to be eaten hot?

9 Which is the safest to cook — a sausage or a haggis?

10 How can we help to ensure good heat penetration when grilling bacon or sausages?

ANSWERS

1 To prevent the multiplication of the organisms, or germination of bacterial spores, by means of high or low temperature controls.

2 A bacterial spore.

3 Foods which are easily able to support the growth of food-poisoning bacteria, e.g. meat and meat dishes, fish, dairy produce (milk, cream, eggs, etc.) or foods containing such produce. 'Meat' would include extracts from meat, etc., such as soups and gravies.

4 No, we cannot. Some microbes (notably bacterial spores) may well survive which is why proper temperature control after cooking is so important.

5 5 °C to 65 °C. Between these temperatures food-poisoning bacteria can multiply. (Of course, neither viruses nor intestinal worm parasites can grow or reproduce within the dead cells of the food.)

6 Cool it as rapidly as possible to below 5 °C.

7 Maintain it below 5 °C. This applies to those foods of a type which are liable to support the growth of food-poisoning bacteria. (NOTE: If the food is to be consumed the same day, it need only be kept below 10 °C.)

8 Maintain it above 65 °C until eaten (or ensure it is eaten within 30 minutes of cooking).

9 A sausage. Because of its shape, the distance from the outside to middle is less than in the case of the spherical (football-shaped) haggis. Therefore, heat penetration will be more efficient in the case of the sausage.

10 Cook them slowly, at medium heat, but turn them often so that heat penetrates to the inside before the outside becomes over-cooked.

PROGRAMME 11

Temperature Control II

1 If food must be cooked but is to be eaten cold, it must obviously be cooled first. It is this cooling process however, that can create dangers for a food consumer. We know that if we employ proper cooking procedures (being especially careful to ensure good heat penetration right through the whole mass of the food), we should be able to kill most of the pathogenic organisms (bacteria, viruses or intestinal worms) liable to be present within the food. We also know, however, that we can never guarantee that some organisms will not survive. Bacterial spores are certainly liable to survive and we can expect such spores to be present in the raw food on many occasions.

Q If we remove the food from the cooking process and allow it to cool slowly, what will happen?

A As the temperature cools to below 65 °C any bacteria which have survived the cooking process will start to multiply. Any bacterial spores which have survived (and the majority will survive) will germinate and the emerging bacteria will then start to multiply also.

---

2 Because it is the number of bacteria in a food that largely dictates if illness will be produced in a consumer of that food, if we can keep the total number of bacteria down to a small (very small) level, we can usually obtain a reasonable degree of safety. Exceptions to this do exist but, for our present purposes, we need not concern ourselves with them.

It is reasonable to conclude that if we can stop any bacteria or bacterial spores which survived the cooking process from multiplying, we can attain reasonably safe food.

Q How therefore, can we stop any surviving bacteria or bacterial spores from multiplying in the food we have just cooked?

A Firstly, we can ensure that the food is eaten quickly, say within half an hour of cooking at most. But this solution to our problem is of no use in the case where the food is to be eaten cold (say for instance, we have cooked a chicken and it is intended for a salad dish). In these circumstances we must ensure that the food in question is cooled below 5 °C as fast as possible.

---

3 Rapid cooling is needed to rob the bacteria of time to multiply to any great extent. The longer the food lies between 65 °C and 5 °C, the longer the bacteria will have to multiply.

Very rapid cooling can be achieved if we put a small quantity of food in a large freezer, but this idea is not as good as it might at first appear to be.

Q Why is it not advisable to cool food rapidly by putting it inside a freezer or fridge?

A There are two reasons why this is not advisable. If you put hot things into freezers or fridges, you increase the air temperature within them. This might not be critical if you had a very small quantity of food in a very large (walk-in type) freezer, but you would in effect cause the outside of the food to ice over before the inside of the food mass cooled. This would actually delay the cooling process.

---

4 We said earlier that, in trying to obtain good heat penetration when cooking food, the problem consists of getting heat right through to the centre of a mass of food. When cooling food, the opposite is the case. The problem now is to ensure that heat gets right out of the mass of food; to ensure that the centre cools down as well as the outside.

Q Why is it that the outside of a mass of hot food cools down faster than the inside?

A Because the inside is insulated by the outside. It is as though the food had an overcoat on. If you imagine a joint of meat, the meat at the centre of the joint is insulated by the meat which surrounds it. In the case of a pan of soup, to take just one example of a fluid type food, the soup cools at the surface (which is exposed to the air) much faster than at the centre or bottom of the pan. The soup at the very centre of the soup mass is insulated by all the soup surrounding it.

---

5 You will recall that the heat penetration process was helped by ensuring that we cooked reasonably sized chunks of food and that fluid foods were well stirred. This same technique could help us to speed up cooling. If we want to ensure that a cooked chicken cools quickly (and remember it must not be a very large chicken that we have cooked, or it must have been split into two before being cooked) we can split it into two (or split the two halves again as the case may be). Small chunks of food cool faster than large ones.

Q How do you think we could help a large mass of fluid food to cool as quickly as possible?

A We must not put it into a fridge or freezer as we now know. What we can do is to split it into smaller lots. For instance, 12 litres (about 21 pints) of soup could be put into three pans with 4 litres (about 7 pints) in each. Even better, we could put it into a large but shallow tray-like dish. This would help it to cool faster because the distance between any point at the centre of the soup mass would now be only a short distance from the surface of the soup that is in contact with the air.

6 Obviously it is essential to put the food to be cooled in a cool place. Ideally a **cooling room** (chill room) should be used. This is very like a 'walk-in' freezer except that the cooling plant inside it is fitted with powerful fans. The air inside the room (or cooling cabinet) is held at about 5 °C so that cooling can be achieved without the surface of the food freezing. Once the food has cooled down throughout its whole mass to about 5 °C, it can be put into a fridge or freezer to complete the cooling process.

It is possible to buy **chiller units** which are small cooling cabinets, usually capable of holding up to 20 kg (44 lb) of food. These are useful pieces of equipment for premises where the use of a large chill room or similar cannot be justified. If neither of these are available then the food to be cooled must be placed in a cold area. Food cooling without a chill room or cabinet is never very satisfactory but, in all cases, we must be careful to protect the cooling food from contamination.

Q Could we cover the food with **tin foil** perhaps, in order to protect it from contamination while it was cooling? (If not, why not?)

A If we covered the food in this way we would delay cooling. Obviously the food must be open to the air because it will only cool effectively if cool air is circulating around it. We must ensure, however, that it is not near open windows or anywhere else where it might become contaminated with airborne organisms, or indeed where people or pests might contaminate it. The food needs to be 'open' (i.e. unwrapped and uncovered) to assist cooling but, in this state, it is obviously liable to contamination which is a risk that must always be guarded against.

7 Once the food has been cooled down below 5 °C–10 °C, it should be kept in a fridge or refrigerated display cabinet, at below 5 °C or 10 °C. Once it has been cooled, it is, of course, cold food and must be treated accordingly.

All types of cold foods that will support the growth of pathogens, must be held below 5 °C until being consumed (or cooked or processed, in the case of cold raw foods).

Q What kinds of foods should therefore be held at 5 °C?

A Highly perishable kinds of food that will readily support the growth of bacteria. These include, especially, meat (and meat products), fish of all types, dairy produce (milk, cream, eggs, etc.) and foods made from dairy produce. Fruit and vegetables are perishable but they will not readily support the growth of food-poisoning bacteria. We can, therefore, be more lax with respect to temperature control of these products, as we can with many types of biscuit, bread or confectionery (unless they contain real or artificial cream), but we should remember that such foods as these are still subject to the ravages of spoilage organisms.

8 We must be careful how we store and display those types of food which will readily support the growth of food poisoning bacteria. How many times have you seen cold meat pies, meat sandwiches etc., displayed in an ordinary cabinet? Such practice is widespread and is also wrong.

Q How, therefore, should foods such as these be displayed?

A In refrigerated (cooled) cabinets. Most of these will reach 5 °C if correctly adjusted. Some will not however, and food businesses should be careful to ensure that the food in the cabinets is kept at 5 °C. In practice, a temperature of 10 °C will be satisfactory so long as the food is to be eaten within a day.

9 The correct use and operation of fridges, freezers and refrigerated cabinets is important. These topics are dealt with in Programme 19 (concerning food preservation). At this stage in our course we need only note that the use of low temperatures is a good way to make food safer to eat BUT it can never be used to kill microbes. We have already seen that although high temperatures can be used to kill microbes, many of them will merely become dormant (go to sleep) at low temperatures and resume activity when their environment warms up again.

Q Ice cream will support the growth of food poisoning bacteria very well but it will probably be melted at 5 °C. At what temperature do you think ice cream should be stored or held for display? (Have a guess. HINT: ice cream will stay solid at −2.2 °C.)

A Legally, ice cream must not go above −2.2 °C. If it does, it cannot be sold unless it is reprocessed. Only a manufacturer can do this effectively. (This temperature limit applies to solid ice cream only, not to 'cold mix' ice creams from special dispensers.)

---

10 Frozen food will 'keep' for long periods of time (if held at −18 °C) or for short periods in an ordinary fridge. Freezing food relies on the fact that bacteria cannot multiply at such low temperatures.

Frozen food does however, present some potential dangers of its own. Take, for example, the case of a frozen chicken. It will have solid ice at its centre and this will act as a very good insulator.

Q Why are we concerned that the ice at the centre of a block, chunk, etc. of food will act as a good heat insulator?

A Because when we cook the food the heat must reach the centre. Remember, that in order to ensure safety, we must get good heat penetration right through the whole mass of food.

---

11 This problem can be eliminated by ensuring that frozen food (that is to be cooked) is FULLY defrosted before cooking it.

While defrosting food we must obviously protect it from contamination. We do not want it to defrost and then be left lying around in a warm kitchen, so that (as it goes above 5 °C) bacteria or bacterial spores in the food start to multiply. We must be careful to ensure proper, full, defrosting in an area where the food will not be exposed to contamination BUT we must not leave the food for so long that it gets warm before we cook it and thereby run the risk of bacteria or bacterial spores multiplying.

Q It is permissible to defrost frozen raw chickens, for example, in a sink full of water? (If not, why not?)

A The raw chicken will almost certainly contain pathogens (picked up either at the farm or slaughter house). If we defrost it in a sink full of water, the sink will become contaminated. The answer therefore, is that such a practice is NOT generally permissible. However, it may be possible to have one sink specially reserved for this and used for NO other purpose. Such a case would be perfectly satisfactory.

12 We must also be very careful that the blood and juices that drip off any frozen raw meat do not contaminate other foods.

Q What is the common way in which this could happen?

A If raw frozen meat is placed above other foods in a fridge. The blood and juices will probably drip on to the food below. Raw food must always be stored BELOW other food. (Preferably separate cold storage facilities should be available for raw and ready-to-eat foods.)

---

13 Once raw food has been cooked and subsequently cooled down, it should not be re-heated. Much controversy exists over the practice of re-heating foods that have been cooked once already. The author's opinion, however, is that it should NEVER be done. It might in theory, be safe to do so in some cases but, on balance, it is not worth the risk.

Food that has been cooked should either be kept hot and eaten hot, or cooled and held cold until eaten.

Q What is the danger of re-heating food?

A We cannot guarantee that all pathogens present would have been killed when the food was originally cooked. Bacterial spores would almost certainly not be killed. Even if we cooled the food carefully (which of course should always be the case), we cannot guarantee that no organisms have had time to multiply. The re-heating process will not be sufficiently hot for long enough to kill either vegetative bacteria or bacterial spores, but it may well allow spores to germinate and allow bacteria to grow. Were the food to be eaten straight away, re-heating would probably be safe, but we now have too many 'ifs' for safety. Certainly re-heating already re-heated food is very dangerous indeed.

---

14 One very useful piece of equipment for any kitchen or similar food area, is a reliable thermometer. ONLY electronic types (with a metal probe) should be used; glass ones may break in the food.

Q What use is a thermometer to us in our attempts to ensure good temperature control?

A We can check the temperature of hot and cold food at the centre, and of food that is being defrosted. The hot food (out of an oven or in a pan of soup, etc.) should have reached 85 °C during cooking, or at least 65 °C–70 °C. Hot food being held hot should be above 65 °C, cold food should be below 5 °C (preferably, or 10 °C if to be eaten the same day). Frozen raw food being defrosted should be above about 10 °C–15 °C before being cooked and ice cream must be below −2.2 °C. A good thermometer enables us to check that our temperature controls are operating correctly.

---

15 We have seen that the use of high and low temperatures can assist us to ensure that the food we handle is safe for consumers. This is so because bacteria of the food poisoning type (our 'greatest enemies'), cannot multiply below 5 °C or above 65 °C. Between these temperatures (5 °C–65 °C) is the 'danger zone' because our 'greatest enemies' can multiply between these temperatures.

KEY FACTS

1. Cooked food that is intended to be eaten cold must be cooled quickly so that any pathogens (and especially any bacterial spores) which have survived the cooking process do not have time to multiply.
2. Cold, perishable, foods should be held below 5 °C until eaten. (Ice cream must be held below −2.2 °C.)
3. Hot food must not be placed in a fridge or freezer because the food would raise the temperature of the food inside the appliance.
4. The problem of cooling hot food is to ensure that the inside of the food mass or volume cools quickly. The outer parts of the food will cool faster than the inner parts.
5. To aid rapid cooling, a solid food mass can be split up (e.g. a chicken or turkey can be halved). In the case of fluid foods they should be decanted into shallow containers.
6. Ideally, a properly constructed cooling (not freezing) room or cabinet should be used to cool down hot food.
7. Frozen foods will 'keep' well if kept frozen, but problems may arise when attempts are made to cook food which has been frozen. Ice-plugs can be formed at the centre of such foods (especially in the hollow centres of chickens and turkeys) and these will prevent proper heat penetration. Frozen foods must be thoroughly defrosted before being cooked so that proper heat penetration can be achieved right through to the very centre of the food.
8. Proper food thermometers should be used in order to check the temperatures of hot and cold foods.

PROGRESS PAPER 11

Try to answer the following questions. Take special note of the model answers and, if you are still unsure, read the whole programme again.

There is no point in going any futher with this book until you have mastered the theory of temperature control.

Don't worry, though; you will master it if you go through the programme carefully a few times.

1 If we remove food from an oven, boiling pan, cooking-range, etc., and let it cool down slowly (perhaps by leaving it lying around the kitchen), what might happen?

2 How can we help a cooked chicken or joint of meat to cool quickly?

3 Could we cool a cooked joint in a fridge? (If not, why not?)

4 Is it permissible to display meat salads in an ordinary cabinet? (Explain your answer.)

5 At what temperature must ice cream be stored?

6 What must we be very careful about when cooking raw food that has been frozen? (Explain your answer.)

7 Is it permissible to re-heat food?

8 At what temperature should stew awaiting service be held in a *bain-marie?*

9 How can we tell if a frozen chicken has been properly defrosted?

10 Is it permissible to defrost frozen raw food in a refrigerator? (NOTE: you will have to think about this question carefully!)

ANSWERS

1 Any bacteria which have survived the cooking process will multiply and may reach dangerously high numbers. Bacterial spores (which will most probably have survived cooking) will germinate and the emerging bacteria will start to grow. Any bacteria which contaminate the food after cooking will also start to multiply in or on the food.

2 Cut or split it, into smaller pieces.

3 No. The hot meat would raise the temperature of the food already in the fridge and cooling would probably be delayed because ice would form on the outside of the food and insulate it.

4 It might be, if the salads were to be eaten within about 30 minutes. Otherwise the salad (containing meat) should be held at 10 °C (if to be eaten that day), or 5 °C within a refrigerated display cabinet.

5 Below −2.2 °C.

6 We must ensure that it has been fully defrosted otherwise ice at the centre of the food mass will insulate it and will prevent thorough heat penetration from taking place.

7 This is controversial; under some circumstances it might be OK, but overall it is not worth the risk. (The safest answer is 'No'.)

8 Above 65 °C.

9 Measure the temperature in the centre of the bird using a metal-probe thermometer. The temperature should be no lower than 10 °C–15 °C. (It can be cooked if its centre is above 10 °C.)

10 Yes it is! You may have thought otherwise, but you should note that this is frozen food: it will normally be at about −18 °C and a fridge's temperature will be higher than this. By using a fridge to defrost deep-frozen food, we can prevent the food from going above 10 °C. In practice, it is best to start the defrosting process in a fridge (if you have space available) and then complete the process by putting the food in a warm (contamination-free) place for a few hours to complete the process. You MUST be very careful of two things however. Firstly, ensure (by using an electronic metal-probe thermometer) that the centre of the food is above 10 °C–15 °C and, secondly, ensure that drips from the defrosting food do not fall on to other food. In practice, defrosting deep frozen food in a fridge is very slow but, if the precautions above are noted, it can be done and it can be useful.

PROGRAMME 12
Cleaning (Decontamination) I

1 We have seen that the three main areas of food hygiene practice are:

Contamination control which consists essentially of steps aimed at preventing food becoming contaminated in the first place.

Temperature control which is aimed at killing microbes in raw foods and preventing the multiplication (growth) of bacteria within a food.

Cleaning (the subject of this programme) which may be thought of as a form of decontamination, that is, removing or killing any microbes which enter the food environment.

Q Where might such contamination (of the food environment, such as working surfaces, utensils, etc.) come from in the first place?

A From raw foods brought into the food areas, from people, pets, pests and from the air (which might carry some contaminants — notably spores of bacteria and fungi).

---

2 Cleaning is, perhaps, one of the most misunderstood aspects of any of the branches of the science of hygiene. To most people, the words 'hygiene' and 'cleanliness' mean exactly the same. By this stage you will have realised that this is not the case. 'Hygiene' refers to all those measures which can be applied to the prevention of microbial food-borne illness and the science of food hygiene certainly involves far more than mere cleanliness alone. It is certainly true that cleanliness has a part to play in food-hygiene controls, but it is not the whole story.

Q Can we always see if a particular work surface, utensil, etc., is 'clean' AND uncontaminated?

A We can see whether it is 'clean', but we cannot see if it is contaminated or not. Microbes are so very small that we cannot see them with the naked eye (we know this already) and, therefore, we cannot 'see' microbial contamination.

3 There is a considerable, and very important, difference between **visual cleanliness** and **microbiological cleanliness**. If we spread soot on to a work preparation surface, it will be **visually dirty**, but the soot will probably not contain any microbes. On the other hand, if we spread bacteria onto a stainless steel table it could look perfectly clean and yet be **microbiologically dirty**.

Q We are concerned, so far as food hygiene goes, with microbiological cleanliness. Why will visual cleanliness not suffice: why is it not good enough?

A Because 'dirt', as such, does nobody any harm at all. It is only when 'dirt' contains microbes that potential danger arises. We can very easily remove 'dirt' but microbes tend to stick to work surfaces, and their tiny size makes it impossible to see them. We must do more than merely remove 'dirt' we can see in some instances and some areas (just where and when will become clear as our discussion proceeds). We need to eliminate the dirt we cannot see which consists, of course, of the microbes which will, in all probability, be contaminating surfaces, utensils, etc.

4 A food hygienist (as you will be if you continue to study and practice food hygiene) never uses the word 'dirt'. We are actually interested in microbial contamination and we must always remember that we 'clean' in order to **decontaminate** a microbe-contaminated surface, utensil, etc.

Q How can work surfaces, utensils, equipment, etc., become contaminated with microbes? (HINT: be careful when you answer this question, you are being asked how the work surface, etc. can become contaminated; you are NOT being asked to name the ultimate sources of contamination.)

A In order to answer this question you must first think about the ultimate sources of contamination and then decide how these sources could do the contaminating. The ultimate sources of contamination are (as we have seen before) man, animals, pests, raw food, air. As far as man is concerned, a food handler, or, of course, a customer for that matter, could contaminate a surface by coughing or sneezing on it, by touching it and so on. For example, a knife that is to be used as an eating utensil, should not have its blade touched by the hands. Food handlers can also contaminate surfaces, etc. because of poor food hygiene practices. Pests, especially flies, can contaminate surfaces, etc. by walking upon them. Raw food, as we know, is frequently contaminated with microbes from source. We have discussed how raw foods may contaminate by the various ways in which cross-contamination can arise (see Programme 9). Microbes, especially bacterial and fungal spores, can be moved around in the air and may consequently land on a surface, piece of equipment, etc.

Contamination may arise in any of these ways (and in other ways which, no doubt, you could think up for yourself by now). The task that we must perform while 'cleaning' is to decontaminate surfaces, equipment, utensils, etc., which may well have become contaminated.

5 We know the real purpose of 'cleaning'. It is to ensure, as far as we can within a practical work situation, that contamination (with microbes) is reduced as far as possible.

Two points need to be noted here. Firstly, it is ALWAYS necessary to prevent contamination from arising when possible. This is not always possible of course, because we have to put raw food on some preparation surface or other, we must allow food consumers to eat with knives and forks and so on. We know that some contamination is inevitable. Having accepted this, we must remember that the contamination which will inevitably arise MUST be reduced as far as possible.

The last five words give us a clue to the second point to note here. It is NOT possible to remove, or kill, absolutely every organism that may be on every surface, etc. at all times. We must, therefore, be content with reducing the degree of contamination as far as practical considerations will allow. If we decontaminate properly we will attain an acceptable level of safety. If we are careless, however, or do not do the right things in the right ways, we will inevitably cause great danger.

Q What is the difference between 'cleaning' and 'sanitisation'? (HINT: don't worry if you cannot answer this yet. Have a guess. It may help you to guess correctly if you remember that a 'sanitiser' is the correct, technical term used in food hygiene for a 'disinfectant'.)

A Cleaning is a process whereby dirt (including any microbes which are present) is washed off a surface, etc. Usually this is achieved by means of water and a degreasing agent (such as a detergent like washing-up liquid). However, no matter how well we wash a surface, some microbes will usually stick to it. ('Surface' could be the blade of a knife, a slicing machine blade, a cup, a table top, and so on.) To 'sanitise' a surface means to treat it with water to which has been added a 'sanitiser', which is a substance intended to kill any microbes that remain on the surface after 'cleaning'.

Sometimes, 'cleaning' will achieve a sufficient degree of safety. In other cases cleaning is not enough and sanitisation (i.e. the use of a sanitiser) becomes essential. We shall discuss these points below as well as discussing what detergents do, and what types of 'sanitiser' should be used in which situations.

---

6 Now that we have a clear idea of the difference between the terms 'cleaning' and 'sanitisation', we can consider when each of these processes should be used and how they should be employed in practice to obtain the maximum effect.

It is of the utmost importance that you always remember that ALL surfaces, equipment, etc., require cleaning but that some require sanitisation in addition.

YOU CANNOT SANITISE A DIRTY SURFACE

This sentence is so very important that you must commit it to memory and always remember exactly what it means. If you apply a sanitiser to any surface which has not previously been cleaned (i.e. degreased), your sanitiser will have little effect.

There are two main reasons why this is so. Firstly, the grease and food particles on the surface may well neutralise the sanitiser before it even has a chance to act on any microbes which are present. Secondly, grease acts like an umbrella, shielding any bacteria beneath it from the sanitiser.

Q How much grease do you think would have to be present on a surface to protect a large number of bacteria?

A Very little. Remember how extremely small the bacteria are and you will realise that a very large number could 'hide' under even a small amount of grease. For this reason we must be very careful indeed to ensure that surfaces to be sanitised are degreased very thoroughly.

NOTE: Whenever the term 'surface' is used in this programme, it means all surfaces with which microbes could come into contact. This would therefore include knife blades, slicing-machine blades, crockery, pans, etc., as well as the more obvious 'surfaces' such as food-preparation tables.

---

7 We can see, therefore, that we will need to perform a lot of cleaning. Sanitisation is a further stage that does not need to be performed on all surfaces on all occasions (this will become clearer a little later in our discussion).

The only really effective cleaning-agent available to us is water but, strange as it may seem, water alone is of no use. It is incapable of wetting many types of surface.

Q Can you explain this rather strange statement? Water is, of course, wet and yet we are saying that it cannot actually wet some surfaces. Have a guess why this is so. (HINT: think of water running off the back of a duck!)

A Water alone will not 'wet' any surface that does not absorb it. A cotton raincoat absorbs water and is therefore wetted by it. A plastic mac does not and the water merely drips off. If you spread water on to a stainless steel surface it will form globules, it won't spread evenly over the whole surface.

This is because water, like all liquids, has a 'tension' at its surface (**surface tension**). This causes it to form globules on any surface which will not absorb it. Grease has the same effect and, in this case, the reason why water alone will not penetrate the grease is due to the molecular structures of the water and the grease.

---

8 Most things are either soluble or insoluble in water as you know. What you perhaps do not know is that molecules of substances can be either **hydrophilic** ('water loving') or **hydrophobic** ('water fearing').

Hydrophobic molecules (such as the molecules of fats and grease from food) repel water molecules, whereas hydrophilic ones attract water molecules. Water cannot get near to grease for the simple reason that the hydrophobic molecules repel the water molecules. In order to allow water to catch hold of grease molecules, we need a substance that is both hydrophobic AND hydrophilic; but how could we have such a substance that is both things at the same time?

Actually, the answer is quite simple. Some substances are **bipolar**, i.e. they have two 'poles' (like the North and South Poles on a compass). Such substances have molecules that are very like a rod — one end is hydrophilic (it loves water and is attracted to it) and the other end is hydrophobic (it repels water but will attract and attach to another hydrophobic molecule such as a grease molecule). If you just use your imagination a little you will soon see that what at first appears to be very complex, is actually very simple. If we add a bipolar substance to water, its water-loving ends will stick to the water molecules. If we now put the water on to a greasy surface, the water-fearing ends of the bipolar water additive will stick to the grease. Now we have managed to hook a water molecule on to a grease molecule (the bipolar water additive acts as our hook). The water can now carry the grease off the surface without any difficulty. The water will also spread all over the surface: its surface tension has been lowered by the bipolar additive which allows the water to 'wet' the surface fully instead of just sitting on it in the form of globules.

Q Do you know of any bipolar water-additives we commonly use to help water degrease a surface?

A You could have said 'soap', which is used to wash greasy hands, but this actually works in a slightly different way which need not concern us here. The bipolar substance usually used is 'detergent' — the stuff that washing-up liquids are made of. By adding detergent to water we can help the water to fully wet a surface and enable it to wash grease and fat molecules off the surface as well.

---

9 Since so many different brands of detergent are available, perhaps we should ask if one brand is better than another. Certainly advertisements would have us believe so, but are the adverts correct? In fact, they are not. So far as degreasing effectiveness is concerned, any good-quality detergent will do. Low-quality brands are not as effective because the concentration of actual detergent in them is lower than in their more expensive counterparts. Commercial, brand-name, detergents (most usually called 'washing-up liquids') have several things added to them to make them appear better. Colours and scents are often used, foaming-agents are usually added so that a thick foam is formed on solution in water. In fact, the thickness or extent of the foam does not indicate that the agent is any better than another. Foaming agents can make a detergent produce more foam than it would otherwise do, and this impresses the user, even though it is of no real consequence. Salt is added to some washing-up liquids to thicken them, the idea being that most people think that a thick liquid is more concentrated than a thinner one. In practice, it is best to buy detergent in bulk (products such as Teepol are readily available) and to purchase the straight detergent rather than pay for more additives which we do not need.

Q Will a detergent kill microbes?

A No, the job the detergent is designed to do is to degrease and so enable water to wash contamination off a surface. The action is therefore one of microbial removal rather than one of microbial killing. Remember that although some microbes will be washed off a surface, some will remain stuck to it.

---

10 The more grease there is on a surface, the more detergent will be used in removing it. For this reason, it is necessary to remove gross contamination (scraps of food, etc.) from a surface before washing commences as otherwise we will be wasting detergent. Having removed food scraps, we can proceed to wash the surface. The detergent manufacturers' instructions regarding the quantity of detergent to use should be followed. About two egg-cup fulls to 4.5 litres (a gallon) of water is sufficient in most cases (unless a very cheap, and therefore very weak, product is used). No advantage can be gained from using more. The detergent should be used in hot water, as it is a far more effective degreasing-agent in hot rather than in cold water. Although not critical, it is best to use water which can just be tolerated by a gloved hand.

Q If the detergent in the water gets used up as it degreases more of a surface (each molecule of detergent is attached to each molecule of grease, only one molecule of grease can be held by one detergent molecule) how can we tell when the detergent/water mixture needs changing?

A Before examining the answer to this question we must first dispel a myth held by many people which can cause problems.

You should NOT merely add more detergent to a detergent/water mixture to 'revitalise' it. The water is becoming progressively more contaminated with microbes as well as grease as you wash out your cloth in it, wash more plates in it, and so on. When cleaning a surface with detergent and water, we are not merely removing grease, we are removing microbial contamination also. Some microbes will remain stuck to the surface, it is true, but many will be removed. If we simply add more detergent, we will allow our water to remove more grease, but we will be washing with highly contaminated water. This is the reason why hands should always be washed in running water and why showering is more hygienic than bathing.

The answer to our question is that we must use the foam to indicate when our washing-water needs changing. If a commercial brand-name detergent is used, this can be misleading as the added foaming-agents allow the foam to persist for far longer than it otherwise would. No such problem arises with Teepol and we can safely say that the detergent and water mixture should be entirely renewed when the foam is clearly breaking down. DON'T wait until it is non-existent, the water and detergent should be renewed when the foam first appears to be lessening.

11 Detergent/water washing will remove a great deal of contamination from a surface, if it is done properly. Therefore we will be greatly reducing the degree of contamination. However, some microbes will still be adhering to the surface, and we now have to decide if this is acceptable or not. It all depends on the surface and what it is used for. As a general rule, any surface with which food does not make direct contact can be cleaned only and does not require sanitising. (The notable exceptions are wash-basins, sinks and conveniences which DO need to be sanitised as well as being washed with detergent and water.)

If, however, the surface is liable to make contact with food, it needs to be sanitised because washing alone will not reduce the contamination to a safe level.

Q We know that a detergent/water mixture washes microbes off a surface. What does a sanitiser do?

A It is a substance that is designed to kill microbes with which it comes into contact. In practice, the different types of sanitiser available do not all do this to the same degree (as we shall shortly see).

12 We must always wash a surface before we sanitise it. Not to do so will result in the sanitiser being rendered ineffective or in the microbes being shielded from the sanitiser by the grease on the surface. It is inevitable that some grease will be present on virtually all surfaces even if we cannot actually see it. In practice we have two different types of 'cleaning' or rather 'decontamination processes' which we must use under different circumstances. These are:

Two-Stage	Three-Stage
(i) Remove gross contamination (scraps of food, etc.)	(i) Remove gross contamination (scraps of food, etc.)
(ii) Wash with hot water/detergent	(ii) Wash with hot water/detergent
	(iii) Apply sanitiser solution

You should notice that the first two stages are the same in each case. It is only the application of a sanitiser that distinguishes three-stage from two-stage methods. We shall discuss each method in more detail in the next programme; for the moment you should memorise the stages of the two methods.

KEY FACTS

1 The food environment (storage and preparation areas, surfaces, preparation tables, utensils, etc.) will readily become contaminated with microbes. Cleaning is a process of decontamination intended to remove the contamination in the food environment and thus make it safe to use for food preparation once again.

2 There is a difference between a surface or area looking clean and being decontaminated. Microbes are so small that we simply cannot see them. We need to attain a state of 'microbiological cleanliness', simple 'visual cleanliness' is not good enough.

3 It is never possible to remove contamination completely; all that can be done is to reduce it as far as possible.

4 Cleaning is a process whereby 'dirt' and grease are washed from a surface. This is achieved by means of hot water and a degreasing agent such as a detergent. Detergent must be added to the cleaning water so that it can cut through the grease.

5 Washing with detergent and water will not kill any microbes; it merely removes some of them. In some cases, this will be adequate. On some surfaces, and with some utensils, it is necessary to obtain a higher degree of decontamination than washing alone can achieve. Chemical substances called 'sanitisers' can achieve this because they kill the organisms which are left after washing has been carried out.

6 It is NOT possible to sanitise a dirty or greasy surface. Careful washing with hot water and detergent must always be done before sanitisation is carried out. Sanitisers cannot cut through grease.

7 Detergent/water mixtures used for washing should be changed often because they soon become contaminated themselves.

8 Two types of decontamination process are used under different circumstances:

Two-stage (for surfaces, etc., which will NOT come into direct contact with food)

(i) Remove gross contamination (scraps of food, etc.)
(ii) Wash with hot water and detergent mixture

Three-stage (for surfaces, etc. which WILL come into direct contact with food)

(i) Remove gross contamination (scraps of food, etc.)
(ii) Wash with hot water and detergent mixture
(iii) Apply sanitiser solution

PROGRESS PAPER 12

Here is another progress paper for you to try. Do your best and remember to attempt each question, even if you only guess the answer. Check your answers with the model answers, but remember that the model answers are sometimes longer and more complex than yours need to be. So long as you get the gist of the answer you are right. Re-read the programme if you do not get all of the answers correct, and cannot understand the model answers.

1 What are the three main areas of food hygiene practice?

2 What is the difference between a surface being 'visually clean' and being 'microbiologically clean'?

3 What are the major sources of contamination for surfaces (including of course, utensils and equipment)?

4 What is the difference between 'cleaning' and 'sanitisation'?

5 What can you NOT do with a dirty surface?

6 Why do we clean a surface before we sanitise it?

7 What is the most commonly used agent that is added to water to help it to degrease or wet a surface?

8 Can detergent kill bacteria?

9 When should we renew a water/detergent solution which we have been using for washing?

10 What are the stages of two-stage and three-stage cleaning?

ANSWERS

1 Contamination control, temperature control and cleaning (decontamination).

2 A surface which is 'visually clean' is one that has no visible dirt on it. Because microbes are not visible to the naked eye it could, however, have microbes on it. A 'microbiologically clean' surface is one where microbial contamination has been reduced to an acceptably low level. (It cannot, in practice, ever be totally cleared of microbes but their numbers can be greatly reduced so as to achieve a level of safety that is reasonable.)

3 Personnel (food handlers, etc.) customers, pet animals, pests (such as insects, rodents, birds), raw foods, water supplies and the air. (NOTE: In those countries, including the UK, where water supplies are treated by means of chlorine, such water is unlikely to be a source of contamination.)

4 Cleaning is a process designed to remove some contamination from a surface and to degrease it. Sanitisation is a process which sometimes has to be used to reduce the degree of contamination even further (after cleaning) by means of a sanitiser (which is a substance designed to kill microbes).

5 You cannot sanitise it.

6 Because the grease and other major contaminants on the surface would probably neutralise the sanitiser and grease would shield the microbes so that the sanitiser could not come into direct contact with them.

7 Detergent.

8 No; it is an agent which helps water to wash away microbes on a surface because it helps the water to wet the surface by connecting water molecules to grease molecules.

9 When the foam obviously starts to break down.

10 **Two-stage** (i) Remove gross contamination (food scraps, etc.)
(ii) Wash with hot water and detergent mixture

Three-stage (i) Remove gross contamination (food scraps, etc.)
(ii) Wash with hot water and detergent mixture
(iii) Apply sanitiser solution

NOTE: if the correct type of sanitiser is used, it will not be necessary to dry or rinse the sanitised surface: it should be left to air-dry. (We discuss various types of sanitiser in the next programme.)

PROGRAMME 13
Cleaning (Decontamination) II

1 We have seen that two-stage cleaning methods (in which a sanitiser is NOT used) can be suitable and sufficient for some applications. A three-stage method must be used in cases where a sanitiser is needed to reduce the degree of contamination of a surface to an absolute minimum.

(REMEMBER: 'surface' includes preparation surfaces (tables, cutting boards, etc.), equipment (slicer blades, etc.), utensils, cups, plates and so on.

Q On which type of surface MUST we use a three-stage cleaning method?

A On those surfaces that are liable to come into direct contact with food.

---

2 The following surfaces are those which must have the **microbial load** (the numbers of microbes present) reduced to an absolute minimum because they come into direct contact with food. The following list consists of examples only, and you may well be able to think of others yourself.

Food utensils
Machinery (e.g. slicers and mixers)
Eating utensils (including plates, cups, etc.)
Trays, etc. (if they come into direct contact with food)
Preparation surfaces
Cutting/chopping boards, etc.
Pans (used for food preparation)
Re-usable containers used for food
Wall surfaces behind or near preparation surfaces
(NOTE: wall areas which are not liable to come into contact with food require two-stage cleaning only)
Handbasins
Sinks
(NOTE: Conveniences also require sanitisation and this topic is dealt with in paragraph 7.)

Q How can we decide whether any particular surface requires a two-stage or a three-stage cleaning method?

A If it is liable to come into direct contact with food, use a three-stage method (i.e. the use of sanitiser is essential). In all other cases a good detergent and water wash (i.e. two stage method) is perfectly adequate.

3 Several different types of sanitiser exist. Some are good; many are not. You should be very careful to select sanitisers that will do the job you want them to do (i.e. to kill microbes) and which can be safely used near food. Having selected the right agent, you must then use it properly (always take special note of the manufacturer's instructions).

We will not discuss all the available types of sanitiser as many are not suitable for use in food premises (or are ineffective for such use) and some, although effective, are too expensive even to be considered. We will restrict our discussion to the **pine-oils, phenol derivatives, quaternary ammonium compounds (QACs)** (pronounced quat-*tern*-ary) and the various **chlorine generating agents.**

Q What types of organism do we wish to kill with sanitisers?

A Bacteria, viruses, fungi and intestinal parasites such as worms.

4 Not all sanitisers will kill all of these. In fact, the parasites and fungi are rather hard to kill with those sanitisers which are safe enough for use near food. Fortunately, bacteria are the biggest problem in food hygiene so we will try to kill them with sanitisers. Some viruses can survive treatment with most sanitisers, and of course fungal spores will be resistant to some extent. The most serious problem is caused by bacterial spores, as they are very resistant indeed to chemical attack.

It can be seen that, however good our three-stage decontamination technique may be, we cannot STERILISE a surface by means of the sanitisers we can safely employ near food.

Q What does 'sterilise' mean? What do you think the difference is between 'sterilisation' and 'sanitisation'?

A To 'sterilise' means to kill all microbial life (including spores). It is a word that is often misused. It should only ever be used when we mean that all microbial life is to be killed, including bacterial spores. This aim cannot be achieved by using food premises sanitisers. Some types of sanitiser are **sterilants** but they cannot be used near food due to their toxic nature. Some sanitisers are, incorrectly, called 'sterilants'; this is a misuse of the word. A sanitiser, on the other hand, is an agent which is capable of killing most types of microbe.

5 We are, therefore, left with the conclusion that, even when we choose our sanitisers most carefully and use them correctly, we cannot destroy all the microbes liable to be present on a surface. We can do nothing about this fact. It is a practical limitation that we must live with.

In practice, fortunately, this limitation should not create too many problems for us, because the sanitisers that are available to use are well capable of creating a sufficient degree of safety. There are two stages or degrees of decontamination. When we only wash a surface and don't use a sanitiser, we reduce the number of microbes on it quite significantly. When we need a greater reduction in the microbial load (the number of microbes present), we can achieve it by using an appropriate sanitiser.

It is true that we will still not be able to kill all bacteria, viruses, or spores, but the level of decontamination achieved will be sufficient for a reasonable degree of safety if our original washing is good enough.

Q Why is it acceptable to reduce the microbial load to a low level, rather than to kill ALL the microbes present on a surface?

A Because it is the number of microbes present that matters (i.e. the microbial load). This was also true in the case of the temperature controls we discussed in Programmes 10 and 11. We simply cannot destroy all microbes (bacterial spores are especially resistant) but we can keep their numbers down. If a few viruses are left on a surface there will be too few to cause disease (you must have a minimum number of them before they can overwhelm the body's defences and cause disease). Any bacteria left on the surface after decontamination will not reproduce. (As long as we have washed and degreased the surface, there will be no food available for them to use for growth, and there will be too few of them on the surface to cause disease, even if they do get on to food).

We can, therefore, feel confident that, so long as we can reduce the number of microbes on a surface sufficiently, we can achieve the necessary degree of safety. We must, however, be extremely careful to ensure that we do reduce their numbers to as low a level as can be achieved in practice.

---

6 Of the many varieties of sanitiser that are available, probably the most common are the pine-oil extracts. These are the pleasant-smelling disinfectants which are freely on sale for domestic use. ('Disinfectants' is a term that should not be used — we refer to 'sanitisers', not disinfectants so far as food hygiene is concerned.) Apart from imparting a pleasant smell to the areas where they are used, these agents are of absolutely no use whatsoever as sanitisers. They are only mentioned here to warn against their use near food. They would be totally ineffective.

Q One reason why 'pine disinfectants' should not be used near food is that they are ineffective sanitisers. Can you think of any other reason?

A The disinfectant would taint food. Sanitisers for use near food, and within food rooms, must firstly be effective but, in addition, they must present no danger to the food either by leaving toxic residues or by tainting food. These requirements greatly limit the possible range of sanitisers we might use in food premises.

7 The substance called **phenol** is one of the oldest disinfectants in use. In the early days of surgical operations and hospital care it made a very great difference to a patient's chances of survival. These dark days have gone and phenol itself has long ceased to be used, primarily because of its toxic properties.

Several different substances can be made from phenol however, which are far less toxic and have a greater power to kill microbes than does phenol itself. Two such substances — the **white fluid** and **black fluid** (commercially marketed by Jeyes) — are extremely effective in medical environments. These fluids cannot, however, be used in food areas because they would taint food to a considerable extent.

There is little doubt, however, that overall, these fluids are the best agents currently available for sanitisation of conveniences. They can be harmful: they are certainly irritating; especially on the skin, and must therefore be used with care (together with protective clothing such as gloves, apron, etc.).

Q How could microbial contamination in conveniences find its way into the food areas or on to food?

A Food handlers must use the toilet sometimes and it is very easy to carry contamination on the hands. Of course, no matter how well-sanitised the conveniences may be, it is still possible for food handlers to contaminate the hands from their own gut. It is still necessary, of course, to ensure that the conveniences are as well sanitised as is reasonably practicable, and it is the white and black fluids that can do this job most effectively.

White fluid is better because black fluid stains the ceramic material of the bowl or urinal. As always, the manufacturer's instructions must be followed and all warnings noted. NOTE: it is ESSENTIAL to ensure that hands are properly washed following toilet use (for whatever reason) no matter how well-sanitised the conveniences may be. (See Programme 14 which deals specifically with the topic of personal hygiene). Never enter conveniences in your overalls, because they will pick up contamination there and pass it on to food.

8 We now know that pine disinfectants should not be used in the food environment due to their virtual total lack of effectiveness, and their tainting characteristics. The phenolic white and black fluids can be used, with very good effect, in conveniences but not near food. Detergents, of the type most commonly used, do not kill microbes but there exist some detergents which *do* have an antimicrobial property. These are the **quaternary ammonium compounds** or QACs. QACs are very good sanitisers if used in the right situations and for the right purpose. They are very effective as skin 'antiseptics'. They are relatively very safe to use and are extensively marketed as **bactericidal detergents** for use in the food environment.

Q These agents are usually sold on the basis of their antimicrobial AND detergent properties. The idea is that you can use them to clean (degrease) and sanitise at the same time. Do you think this is advisable? If not, why not?

A Remember that we have stressed that you cannot sanitise a dirty surface. QACs have both detergent and bactericidal (bacteria-killing) properties. It is very convenient to be able to use one agent to do both things and therefore to save both labour and effort.

Unfortunately, life is rarely that simple, and claims for these agents are often exaggerated. To have most effect, a QAC should be used as a cleaning agent first and then fresh agent should be used as a sanitiser. This negates their advantage and, as they are somewhat expensive, we would increase our costs if we used them in this manner. All in all, the golden rule still holds true — you cannot sanitise a dirty surface.

9 In fact there really is no short-cut to good hygiene and proper results will only be achieved after effort. QACs are very good for some applications but far less good for others. They do have the serious drawback that they are NOT very effective against a family of bacteria known as the enterobacteriaceae to which our arch-enemies the Salmonellae belong. As it is this group of organisms that causes us most problems in the food environment, there is little point in using an agent that is not very effective against them.

QACs have little effect on viruses or fungi and none against bacterial spores. We are left with the conclusion, therefore, that these agents are not ideal for our purposes.

Q What properties do we want a sanitiser to possess if we are to use it within the food environment? What do we want it to be able to do?

A Ideally, we want it to kill a wide variety of organisms, we want it to be safe near food (to be neither toxic nor tainting), and we want it to resist being **denatured** (having its properties changed) by organic material, (grease, etc.) which may be present on a surface.

(NOTE: 'organic material' means food, food scraps and particles, grease, fat, etc.)

---

10 Unfortunately, there is no ideal sanitiser available and we must make do with the best compromise we can get. QACs are ideal for washing and sanitising glasses, table cutlery and crockery (in automatic dish washers for example) but they are not much value elsewhere in the food environment.

We are forced, therefore, to accept a compromise as far as sanitisers for use within food environments are concerned. We don't have a perfect agent available so we must use the very best that IS available.

Fortunately there is one type of sanitiser that does possess extremely useful properties from the food hygiene point of view. Those agents which release chlorine into solution when mixed with water are not perfect but they are very useful.

Q Can you think of somewhere else, besides food premises, where chlorine is used as a sanitiser?

A The water recirculated in swimming baths is usually sanitised by means of chlorine. The vast majority of mains water is also made safe to drink by means of a series of purification processes which always includes treatment with chlorine.

---

11 Chlorine is so very effective as a sanitiser when dissolved in water, that it can be recommended for use in virtually all areas used in connection with food storage, transport and handling. It is effective against most varieties of bacteria liable to present a risk of either food poisoning or food spoilage. It is less effective against fungi and viruses, but it does have some useful killing potential against many varieties of these organisms. It can even kill some spores BUT it must be applied in concentrations far too high for use near food to be of any use in a food environment as a spore-killer.

Q We have seen that chlorine dissolved in water is very effective as a sanitiser. A sanitiser's ability to kill microbes is only one of its properties of interest to us. What other properties must we consider before we can conclude that chlorine in water can be used near food?

A We should remember that it is intended to use the agent near food and therefore, it must not leave toxic (poisonous) deposits which could get on to the food. It must not taint food and it should be resistant to being made ineffective by organic material. Preferably it should be capable of wetting a surface evenly.

12 Chlorine, when dissolved in water, is an extremely good sanitiser for use in the food environment but, as we have shown, it is not perfect. It will not leave toxic residues which might get on to food IF it is used carefully. It will not taint food either (despite its strong smell when used in swimming baths) so long as it is used according to the manufacturer's instructions. It is very effective at killing a wide variety of microbes if, once again, it is correctly used.

It is not perfect because of two properties it does NOT possess. Chlorine is highly susceptible to being made ineffective if it comes into contact with organic matter, or if it is left exposed to the air for a few hours, and it does not 'wet' a surface very well (it will not cut through grease at all).

These two shortcomings mean that it is not very effective as a sanitiser in conveniences, and cannot be used on any surface that is not already degreased to a considerable degree.

Q How could we effectively degrease a surface before applying a chlorine/water solution?

A We should carefully wash the surface with a detergent/hot water solution having first removed gross contamination (such as food scraps).

---

13 We already know that we must degrease a surface and make it visually clean before we use any sanitiser (you cannot sanitise a dirty surface), so the fact that this process is essential before using a chlorine sanitiser should come as no real surprise. When such sanitisers are used, however, our preliminary cleaning must be excellent. It MUST be very carefully carried out if the chlorine agent is to be as effective as possible.

You should note at this point that proper standards of food hygiene can only ever be attained and maintained if we expend suitable and sufficient effort. No 'magic' agents or short cuts exist. Good food hygiene standards (which we know are both essential and well worth the effort) are only ever obtained if we are both diligent and careful.

Q What do you think 'suitable and sufficient effort' means in the last paragraph?

A 'Suitable' means doing the right things at the right times. 'Sufficient' means that we must give as much effort as we can to achieve the desired result of ensuring that the food our consumers eat is as safe as we can make it.

---

14 Chlorine in water is therefore the very best sanitiser we can use in a food environment. Like all chemicals it must be respected and be used carefully. If we are not careful with it not only will it be less effective than it should be, but in addition, it may well present a danger to us or to the consumers of our food.

Chlorine-generating agents come in many forms — liquids (such as highly concentrated Domestos and the more dilute Milton), crystals (such as Milton crystals), and tablets which dissolve in water (such as Maws, Boots tablets which are usually termed 'sterilising tablets' by the manufacturers).

The tablets are more effective than the liquids, they are safer to use and they retain their effectiveness for longer periods during storage (but they MUST be kept dry). ALWAYS follow the manufacturer's instructions exactly when using these agents. It is not a good idea to use a larger number of tablets than the manufacturer recommends as such a practice will NOT be more effective. In fact, you may even run the risk of tainting a surface.

Q We know that we must 'clean' a surface to be sanitised. We also know that hot water must be used with detergent. Should hot water or cold water be used with a sanitiser?

A Hot water increases the effectiveness of the sanitiser and in the case of chlorine generating tablets, it also helps the tablets to dissolve.

15 If the chlorine-based sanitiser is to have its greatest effect, it is essential to use it in the correct way. The following procedure should ALWAYS be followed:

(i) Clear all gross contamination (food scraps, etc.)
(ii) Clean (degrease) by means of a hot water/detergent solution.
(iii) Mix the sanitiser in hot water (as hot as can be tolerated with a gloved hand) in the concentration recommended by the manufacturer.
(iv) Ensure that you are wearing proper protective clothing (especially gloves and a waterproof apron to protect your from splashes).
(v) Apply the sanitiser solution to the surface (or immerse utensils, etc., into the solution) and leave it in contact for at least 30 minutes.

Leaving the solution in contact for at least 30 minutes is called the **contact time**. Microbes exposed to a sanitiser do not all die instantaneously. We must give the sanitiser time to work. When we are immersing utensils into a sanitiser we can leave them for 30 minutes. When washing sanitiser solution on to a surface, it is essential to get a lot on to it (a quick 'wipe over' with a cloth, etc., is NOT good enough). Be careful not to splash it around, of course, but make sure you really wet the surface with the sanitiser, then leave it to dry naturally (i.e. to 'air-dry').

When chlorine agents are used it is NOT necessary to rinse the surface off. You can simply let it dry naturally which will allow the agent enough time to work properly. NOTE: if a surface is to be used within a short time of being sanitised, it may be advisable to rinse it off before use, in this case, the sanitiser MUST be left in contact for at least 30 minutes before being rinsed.

If a chlorine agent is used inside any food-processing equipment (e.g. mixers, vending machines, etc.) the agent MUST be rinsed out (after 30 minutes contact time), because the sanitiser could lodge in high concentrations inside any pipes, channels, etc., of the equipment.

Q If we misuse a sanitiser we might run the risk of harming the food we produce. (We could taint it, for example.) What other kind of harm could we do?

A We could injure ourselves! This is why it is essential to use all sanitisers ONLY in accordance with the manufacturer's instructions and especially why all safety rules relating to their use MUST be obeyed.

---

16 You must remember to use fresh sanitiser each time you start a cleaning cycle — once mixed in water, it does not 'keep' for long because the active ingredient evaporates. Use disposable cloths or CLEAN mops, otherwise you will only be adding more contamination than you will remove.

NOTE: chlorine-generating tablets can most usually be recognised by the fact that they contain the following chemicals — **sodium dichloro-s-triazinetrione,** or **sodium dichloroisocyanurate.** A little detergent can be added to the water used for mixing. This will increase the efficiency of the sanitiser because it allows the sanitiser solution to wet the surface more easily.

Q When using a sanitiser, are we using a two-stage or a three-stage cleaning method?

A A three-stage method, i.e. removing gross contamination (scraps, etc.), then degreasing (very well) with water and detergent and, thirdly, applying the sanitiser solution.

17 The many operations performed in connection with the preparation, service, and sale of food must be well organised if they are to be performed efficiently. Such organisation must include all necessary cleaning performed in operating a business on food premises.

It would be extremely inefficient if we merely cleaned different areas of food premises as we felt like it. **Cleaning schedules** are devices to help us plan what to clean and when to clean it (and whether to clean by a two-stage or three-stage method).

Such schedules consist of lists of areas and items to be cleaned, together with information on the frequency of cleaning (after use, daily, weekly, etc.), along with details of cleaning methods to be used and agent(s) to be employed.

Q Cleaning schedules detail the formal, routine cleaning that must go on within all food premises — is this the only cleaning we need? (Explain your answer.)

A No. We must never forget that cleaning is really a process of decontamination. If we relied only on our cleaning schedules, we would run the risk of contamination building up. This would increase the risk of food contamination arising and would also make cleaning more difficult.

The rule to remember is that 'dirt', 'waste', and all forms of decontamination MUST be kept down to a minimum. The only way to do this is to 'clean as you go'. This means wiping up spillages as they occur, washing utensils, etc., as soon as they have been used, and generally preventing the accumulation of waste, grease, food scraps, etc.

18 One special form of cleaning deserves special mention. The washing of crockery and eating utensils is more efficiently carried out by means of automatic washing machines. These usually include a sanitisation cycle after a detergent/hot water wash. Finally, a hot water rinse completes the process. The sanitiser used is frequently a quaternary ammonium compound which is most suitable for such a purpose.

All crockery and utensils should be left to **air-dry** and should NOT be dried with cloths (which could add contamination to the cleansed dishes, plates, etc.).

When an automatic dishwasher is not used (it cannot be used for pans for example), it is, of course, then necessary to use sinks. When sinks are used, the **two-sink method** should be adopted.

This consists of two sinks, one containing a water/detergent mixture and the other a water/sanitiser solution. The water in each case should be about 80 °C (at this temperature it can just be tolerated by a gloved hand). The articles to be washed are first cleaned in the water and detergent and then rinsed in the sanitiser solution. They should then be left to air-dry and should not be dried with a cloth. If any articles must be dried quickly, DISPOSABLE paper towels should be used. Care must be taken to cleanse and sanitise dishcloths, scouring pads, etc., after use. (Wash them well in water and detergent, and then stand them in a water/chlorine-generator solution for 30 minutes.) Failure to observe these precautions will only serve to create a risk of contamination from the dishcloth, scouring pad, etc.

Quaternary ammonium compounds are also suitable for use as the sanitiser in the second sink in the two-sink washing method.

KEY FACTS

1. In most cases, it is not possible to kill all the microbes that may be present on a surface or on utensils. Usually it is perfectly adequate to reduce their number to a minimum but, in order to do so, it is absolutely essential to clean carefully and well.
2. Many types of sanitiser exist, but only a few of them can be used near food. Some may be poisonous if they get on to food and others may taint the food.
3. There are no short-cuts to food hygiene and 'one-stage' sanitisers are not good enough for our purposes.
4. Great care must be taken to allow surfaces, utensils, etc., to dry naturally (to air-dry) following cleaning and sanitisation. Cloths and floor mops can be a source of contamination. Disposable cloths should be used and mops must be cleaned *and* sanitised after use. If you must use dishcloths, sanitise them carefully after each use.
5. It is always necessary to use strong disinfectants in conveniences. Special attention should be paid to the under and upper sides of toilet seats, to door handles, etc.
6. Many sanitisers can be dangerous to use. ALWAYS follow safety instructions and NEVER mix different sanitisers together (poisonous fumes could be given off if you do).
7. Cleaning schedules should be used to enable us to ensure that all areas, utensils and equipment receive proper cleaning.
8. It is best to 'clean as you go' as far as possible so that the contamination load within the food premises is kept to a minimum.

PROGRESS PAPER 13

Now try to answer the questions below. Check your answers with the model answers and remember to revise the programme if you feel that you have not completely understood and learned its contents.

Your answers need not be exactly like the models, or as detailed in many cases. So long as you get the 'gist' of the answer, that will be perfectly sufficient. As always, write all your answers on a separate sheet of paper before looking at the model answers.

1 What types of surface must have a three-stage cleaning process (including use of a sanitiser) applied to them? (Give examples).

2 What is the difference in meaning between the terms 'sanitisation' and 'sterilisation'?

3 Is it possible to kill all the microbes on a surface by means of sanitisers?

4 Why can't we use a strong-smelling sanitiser (a disinfectant) in a food environment?

5 What must we always do to a surface before we apply a sanitiser to it?

6 What type of sanitiser is the best for use in conveniences?

7 What types of sanitiser are the best for use in the majority of areas in food premises (e.g. the food-preparation surfaces)?

8 Why is it important always to follow the manufacturer's instructions very carefully when using a sanitiser?

9 What is meant by the 'two-sink' method of washing up?

10 What must be done with dishcloths to make them safe to use?

ANSWERS

1 Those surfaces with which food is liable to come into direct contact. For example: food utensils, machinery (slicers, mixers, etc.); eating utensils; trays; etc.; preparation surfaces; cutting/chopping boards; pans; wall surfaces (but only those parts liable to come into direct contact with food, e.g. those behind preparation tables); re-usable food containers; handbasins, sinks. NOTE: in addition, conveniences also need to be sanitised.

2 'Sterilisation' means that ALL the microbes on a surface are killed. This can only be reliably achieved in a laboratory. We can attain a suitable degree of safety in the food environment if we 'sanitise' surfaces, etc., which means treating them with an agent that will kill a large number of the microbes on the surface but cannot kill all of them.

3 No, it is not. We can kill a large proportion of them, however, and this will enable us to attain a sufficient level of safety if we use the right sanitiser in the right way.

4 Because residues of the agent would be left on surfaces and, if picked up by food, such residues might prove to be toxic to consumers or would be liable to taint the food.

5 We must ensure that it is degreased to a high degree (by using a hot water/detergent solution after having removed gross contamination such as food scraps).

6 White fluid (e.g. Jeyes white fluid).

7 Chlorine-generating agents, especially the soluble tablets.

8 Because, otherwise the agent may not be effective or danger may be created to us or to our food consumers.

9 First wash in a hot water/detergent solution then rinse in a sanitiser/water solution. (Leave items to air-dry as far as possible, but if it is essential to wipe dishes, etc., always use disposable paper.)

10 Wash them well in hot water/detergent solution then soak them in hot water/sanitiser solution (chlorine-generating type) for 30 minutes. Wring them out and allow them to dry.

PROGRAMME 14

Personal Hygiene

1 Television, radio and press advertisements frequently warn us of the dangers of bad, or even just inadequate, personal hygiene. The 'dangers' in the mind of the advertiser however, are concerned with what can most aptly be called 'social' consequences, i.e. if we do not bathe regularly (preferably with 'Brand X' soap of course), or use 'Brand Y' deodorants, perfumes, aftershave, etc., it is likely (or so the advertiser would have us believe) that we shall become social outcasts. No doubt there is some truth in such claims but, so far as food hygiene is concerned, the topic of personal hygiene concerns itself with matters of far greater importance than merely ensuring that we smell nice.

Human beings are a rich source of potential contamination of food. Personal hygiene, as far as food hygiene is concerned, consists of essential measures aimed at preventing human beings themselves from contaminating the foodstuffs others will eat. Social niceties may well be important, but social health is vastly more important.

Q Where, on or in a human being, do you think we might expect to find any micro-organisms?

A Microbes (including bacteria, fungi and viruses, together with metazoan and protozoan parasites sometimes) can be found in many parts of the human body. The main sites are:-

Skin — bacteria and fungi mostly

Mouth — (perhaps also lungs and throat) — bacteria, fungi or viruses

Nose and nasal passages — bacteria, fungi or viruses

Genital area — bacteria, fungi, viruses and (possibly) protozoa

Gastro-intestinal tract (gut) — bacteria, fungi, viruses and protozoan and metazoan parasites

Undoubtedly the nose, mouth and gut are the most important sites for microbes, but it must always be remembered that, although most of the microbes normally living on the skin are harmless, the skin (especially fingers) can transmit contamination from one surface or food to another very easily.

---

2 When considering the potential risks of humans contaminating food, either directly or indirectly, we must remember that our customers as well as ourselves represent potential sources of contamination. In this programme we will be concerned with the risks that food handlers themselves may present to food and how proper personal hygiene practices can help to prevent food, and the food environment in general (such as work surfaces, utensils, etc.) from being contaminated from the humans in that food environment.

The possible consequences of poor personal hygiene standards and practices can be serious. Many an outbreak of food poisoning has been traced to errors in the personal hygiene of food handlers. Remember also that, as with many areas of food hygiene, what at first may appear to be a very simple, even obvious, topic, turns out to be more involved than we might think once we study it in detail.

Q How might customers present a risk of contamination to food and how can we guard against such risks?

A They could cough or sneeze over open (unwrapped) food or could contaminate it by touch. We should be careful always to enclose open food within total enclosures (closed, clear plastic cabinets, for example) or to display only wrapped food. Note that even plates of salad can be covered with Clingfilm to protect them and also note that many 'display cabinets' are not totally enclosed. Badly fitting flap doors are frequently used, or the sides are open. Worse still are the clear plastic or glass screens often seen in use. These will protect the food against direct contamination but nothing more.

Problems of customers touching open food ('helping themselves' but later changing their minds and picking up some other food article) are harder to deal with. If you must have a self-service system it is best to ensure that foods are wrapped. Even the provision of tongs or scoops for customer use is not a satisfactory solution because, even when they are obviously provided customers rarely use them.

---

3 Many of the evils of poor personal hygiene are well known and obvious. Licking fingers (especially dipping fingers into food to taste it), smoking (which inevitably entails touching the lips, and therefore possibly transfering microbes to the hands and then later to food), spitting, nose-picking, blowing into paper bags, touching or picking up ready-to-eat foods with the hands (rather than with tongs or scoops) are all well known and, of course, they are absolutely taboo for any food handler.

Less well known are some of the other 'bad personal habits' which can present dangers to all concerned. Because the human skin has large numbers of microbes on it, any contact with the bare skin can present hazards to food. Obviously a food handler must touch food but the hands MUST always be clean before doing so. If you scratch an itch you should wash your hands before touching food again.

We cannot help sneezing or coughing sometimes, but a food handler MUST be especially careful to 'catch germs in a handkerchief'.

Q Although you must never sneeze or cough directly on to food, catching germs in a handkerchief could also present danger. Can you suggest why?

A The handkerchief itself could be a potent reservoir of 'germs'. Imagine what could happen if a cotton handkerchief is taken quickly from the pocket. The 'germs' on the handkerchief would be swept into the air. Food handlers should always use disposable tissues ONLY and dispose of each one safely after use (keep some in your pocket for when you need them). The hands MUST be carefully washed following a sneeze or cough, or whenever a tissue has been used.

---

4 Hands are a potent source of contamination for food. Foods should be touched by hand as little as possible — use tongs, scoops, forks, whenever possible. The wearing of cotton gloves (popular in some catering establishments) is NOT a good idea. The gloves will inevitably pick up contamination just as easily as the hands can but the hands can be washed more often and more easily.

Hand washing is a basic precaution for food handlers and MUST be done whenever the hands might have become contaminated.

Q Name the major ways in which food handlers' hands can be contaminated.

A Following toilet use. Microbes of many types are present in the gut and they can easily pass through toilet paper to the hands. We can live with our own microbes (usually) but they could make someone else very ill if they get on to their food. Even after urinating, the hands could be contaminated and most areas of a toilet (door handles etc.) could be contaminated. It is essential to wash the hands properly after toilet visits. Another point needs to be noted here. Exits from conveniences should always be of the 'push open' swinging-door type so that a food handler does not have to touch the door after washing the hands.

Nose-picking, skin-scratching, handkerchief use, finger-licking, touching the lips during smoking or eating are the other main ways of contaminating the hands.

In addition, we must not forget that microbes can be readily transferred to the hands during the handling of raw foods (meat and vegetables especially) or when handling waste foods, emptying dustbins, etc. In all cases, the key to safety is to wash the hands diligently and properly.

5 You may think that the hands can only be washed in one way and that it is impossible to wash them incorrectly. You can be forgiven for thinking this but, in fact, you are completely wrong!

Surgeons and other members of surgical teams wash their hands correctly, but the vast majority of people do not. To understand why this is so, we need to consider carefully exactly what it is we are attempting to do whenever we wash our hands.

Q What are we (as food handlers) trying to do when we wash our hands?

A Most people would probably answer that we are attempting to 'clean' the hands. You should, by now be able to distinguish very clearly between 'cleaning' and 'hygiene'. You will recall from the discussion in earlier programmes that there are two types of 'clean' — 'visually clean' and 'microbiologically clean'. When washing the hands, therefore, we are attempting to make them microbiologically clean, that is as food handlers, we are, like a surgeon, attempting to decontaminate them.

6 In fact, such an aim cannot be fully achieved — not even by a surgeon — but we must be careful to ensure that we DO decontaminate our hands as much as we can. To do this we need the right equipment and this consists of:-

(i) Soap (preferably liquid soaps, as these are convenient and have good, degreasing properties but NOT scented soaps as these may leave food-tainting residues on the skin).

(ii) Running, warm, water. If we fill a bowl with water and wash our hands in it, we will be rinsing our hands in contaminated water.

(iii) Wash basins of a type designed for food handlers. These should have warm water mixer taps (so we can get warm, rather than boiling hot running water) which are operated by a foot pedal so we don't have to touch the taps (which could be contaminated from other users). The wash basin should NOT have a plug as we should never be filling it with water. You must NEVER wash your hands in a sink because you will contaminate the sink.

(iv) Hand drying facilities — preferably hot air blowers. Disposable paper towels are the second-best method, and, if used, we need covered bins to dispose of them. **No other form of hand drying should ever be used in any food establishment.**

These requirements apply to ALL hand-washing facilities in a food establishment, whether they are in conveniences or in food or ancillary areas.

Q One piece of equipment, essential to proper hand-decontamination, has been left out of the above list. Can you name it?

A A nail-brush to decontaminate under the nails. This is a legal requirement, but the use of nail-brushes can also present dangers. We will discuss these, and how they can be overcome, below.

---

7 In order to decontaminate the hands properly (and remember that, as a food handler, you MUST do everything you can do to protect those who will consume the food you prepare, serve and handle), you will need to follow the procedures set out below:

(i) Wet the hands with running water.

(ii) Put a little liquid soap into one palm and rub hands together in the normal hand washing manner.

(iii) Continue to 'wash' the hands this way, ensuring that you cover every square inch of hands, fingers (and forearms and wrists if necessary). You should continue spreading the soap over the skin for at least three minutes (this is a much longer time than you might think — try counting to 180, slowly, while washing your hands). It might be necessary to put a little more water on to the hands to make the soap solution more manageable.

(iv) Rinse the hands thoroughly with running water.

(v) Take YOUR nail-brush (you should have your own nail-brush, as explained later) and wet it under running water. Put some liquid soap on the bristles.

(vi) Scrub under the nails carefully and well. Once again, you should be careful and meticulous — don't rush it — someone's life might depend upon your care.

(vii) Rinse the nails (and later the nail-brush) under running water.

(viii) Dry the hands thoroughly.

All of this may sound very fussy, but you will soon get used to it. Memorise these steps and get into the habit of following them. It is almost certain that you don't wash your hands properly at the moment (most people don't), but it is equally certain that if you want to be a good, safe food handler, you will have to wash them properly in the future. Only by scrupulously following these steps can you ever hope to do so. In addition, remember that nails should always be short and well manicured to facilitate proper hand washing.

Q Why do you think that a food handler should have his or her own nail-brush?

A To answer this question you really need to consider what it is that the nail brush is intended to do. It is, after all, only a brush designed to sweep microbes (and dirt) from under the nails. The microbes will, however, stick to the bristles very easily. If a nail-brush is left on each wash basin for anyone to use, the bristles are bound to collect microbes. We will end up with a brush that adds more contamination under the nails than it removes.

One way to avoid this is to use a personal nail-brush. In this way we can at least ensure that we wash it (in hot water and detergent) regularly and that we rinse it off after use. It is our own personal nail brush and therefore we must look after it carefully. Having rinsed the nail brush (or washed it thoroughly, which we must do at least once a day), we should dry it well on disposable paper towels or tissues. We should then keep it in our pocket ready for use again. Do NOT put it into a plastic bag because it will remain wet and contaminating microbes may multiply on it.

Of course, the nail brush must be made of plastic so that it can be easily cleaned.

---

8 We have considered hand-washing in some detail, but it IS an important topic and is one that many people know little about.

Hand-washing is very like washing a food-preparation surface in that we will not be able to kill all the microbes on the skin by washing with soap. Many will remain because they stick to the skin surface and lodge within pores to a considerable degree. So long as we perform hand-washing and nail scrubbing properly however, we will achieve an adequate reduction in the number of microbes present on the skin. As is often the case with food hygiene, it is not possible to eliminate ALL the microbes that may be present but it IS possible to reduce the total number to a safe level. This will only be achieved however, if we follow the 'rules' of hand-washing discussed above. A quick wash over in a bowl of water is NOT adequate under any circumstances.

Q How about nail polish and jewellery — do you think these could affect hand-washing efficiency?

A Nail polish, whether coloured or clear, should never be worn by a food handler while at work. It is inevitable that constant washing will cause it to flake sooner or later and food consumers are liable to be upset if they find flakes of plastic in their food.

Similarly, jewellery should not be worn either. Rings containing stones are definitely not permissible as the stones could become dislodged and enter food. Bracelets, and wrist-watches, make hand-washing difficult (the wrists require washing just as much as the hands) and a watch could become damaged or caught in food-processing machinery. Even earrings can present a potential hazard because they could fall into food (this has been known to happen on more than one occasion).

Strictly speaking, even plain gold rings such as wedding rings, should not be worn either. Food particles and contamination of various sorts can easily get lodged under the ring and are later released into food. It is recognised, however, that married women do not usually like removing their wedding rings and many have worn them continuously for so long that they simply will not come off. So long as the ring contains no stones it is acceptable for it to be worn, but special precautions MUST be adopted.

When washing the hands with a plain ring on, it is essential to move the ring up the finger a little so that you can wash behind it. If this precaution is taken, the wearing of a plain ring (not containing any stones) should present no major risks to food hygiene.

---

9 The skin, especially on the hands, can act as a medium of contamination to food. This is why hand-washing (and washing of wrists and forearms, when necessary) is so very important. The skin can sometimes harbour extremely dangerous microbes and, in such cases hand-washing will not achieve an adequate level of safety.

Skin lesions, such as cuts, boils, etc., are frequently infected with a type of bacterium called *Staphylococcus aureus* which can produce food poisoning if it gets on to food. We shall discuss this type of food poisoning in Programme 17. For now, we shall consider how personal hygiene can prevent our customers from being infected by it.

All cuts and skin lesions, must receive first-aid treatment. This is an obvious precaution designed to protect your health. Cuts and other skin lesions that do not heal properly must receive medical attention as must severe lesions and cuts — this is an obvious precaution designed to protect personal health.

In addition, all such lesions and cuts MUST ALWAYS be covered with a waterproof dressing. This dressing must be entirely waterproof and must not be ventilated at all. Such a precaution is necessary to ensure that any microbes in the lesion do not get into food, the idea is not to prevent water from getting into the cut although, if contaminated water or blood from raw meat, etc. did get into the cut, matters could be made worse. It is especially dangerous to get soil from vegetables into such a lesion. A waterproof, unventilated, dressing will therefore protect both food handler and food consumer.

Q What kind of dressing could you use on a small cut? What kind could you use if you had a bandaged hand or finger?

A A waterproof, unventilated sticking plaster can be used on a small cut. These should be of the blue-coloured variety sold for food handler use. These will show up clearly if they fall off and get into food, whereas flesh-coloured varieties would not.

Waterproof finger-stalls can be used on bandaged fingers, but if the hand is bandaged it would be necessary to wear surgical gloves obtainable from large pharmacies (chemist shops). In the case of some skin conditions, it would be unwise to prepare food in any case until the condition has cleared. Medical advice should be sought in cases of doubt.

It should be noted that all cuts and lesions should be treated with appropriate antiseptics (or in accordance with medical advice).

If you wish, you can, of course, remove the dressing once you have finished work.

Burns are especially hazardous and must be kept clean. Once again, a waterproof dressing will be needed for work and, as always, medical attention must be sought in any cases of doubt.

---

10 So far, we have considered personal hygiene practices but it is equally important to consider the clothing that food handlers wear while at work.

Ordinary, everyday clothing can pick up an awful lot of contamination. Obviously, food must be protected from this which is why clean, washable overclothing MUST be worn by all those who come into contact with food storage, preparation or handling areas, and by cleaners and washers up who could otherwise contaminate the food environment by means of their outside clothes.

Exactly what type of overclothing is worn depends on the food handler's job (remember, that as far as food hygiene is concerned, cleaners, waitresses, barmen, washers-up, etc. are all food handlers). Overclothing can range from a waitress's uniform to a chef's 'whites', but the important thing is that the overclothing worn in food rooms must NOT be worn outside where it might be contaminated.

The overclothing must be clean, if it becomes contaminated (or dirtied during use) it must be exchanged for clean. Spare sets of overclothing should be kept available to allow this to be done because it is very easy to spill something on overclothing while working. All too often, food businesses and similar operations will budget for a weekly change or wash of overclothing without taking into account that overclothing needs to be changed when it becomes dirty — which can happen more frequently than once a week. It may be necessary to have a DAILY change available. It is about time that the food industry as a whole realised this.

Q What items of overclothing are needed for a chef or cook?

A A white coat (and possibly over-trousers), capable of being easily washed, hair-covering and shoes.

---

11 When considering what overclothing should be worn by any food handler it is necessary to bear in mind that the purpose of the overclothing is to prevent contamination on outside clothes from getting on to food, surfaces or utensils. Waitresses, barmen, etc., are usually provided with a uniform. This is fine so long as it is worn only inside the food premises. Hair-covering is not essential for such staff, but it must be worn by those who handle food and it is wise for washers-up to wear it too to stop hairs getting on to plates, etc. Neck coverings are needed if raw food is liable to come into contact with the neck (as when joints or sides of meat, etc., are carried).

In general, the following overclothing will usually be required:

Coat or overall with tight-closing cuffs. It may be necessary for a waterproof apron to be worn also (by washers-up and cleaners) and over-trousers may be useful as well.

Head coverings which must always ENTIRELY enclose the hair. The vast majority of head-coverings used in food premises are virtually useless because they do not entirely enclose the hair. Chefs' hats for men and headscarf-type head-coverings for women are needed. Hair may need to be tied or clipped back to enable it to be completely enclosed. It is ESSENTIAL to completely enclose the hair, even a small fringe at the front is not acceptable. Keep the hair totally enclosed. 'Keep it under your hat' is the phrase to remember.

Shoes — of all the items of overclothing which may become contaminated from outside, none are more liable to such contamination than shoes. Imagine walking dog excreta into a food room! A pair of stout shoes (NOT with open toes as these cannot protect you if something falls on your foot) should be kept for use in food rooms. These should be kept clean and be worn in the food rooms and NOWHERE else. It is now possible to obtain good, attractive-looking, safety shoes in a variety of styles for both men and women. You are strongly advised to wear these. Not only do they provide foot protection, but they also provide good slip-resistance and you will find that soft, unsuitable shoes will soon add to fatigue if you are on your feet all day long.

Q What should you do when you finish work or before leaving the food premises?

A Before leaving the food premises, for whatever reason (even if only going out shopping), you must ALWAYS change out of the overclothing (including shoes) as otherwise the overclothing will become contaminated from outside, defeating the object of wearing it in the first place. Similarly, always change back into the overclothing (including shoes) before entering a food area.

---

12 Each year, a large number of cases of food poisoning are traced to food handlers who are carrying a food-poisoning disease. It is ABSOLUTELY ESSENTIAL that you always inform your manager if you have suffered symptoms of illness. Even if you had slight symptoms only, perhaps over the weekend or on your rest days, and even if you think that it was simply due to over-indulgence, REPORT THE SYMPTOMS. This is necessary so that the health authorities can check whether you are carrying an infection that could be passed on to food. If so, you should be laid off work until you are free from infection. This will be essential if the food consumers are to be protected.

The symptoms to report are:

Diarrhoea — even if only a little 'looseness'
Abdominal pain
Vomiting or feelings of nausea
Fever
Sore throat
Colds, 'flu or cough symptoms

As long as you report these to your manager, advice can be sought from the health authorities and everyone can be sure that you do not become a risk to food consumers. If you have had these symptoms, PLEASE report them. Not to do so is to risk injuring your customers. You are not a 'leper' and no one will treat you like one, but you ARE a food handler and it is your duty to protect your consumers as far as you can.

KEY FACTS

1 Microbes of one kind or another can be found on or in many parts of the body — notably the skin, mouth, nose, genital area, and the gut.

2 Food handlers must always be especially careful with their personal hygiene or otherwise they can contaminate food with the possible result that food poisoning occurs.

3 Food handlers, especially, should cover all skin cuts, abrasions or lesions with waterproof dressings, not touch parts of the body and then handle food without first having washed the hands, wash the hands often, but particularly after using the toilet or handling raw food.

4 Food handlers must not cough or sneeze over food. Only disposable tissues should ever be used, NOT handkerchiefs, and they must be properly disposed of in a lidded bin after use. Food handlers must wash their hands after using a tissue.

5 Food handlers should always have their own nail-brush which is kept clean and sanitised.

6 Neither nail polish nor jewellery should be worn by food handlers at work. It is difficult to wash the hands properly if jewellery is worn and nail polish can flake off and enter food.

7 Food handlers should wear clean, washable overclothing at work. The clothing and shoes worn in food rooms should not be worn elsewhere. Outdoor clothing and shoes must not be taken into a food room because they will carry contamination with them.

8 Symptoms of illness must be reported to superiors as soon as possible (even if they occurred when a food handler was off-duty). Special care must be taken to report symptoms of:

Diarrhoea (even if only a little 'looseness')
Abdominal pain
Vomiting or feeling sick
Fever
Sore throat
Colds and 'flu or cough symptoms

PROGRESS PAPER 14

Attempt the following questions and then check your answers against the model answers. Remember that you should mark your answers right if they are essentially the same as the model answers. They do not need to be exactly the same, as the models answers often contain more information than is necessary — they are designed to help you revise the main points of the programme. Re-read the programme if you cannot answer any of the questions below or if you get any wrong.

1 What is the purpose of personal hygiene as far as food handlers are concerned?

2 Who are food handlers? (HINT: does this term refer only to chefs and cooks?)

3 What parts of the human body usually harbour microbes of one kind or another?

4 How can customers present a risk of contamination to food and how can we avoid that risk?

5 Name some of the most common and well known, bad personal habits that can give rise to a food handler contaminating food.

6 Explain how hands should be washed in order to decontaminate them properly.

7 What must a food handler do with a skin cut?

8 What must a food handler do before entering a food area?

9 What kind of head-covering must a food handler wear? (NOTE: this means a food handler who is actually engaged in handling or preparing food).

10 What symptoms of illness must a food handler (of all types, i.e. chef, cook, waiter, bar staff, cleaners, etc.) report to the management?

ANSWERS

1 It is intended to prevent, as far as possible, food handlers themselves contaminating food or the food environment.

2 A food handler, as far as food hygiene is concerned, means anyone who comes into contact with a food preparation, storage or handling area or who serves food, washes utensils, equipment or food areas. The term therefore includes chefs, cooks, bar staff, waiters, waitresses, porters, servery staff, cleaners, washers-up and so on.

3 The skin (especially skin lesions), nose, mouth and throat (including the lips), gastro-intestinal tract (gut) and genital area.

4 They could cough or sneeze onto food, or touch open (i.e. unwrapped) foods with the bare hands. Food displayed for sale should be totally enclosed or wrapped. Foods intended for customers to serve themselves should be wrapped in some way (by Clingfilm stretched over a plate of salad, for example).

5 Finger-licking; licking a spoon, etc. to taste food and then using same spoon again; smoking in a food room; spitting; nose picking; blowing into paper bags; touching ready-to-eat food with the fingers (always use scoop, tongs, fork, etc.), scratching the skin (wash the hands afterwards), coughing or sneezing over food or food surfaces (catch germs in a tissue handkerchief, wash the hands well afterwards and dispose of the used tissue in a bin). Finally, failure to wash the hands properly — especially after toilet use, after handling raw foods and before handling any food — constitutes a serious danger to consumers.

6 (i) Wet the hands with running water.
(ii) Put a little liquid soap into the palm.
(iii) Wash the hands with soap as normal but make sure that each square inch of hands, fingers, etc., are washed. You may need to use a little more water at this stage; continue rubbing the soap over the skin for at least three minutes.
(iv) Rinse the hands thoroughly with running water.
(v) Wet your personal nail-brush in running water and put some soap onto it. Scrub the finger nails carefully. Don't rush this job — be meticulous.
(vi) Rinse nails under running water.
(vii) Dry hands with hot air blower (or paper towels, remember to put used towels in bin after use).

NOTE: remember to keep nail brush clean and keep it with you, don't leave it hanging around anywhere to pick up contamination.

7 Have the cut treated with antiseptic (consult a doctor if it is serious, or if it fails to heal). Always keep the lesion covered with a waterproof, unventilated dressing while at work.

8 Change out of outside clothing (including shoes) and into overclothing (including shoes) before entering. In addition, all food handlers should get into the habit of properly washing the hands as soon as they enter a food area from elsewhere.

9 One which completely encloses the hair, (e.g. chef's hat, headscarf or head square — each of which must be properly worn so that the hair is completely enclosed. Long hair may have to be tied back to facilitate this).

10 Diarrhoea — even just slight 'looseness' of the bowels
Abdominal pain
Vomiting or nausea
Fever
Sore throat
Colds, 'flu or cough symptoms

PROGRAMME 15

Food-Room Design and Construction

1 We know that food hygiene consists of two main aspects. Firstly we must ensure that food is stored, handled and transported so as to protect it from contamination and to help prevent the risk of food consumers falling victims to food poisoning. We know that areas in which food is present, prepared, or served must be kept clean, as must all equipment with which food may come into contact.

Q All of these things can be termed 'food hygiene practices'. What is the other main aspect of food hygiene?

A We must ensure that the food rooms in which food is stored, handled or sold are designed and constructed to facilitate good food-hygiene practices. It would obviously be extremely difficult to keep a wooden shack 'clean' and such a structure will inevitably make the attainment and maintenance of proper food hygiene standards extremely difficult.

---

2 Although food hygiene practices must be considered to be THE most important aspect of food hygiene, good practice cannot be carried on in poor premises. The design and construction of food rooms, the equipment used in them, and the surfaces on which food is handled, must all facilitate good hygiene practice.

Q What is the MOST important property that a food room should possess?

A It must be capable of being effectively cleaned. This is not the end of the story of course. It must also be well lit, well ventilated, be rodent- and insect-proofed, etc. (as we shall discuss shortly), but the main criterion is that food rooms, and all the equipment, tables, etc., within them are capable of being effectively cleaned. In practice, the easier they are to clean, the better.

3 Before we even begin to consider the construction of food premises (i.e. what the walls, floors and ceilings should be made of and so on), we need to consider the design and layout of the premises. All too often little thought is given to this aspect of food hygiene. It is often presumed that all that is necessary is to obtain a building which is partitioned off into rooms. We then position equipment, servery, storage areas within these rooms as best we can. It is obvious that this is the wrong way to go about things.

Q If this is the wrong way, what is the right way?

A The whole food premises should be designed with a view to facilitating the attainment and maintenance of good food hygiene practice. This means that we must firstly consider how much space we need, where we need it, and what we will use it for. One of the biggest mistakes ever made in connection with food-premises design, is to allow too little space for people to work in and far too little space to store food in. Of course, it may be that available space is limited but, at least, a little thought and care help ensure that the space available is used to the greatest advantage.

---

4 Two aspects of food premises design are of paramount importance. There is neither space nor need to consider design in detail in this book, but you will need to know general points. Design is a complex matter, especially when, as is all too often the case, the premises have not been specifically built as food premises, or when you have to make the best of premises already designed and built. Even in these cases however, a little thought and application of common sense, by perhaps rearranging the tables a little, etc., can often improve matters greatly.

Q One of the first, and most important, principles of food room design is that there should be 'clean' and 'dirty' sides. This sounds somewhat strange as no food room should be 'dirty'. What do you think it means?

A The 'dirty' side referred to does NOT mean that we can tolerate a 'dirty' food room. What it does mean is that raw ('dirty', i.e. already contaminated) food and ready-to-eat ('clean' and, hopefully, uncontaminated) food be kept separate. This is best done by having separate raw food and ready-to-eat food rooms. Alternatively, it is possible (though far less satisfactory) to have separate tables for raw preparation and ready-to-eat preparation. In all cases a work-flow should be designed in which raw food is prepared and passed on to cooking processes and ready-to-eat food comes 'out the other side'. On no account should any back flow occur as this will only encourage cross-contamination.

5 The 'golden rule' therefore, is to design food premises, arrange the layout of the rooms, and organise the handling of the food in such a way that cross-contamination does not arise. A little common sense will show you how this can be done. Similarly, you will see many food premises in which the simple principle of keeping 'dirty' and 'clean' sides separate has simply not been followed. This is one reason why cross-contamination is so liable to arise in food premises. A simple, and yet most important, principle of design has been ignored.

Raw vegetables present a special risk to food. They are usually covered in soil (which usually contains bacterial spores) and the soil can so easily become airborne and bring about contamination of foods. One special point is that raw vegetable preparation areas should be TOTALLY separate from other food rooms. Once the vegetables have been peeled/washed they can then safely enter other food rooms.

Q What are the main points to look out for in food-room design?

A The premises/rooms should be designed to allow sufficient space for working and food storage and, especially, to allow raw and ready-to-eat foods to be kept separate ('clean' and 'dirty' sides). There should be such a work flow that there is a natural progression from 'raw' foods to finished product — no back-flow should arise as this will facilitate cross-contamination.

6 The most common fault found in food premises design is that far too little regard is paid to the question of making cross-contamination unlikely. So far as the actual construction of food rooms is concerned, the most common fault concerns the use of inappropriate materials in inappropriate places.

Obviously we need floor, wall and ceiling surfaces that are easy to clean. In addition, they must remain unharmed by water, condensation, fats and cleaning materials (detergents and sanitisers). All this is a tall order and comparatively few materials are suitable. Most food rooms receive fairly heavy use; they must be constructed so as to be able to resist this use and, in some cases, to resist abrasion or even the possibility of percussion damage (e.g. a trolley knocking into a column, wall, door, etc.).

Q Considering these requirements, what are the main properties that a surface should possess if it is to be used in a food room?

A It should be capable of being easily cleaned, and be unaffected (undamaged) by oils, fats, water, sanitisers and cleaning-agents. It should be tough enough to 'last' and may need to be capable of resisting bumps (by trolleys, etc.) and abrasion.

7 No ideal floor, wall or ceiling surface exists. We must therefore accept compromise. Not all food rooms receive the same degree of heavy use or abuse, and we may be able to use particular surfaces in some situations and yet not in others. Let us look at the choices available.

Floors need to be hard-wearing; they must be capable of being effectively cleaned and should, as far as possible, be non-slip. We immediately have a problem. No floor surface is ever totally 'non-slip' so we must see whether we can find one that is slip resistant. We can, but they usually have a roughened surface which makes them hard to clean. In practice we must choose a smooth floor that is capable of being easily cleaned and sort out the problem of slipperiness by means of the use of appropriate footwear. Mopping-up spillages as they occur will go a long way to making a floor safer to walk on, and many varieties of safety shoe are now available which greatly reduce the risk of slipping.

Q What are the main properties we want a floor surface in a food room to have?

A It should be hard-wearing, capable of being effectively cleaned and, as far as possible, slip resistant.

8 To be capable of being effectively cleaned, a floor must be impervious to moisture, unaffected (undamaged) by oils, fats and cleaning materials, and hard. In areas which are not used much, vinyl sheets (the heavy-duty industrial varieties) may suffice. Elsewhere, a hard **composite** floor is needed. These are floor surfaces that are made up of cement and aggregate. One of the best is a **granolithic** floor which is made of cement and granite chippings. In all cases, the vinyl sheet, or granolithic floor should be whole. Tiles are available, but considerable problems arise with regard to the joints between them. These inevitably accumulate grease and dirt and make cleaning difficult. Granolithic (cement and granite) floors are laid in large bays and joints can be well sealed (joints are in any case, kept to a minimum).

If the floors are of wooden construction (suspended floors) it may be possible to use only vinyl sheeting. In such cases, sheets (not tiles) should be used, and these must be of the heavy-duty type. Ordinary vinyl sheet (intended for home use) is too thin and too easily damaged.

Finally, the floor to wall junction should be **coved** (curved) to facilitate cleaning. This can be easily done with a granolithic floor or special coving tiles can be used. (NOTE: such coving must be wide, going at least six inches up the wall and six inches across the floor).

Q What are the main properties that a food room wall surface needs to have?

A It should be impervious to moisture, smooth, and have few joints (these features make it easy to clean). It should be unaffected by cleaning materials and, in some cases, capable of resisting percussion or abrasion damage.

9 Unfortunately, no wall surface possesses all these properties. Once again we must choose a compromise. The traditional surface for walls is glazed wall-tiles. Unfortunately, these have disadvantages. One is that, they contain many joints and, although these can be **grouted** (filled) with waterproof grout, they can still make the wall difficult to clean.

Special hard plastic wall boards are available that are very good indeed as they have only vertical joints (few in number) which can be effectively sealed. Care is needed in choosing such boards, however, as many poor ones are on the market. In some areas (where condensation, steam and abrasion are not a problem), the walls could be covered with plaster painted with washable emulsion paint. Any wall area that is subject to percussion damage (especially likely at columns or wall angles) can be protected by aluminium sheeting. Wall-to-wall angles should be coved to facilitate cleaning. This can easily be done if plastic-type wall boards are used. (NOTE: once again the coving must be wide).

Q What are the main properties we want of a ceiling in a food room? (Be careful here, think what can happen to a ceiling.)

A The answer in this case is that it depends where the ceiling is. If it is liable to get hot (above an oven for instance), it will have to resist that heat. If it is in a steamy atmosphere, it should resist condensation. In all cases, it should be capable of being cleaned and redecorated. We cannot normally use an impervious ceiling as condensation will form on such a surface and fall on to food. We should use a slightly pervious ceiling material that will readily dry out and can be redecorated at regular intervals. The overall compromise is a plaster and emulsion paint surface. Condensation can be reduced by means of good insulation above the ceiling itself. So called 'anti-condensation' surfaces and paints are available, but they simply do not work. Wall-to-ceiling junctions should be coved.

10 All equipment, tables, etc., must be capable of being easily cleaned. Those made of stainless steel or aluminium are best. Even sinks and handbasins are best made of these materials. Ceramic handbasins are especially unsuitable as they are highly likely to become fractured.

We should also remember that we need to have clean hot and cold water available, and that we need washing-up sinks and handbasins. We should have enough handbasins to make it easy for food handlers to reach one. It is better to have too many than too few as, if handbasins are obviously available, this encourages food handlers to wash their hands often.

Equipment and fittings must be arranged so that we can clean around, behind and under them. This is best arranged if we have 'island' sites, i.e. equipment should be sited so that we can get around it easily for cleaning purposes.

Q What about food storage facilities — what are the main requirements we should be concerned with?

A We should have enough storage facilities available to enable us to separate raw and ready-to-eat foods. The storage facilities (like all other food rooms) must be insect- and rodent-proof and must be capable of being easily cleaned. Remember that raw vegetables should be stored separately from every other food and that storage shelves must be capable of being easily cleaned. Facilities must be available for cold storage and display and for hot display (temporary storage prior to service) so that proper temperature controls can be exercised.

11 Food rooms should always be well lit. This not only facilitates safe working, but also enables cleaning to be properly performed. It should be noted that too much light can be as bad as too little. Lighting needs to be carefully designed so that a balance between too little and too much can be struck.

Q What about ventilation — why is it necessary to ensure good ventilation of food rooms?

A There are three reasons. Firstly, good ventilation reduces condensation problems (condensation can damage surfaces very easily, especially plaster and paint). Secondly, good ventilation makes the environment more pleasant to work in (which reduces mistakes — you cannot work well in an uncomfortable room). Thirdly, good ventilation reduces the number of airborne microbes in the room and, remember that the people in the room will be breathing microbes out into the air all the time.

---

12 There are two types of ventilation. **Natural ventilation** consists of open windows. This is not efficient as outside weather conditions will greatly influence the number of changes of air that the room receives each hour. In addition, open windows permit flying insects to enter. If you must have open windows (some people like open windows even when mechanical fans are also used), they must be screened with fine, plastic mesh (which can be washed) to prevent insects flying in.

Mechanical ventilation (the second type of ventilation) is by far the best. This consists of extractor fans or an 'air conditioning' system which pulls air out, cools or heats it, purifies it and then pushes 'conditioned' air back in. Often, such air is both fresher and purer than outside air.

It is especially important to provide ventilated (extract) hoods above all cooking ranges, boilers, etc. If we can remove heat, condensation and fumes from the source in this way, we will automatically obtain a better overall standard of ventilation. Such hoods must be connected to extractor fans; they must be capable of being easily cleaned, (aluminium is best) and must be fitted with filters to trap the grease which evaporates from cooking processes. These filters must be cleaned regularly as otherwise the condensed fat will burn and create a fire risk.

KEY FACTS

1. Proper food-room design and construction assists good food hygiene practices.
2. All food rooms, and all surfaces in them, must be capable of being effectively cleaned.
3. Food areas and premises should be designed and arranged so that there is a work flow — from raw food, through cooking and preparation, to ready-to-eat food. No crossing back or cross-over should occur so that cross-contamination is avoided.
4. Also to stop cross-contamination, it is necessary to ensure that all food areas (containing raw meat, fish or poultry or root vegetables) are separate from ready-to-eat food areas.
5. Floor and wall surfaces should be hard-wearing, impervious to moisture and capable of being easily cleaned.
6. Wall-to-wall, wall-to-floor, and wall-to-ceiling junctions should be coved at a wide angle to facilitate cleaning.
7. All equipment, tables, etc., must be capable of being easily cleaned. Wood should not be used because it is pervious to moisture and cannot, therefore, be easily cleaned.
8. Food rooms must be well lit and well ventilated. Good lighting enables dirt to be seen clearly. Ventilation removes germs from the air, it removes steam which can condense on to surfaces and damage them, and it makes cooking areas easier and more pleasant to work in.

PROGRESS PAPER 15

Now, as before, have a go at the following questions. Check your answers against the model answers. (Remember that your answers need not be exactly the same.) Read the whole programme again if you get any question wrong or if you cannot answer any question.

1 Apart from food hygiene practices, what is the other main aspect of food hygiene?

2 What is the most important property that a food room should possess?

3 What is the main principle of good food-room design?

4 What is the most common fault of food-room design with respect to space?

5 What is the most common fault of food-room design with respect to layout?

6 What kind of surface would you recommend for use as a food-room floor?

7 What kind of surface would you recommend for use as a food-room wall?

8 What kind of material should a food-preparation table be made of?

9 Why should cooking ranges and boilers be covered with extract hoods?

10 Why should a food room be well ventilated?

ANSWERS

1 The design, layout and construction of food premises and food rooms, to facilitate good food hygiene practices.

2 It should be capable of being easily cleaned.

3 Ensure that cross-contamination is discouraged. (It should have a good work-flow from raw to ready-to-eat foods and have no back-flow. It should have sufficient space to facilitate ease of working and have separate raw and ready-to-eat food preparation areas.)

4 Too little space is allowed to enable proper separation of raw and ready-to-eat food storage and handling areas.

5 Proper separation of raw and ready-to-eat food areas is not allowed for.

6 A surface that is impervious to moisture, smooth and with few joints — i.e. one that is capable of being easily cleaned. Examples are heavy-duty vinyl sheet and granolithic floor surfaces.

7 One which is capable of being easily cleaned. Special-purpose plastic-type wall boards are best.

8 Stainless steel or aluminium. It must be impervious to moisture and smooth so that it can be easily cleaned and must resist abrasion.

9 To remove heat, steam and fumes before these can create discomfort or damage to surfaces.

10 To remove steam and therefore help prevent surface-damaging condensation; to remove heat and steam which make working conditions unpleasant (and can lead to mistakes being made); to remove airborne microbes which food handlers are breathing into the food room atmosphere.

PROGRAMME 16
Food Poisoning I

1 Most people have heard of 'food poisoning' but few know what it is. Many people think it is an illness you 'catch' after eating rotting food. This is not strictly true. You can eat rotting food sometimes without becoming ill, but at other times you could end up very ill indeed. It all depends upon whether or not **food poisoning microbes** are present in the food.

Three major classes of food poisoning exist, but we are primarily concerned with only one of them.

The three major classes are:

(i) Illness produced after eating poisonous foods (such as mistaking poisonous toadstools for edible mushrooms).

(ii) Illness produced by the consumption of food that has been accidentally contaminated with toxic chemicals.

(iii) Illness produced by those microorganisms (especially, but not only, specific types of bacteria) which are capable of producing food poisoning if given adequate time and suitable conditions to grow in food.

Certain individuals can also suffer symptoms of **gastro-enteritis** if they eat foods to which they are allergic. This is an unusual allergy reaction rather than food poisoning in the true sense. So far as food hygiene is concerned, we are primarily interested in the microbial-type food poisoning as this is by far the most common type and is the type we can control by means of good food hygiene practice.

Q Can you tell if any food will cause 'food poisoning' by simply looking at it, smelling it or tasting it?

A No, you cannot. Food can look, smell and even taste perfectly normal and yet still produce food poisoning in anyone who eats it. This is why it is so very important to employ proper food hygiene practices at all times. You will never be able to tell whether any food is definitely safe to eat. Only the exercise of good hygiene practices can ever reduce the possibility that food poisoning will occur.

2 **Microbial food poisoning** is an infectious disease spread by food. This means that it is a disease which can be passed from person to person through food. Its infectious nature is due to its being produced by a pathogenic disease-producing microbe.

Q Food poisoning produced by microbes is said to be 'food-borne' (i.e. passed on through food); can you think of any other ways in which an infectious disease may be passed on to a victim?

A Of all the many varieties of microbe that exist, only a comparatively small number are capable of producing disease. Each type of pathogen produces a particular type of disease (some can produce a few different types of disease, depending upon the circumstances). Each food-poisoning pathogen is usually passed on through food. The food is then said to be the **transmission medium** for the food-poisoning germs. Other types of pathogen have other types of transmission medium, e.g.

Water-borne	— caught by drinking contaminated water (e.g. typhoid fever)
Airborne	— caught by breathing contaminated air (e.g. colds and 'flu)
Zoonose	— caught from an infected animal (e.g. rabies from a dog bite)
Arthropod-borne	— caught after a bite from an infected insect (e.g. malaria)
Contact	— caught by direct contact (e.g. venereal disease)

3 Merely eating food that contains a type of microbe which can produce 'food poisoning' does not, automatically, mean that the person concerned will become ill. We can tolerate a small number of such microbes, but a large number will be able successfully to infect the food consumer. The minimum number of organisms needed to produce disease is called the **infectious dose** or **challenge dose** (because it is large enough to 'challenge' the body and successfully to infect it).

Q What do you think is the average challenge dose for most food-poisoning bacteria — hundreds, thousands or millions?

A In most cases it is millions. This sounds a lot, but you should remember that bacteria are extremely small, they reproduce (multiply) very quickly and even a small meal could easily contain thousands of millions.

The fact that we can tolerate a few bacteria in our food is the reason why temperature control can be used to ensure that food is safe to eat. Correct temperature control can prevent microbes from multiplying and will therefore keep their numbers in food down to below the challenge (infectious) dose.

4 Those bacteria which produce food poisoning can be divided into two main classes — the **invasive** type and the **toxin** type. They differ in the way in which they produce disease in the victim (who is called a 'host').

Invasive organisms produce symptoms of food poisoning by infecting the gastro-enteric tract (the gut and intestines). They 'invade' it and produce an inflammation of the gut wall (gastro-enteritis = inflammation of the gut). It is this effect which is responsible for the symptoms of food poisoning.

Toxin type organisms produce food poisoning by multiplying in the food and, in so doing, producing a toxin which they excrete into the food. It is this toxin which is responsible for the food poisoning.

Invasive organisms must survive all processing and be eaten alive by a consumer (in sufficient numbers) to cause disease. In the case of toxin varieties, the organisms must multiply in food sufficiently to produce enough toxin to cause disease symptoms when the food is eaten by a consumer. Once enough toxin has been formed, the organisms producing it could be killed and yet disease still result — it is the toxin that causes the problem, not the organisms in the gut. Toxins can be destroyed by heat, but it takes a temperature of about 65 °C for about one hour to do so and, even then, some types of toxin are more heat resistant than others.

Toxins which are excreted outside an organism are called **exotoxins** ('exo', like the word 'exit' = outside). Some other organisms have toxins also, called **endotoxins** ('endo' — inside); these are contained inside them and are not excreted except when the organism dies. Endotoxins do not produce food poisoning but they can produce a life-threatening shock if a large number of endotoxic organisms enter the bloodstream and die there.

(This is not food poisoning as such but it is a possible, often fatal, consequence of infection with some types of invasive food-poisoning organisms. Fortunately, fatalities from such causes are not common although they certainly do occur.)

Q We now know that food poisoning bacteria (of different types) can produce food poisoning in different ways. How, do you think, can viruses and fungi produce gastro-enteritis or food poisoning? (HINT: remember that viruses can only 'live' when inside a host cell, and that fungi do not normally produce food poisoning in the traditional sense).

A Viruses must invade the gut wall before they can produce symptoms of illness. When outside a living host cell, viruses do nothing at all. They certainly do not reproduce and certainly do not produce any toxin. Food cells are, of course, dead cells, and therefore the viruses cannot reproduce inside them. The only thing a virus does do in food is to wait patiently until it is eaten by a susceptible host.

Fungi can produce toxins called **mycotoxins** ('myco' = fungi). These are currently the subject of much controversy. It is known that some mycotoxins can produce cancer in humans. The current recommendation that mouldy food is safe to eat so long as the mould is cut off could be changed in the future. At the time of writing, more research needs to be done into this question. Certainly, fungi do not produce food poisoning as we know it. If it is discovered that moulds commonly found in foods can produce **carcinogenic** (cancer-producing) mycotoxins, it will obviously be necessary to amend our views regarding the safety of, for example, cutting mould from blocks of cheese and eating the remainder.

5 All infectious diseases have certain characteristics by which we can usually identify them. The main ones to note are the symptoms of illness and the **incubation period**. The symptoms of food poisoning usually consist of diarrhoea and/or vomiting, but variations on these general themes do exist (as we shall see later).

The incubation period is the time between someone being infected by a pathogen and the first sign of symptoms. In the case of *Salmonella* food poisoning for example, the incubation period is usually 12–36 hours, with a range of 6–72 hours. This means that you could start to show symptoms of *Salmonella* food poisoning between 6 and 72 hours after eating a meal contaminated with *Salmonella* bacteria. Most usually you would experience symptoms (diarrhoea, vomiting and fever in this case) from 12 to 36 hours after consuming such a meal.

Nearly all infectious diseases have two ranges of incubation period — the outermost limits (6–72 hours in our example) and the usual, or average, time (12–36 hours in our example).

Q Do you think that the incubation period for toxin-type food poisoning will be longer or shorter than for invasive types?

A Exotoxic type food poisoning usually has a short (a few hours) incubation period. As it is produced by the consumption of a ready-formed toxin, symptoms will arise as soon as the toxin gets into the stomach and gut. Food poisoning produced by invasive organisms takes longer to produce symptoms (that is, the incubation period, or the time taken for symptoms to show, is longer) because, in these cases, the pathogen has to invade the gut and establish infection there before symptoms will arise.

6 You will have to memorise some symptoms and incubation periods of the common types of food poisoning. We will look at these in Programme 17. For now, we can generalise by saying that toxin-type food poisoning usually produces symptoms within a few hours, whereas the invasive type usually takes about one or two days for symptoms to show.

Not everyone who is infected with food-poisoning organisms will show symptoms of the disease. Furthermore, not everyone who does have symptoms will have them to the same degree or severity. This is a peculiarity of all infectious diseases.

Q If you catch a cold, does every other member of your family catch it too?

A The usual answer to this question is no, they do not. This is because each individual has a different susceptibility to the disease in question.

Sometimes we build up an immunity to a particular infectious disease. This can be lifelong (we don't usually catch chicken-pox twice) or it may last for a very short time. For reasons which we need not go into here (they are actually quite complex), you cannot form an immunity to bacterial food poisoning of either the invasive or the toxic type. You could get a 'dose of food poisoning' time and time again without becoming immune to it.

7 The fact that it is possible to be infected with a food poisoning germ and not show symptoms, is a very important one. This leads to problems caused by **carriers** of food-poisoning diseases. A 'carrier' is someone who is infected by a pathogen but who does not show any symptoms. If a food handler shows any symptoms at all of enteric illness (diarrhoea, bowel looseness, nausea, vomiting or even fever), they MUST report to the manager who should lay them off work until a faeces sample can be tested to see whether they have a disease that could be transmitted through food. It is obviously very dangerous indeed to have someone in a food establishment if they have a food-poisoning microbe inside them.

Carriers cannot inform anyone because they do not have any symptoms. It is easy for even the best food handler to slip up and if they are 'carriers' of food-poisoning microbes, any slip up in personal hygiene (after visiting the toilet) will be likely to pass on microbes to the food.

It is obviously preferable to exclude someone from working as a food handler if they have a food-poisoning microbe inside them. Carriers do not realise they have any infection and can therefore present real hazards to food. Many outbreaks of food poisoning have been traced to food handlers who were carriers.

Q If food premises are involved in a case of food poisoning what should be done? (Think about this carefully and then have a guess).

A It will be necessary to try to trace where the infection came from so that it can be prevented from spreading and, hopefully, from recurring in the future.

What usually happens is that the Environmental Health Officer (EHO) of the Local Authority will get a report from a doctor that a patient is suffering from food poisoning. The patient will be asked to put some faeces into a sample pot. This is analysed by the Public Health Laboratory and (hopefully) the microbe responsible is identified. The EHO will visit the patient and take details of where and what they ate, where the food came from and when it was eaten. The EHO then attempts to trace the source of the organism concerned.

Sometimes several people have the disease and it is then possible to say whether a common food was eaten by them all. The EHO then visits the source of that food (shop, restaurant, etc.) and takes samples of food, swabs from preparation surfaces and perhaps asks staff to provide faeces samples. This is necessary so that the outbreak can be stopped and prevented from happening again.

If you are ever involved in an investigation such as this PLEASE co-operate, remember that the EHO is trying to combat a disease that could kill people. The EHO can only hope to be successful if everyone co-operates.

KEY FACTS

1 Three main classes of food poisoning exist:

(i) Eating inherently poisonous foods

(ii) Eating food that is contaminated with toxic chemicals

(iii) Food poisoning produced by specific types of pathogenic microbe

In addition, some people are allergic to certain foods. They may well suffer symptoms of gastro-enteritis (as well as other possible symptoms) if they eat such foods.

2 It is not possible to tell if food is fit to eat by its appearance, smell or taste. If food is obviously 'off', then no one should eat it, but food can look, smell and taste perfectly normal and yet still produce food poisoning.

3 Those groups of bacteria which can produce food poisoning (only a few groups can do so), can be divided into two main classes — invasive and toxic. The invasive types produce symptoms because they grow in the gut and cause a disturbance inside it. The toxic varieties produce chemical toxins (poisons) when they grow in a food and it is when these toxins are eaten, along with the food, that symptoms of illness arise.

4 Enteric viruses do not perform any reactions with food at all. They use food merely as a transmission medium in order to gain entry into a host's digestive tract. Once there, they invade the cells of the gut to produce gastro-enteritis. Fungi do not produce food poisoning in the normal sense, but some varieties do produce mycotoxins which may produce tumours in humans.

5 Two main features of any infectious disease are the symptoms of the disease and the incubation period. (NOTE that bacterial food poisoning and viral enteritis are both infectious diseases.) The incubation period is the time between becoming infected with a pathogen and the first signs of symptoms.

6 A carrier is someone who is infected with a particular pathogen but who shows no symptoms of disease. Carriers can pass on infection to others.

7 If food premises are involved in any case of food poisoning or it is thought to be possible that they are, a report should be sent to the local Environmental Health Department without delay. This is necessary so that a possibly large outbreak of disease can be stopped. (Environmental Health Departments can be found at the local Town Hall or Council Offices.)

PROGRESS PAPER 16

The programme you have just read is one of the most complex in this book. Despite this fact, it is important. Have a go at the following questions and try your best to answer them. Having answered, or attempted to answer, all the questions, compare your answers with the model answers (always remembering that your answers do not need to be exactly like the model answers which sometimes provide additional information). So long as you get the gist of the answer you can mark your response as correct.

You will not be able to understand Programme 17 unless you have fully understood Programme 16. Therefore, for your own sake, if you cannot answer any of the following questions, or if you get any wrong, or even if you are unsure about any point read the programme again before you continue. Write your answers on a separate sheet of paper.

1 What are the three major types of food poisoning?

2 Which of the three major types of food poisoning is of most concern to food hygiene? Why is this type of most concern?

3 Can you tell if any particular food is liable to cause food poisoning by its smell, looks or taste?

4 Will food that is obviously 'off' or rotting always produce food poisoning?

5 What is meant by the 'infectious' or 'challenge' dose?

6 What is meant by invasive food poisoning? What is meant by exotoxic food poisoning?

7 What is a mycotoxin? What harm can it do?

8 What are the main symptoms of food poisoning?

9 What is meant by the term 'incubation period' (so far as food poisoning is concerned)?

10 What is a symptomless carrier of an infectious disease?

ANSWERS

1 Consumption of toxic foods (e.g. mistakenly eating poisonous toadstools instead of edible ones). Poisoning caused by eating food which is accidentally contaminated by chemicals (e.g. if fruit is boiled in a copper pan, the acid in the fruit dissolves the copper which will produce symptoms in anyone who eats the fruit). Microbial food poisoning caused by eating food that has been contaminated by microbes of a type that can cause food poisoning. (Remember that only certain types of microbe produce disease — these are the pathogens or pathogenic varieties. Only certain types of pathogens produce food poisoning.)

2 Microbial food poisoning — because it is the most common type and because it can be controlled by means of good food hygiene practice.

3 No. Food can look, smell and taste perfectly normal and yet could still produce food poisoning (because it contains food-poisoning germs or toxic chemicals).

4 No. It depends upon whether or not it contains any food-poisoning microbes. It will be rotting because it contains microbes that can rot it (spoilage organisms) but these do not usually produce disease. The fact that it is obviously 'off' tells us, however, that microbes have been able to grow in it. If it contains pathogens, they too will have been able to multiply (perhaps to dangerous levels) as well as the spoilage organisms. For this reason it is unsafe to eat food which is obviously 'off'.

5 It is the minimum number of pathogens that must enter the body in order to produce disease.

6 Some pathogens that can cause food poisoning do so by growing in the gut wall — they are 'invasive' because they invade the gut. Other types of food-poisoning microbe produce food poisoning because they multiply (grow) in food and produce a toxin in the food. It is this toxin which is responsible for the food poisoning caused by this variety of microbe. Because the toxin is excreted out of the microbe it is called an Exotoxin. ('Exo', like 'Exit', means 'outside').

7 It is a toxin produced by a fungus (especially a mould). It is known that some mycotoxins (especially **aflatoxin** from peanuts — a mould grows on the shells) can produce cancer in man. It is thought that other fungi may produce such toxins too, when growing on grains, cheeses, etc. This is a question that is controversial at the moment, more research is necessary to establish all the facts.

8 Diarrhoea and vomiting. You should note however, that the severity of the symptoms can differ greatly, from a little looseness to watery diarrhoea, from simple nausea to severe vomiting. This can be so even when the same variety of microbe is causing disease in two different people. Some varieties of food poisoning present additional problems, such as fever and abdominal pain, as we shall see in Programme 17.

9 It is the time between eating a food (which is contaminated with food poisoning microbes or toxins) and showing the first signs of symptoms. The incubation period is characteristic for each variety of microbial food poisoning although it usually has a range of time (e.g. 6 to 72 hours, 1 to 4 hours, 2 to 21 days, etc.)

10 A 'symptomless carrier' (or 'carrier') is someone who is infected with a pathogen but suffers no symptoms of disease.

(We have used the term 'carrier' in the programme, but a more correct term is 'symptomless carrier' as used in this question. Both terms are correct.)

PROGRAMME 17

Food Poisoning II

1 The term 'food poisoning' is a bad one. It is used as a general term for a group of conditions with numerous causes. It sounds as though it should mean that food is 'poisoned' although the most common form of food poisoning is actually produced by consumption of food which is contaminated by particular types of microbe (especially certain bacteria) and it is, in this case, an infectious disease.

Q Besides infection by food-poisoning microbes, what else can produce food poisoning?

A Consuming something that is actually poisonous (mistaking poisonous toadstools for edible ones, for example) or the consumption of food which is contaminated with toxic chemicals.

---

2 In this programme we are concerned with microbial food poisoning, i.e. the form of this disease which is produced following the consumption of food that is contaminated with specific microbes of a type that can produce food poisoning. We concentrate on this type of food poisoning because it is the most common variety but also because it is the type that is easiest to control.

Q How can microbial food poisoning be controlled?

A By the exercise of proper food hygiene practices at all times.

---

3 Unfortunately the topic of microbial food poisoning is one that most students of food hygiene find the most difficult. We must learn the names of several different types of microbe (such names are based on old Latin and Greek and therefore they seem strange when you first meet them). We must learn where these organisms are most likely to be found and what symptoms they produce. In addition, we must commit to memory the 'incubation periods' for each disease. All this seems very hard at first, and many students of food hygiene dread this topic. There really is no need to do so, however, as eventually you will remember. We will simplify matters as much as we can, but eventually you will have to read the summary of key facts at the end of this programme over and over until you can memorise them. Don't panic, however, as the vast majority of students do remember them in the end.

Q What is meant by the term 'incubation period'?

A It is the period of time (hours, days or weeks in some cases) between someone becoming infected by a particular pathogen (disease producing microbe) or its toxin and the first sign of symptoms appearing.

---

4 The symptoms of any disease are the signs that indicate that someone is actually suffering from the disease. The symptoms of 'flu include headache, fever, aches and pains, running nose, etc. It is NOT possible to diagnose any infectious disease from symptoms alone. The pathogen must be found in the body and identified as the type of pathogen which produces the kind of symptoms being suffered. So far as microbial food poisoning is concerned, the pathogen will usually be found in the faeces. Samples of faeces are obtained from a sufferer and the pathogens in it can be identified in the laboratory. Some types of microbial food poisoning do not cause any pathogens to be excreted but, in these cases, the pathogen can be found in a sample of the food eaten by the victim. If this cannot be done, then a diagnosis of food poisoning has to be made on the strength of the symptoms' evidence alone. In these cases, the diagnosis can only ever be a good, educated guess.

Q Will everyone who is infected with a particular food poisoning pathogen suffer the same symptoms?

A No, they may not. It is possible to be infected and yet not suffer any symptoms at all (for 'symptomless carriers' see page 148). It is also possible for the severity of symptoms to differ greatly. Some people suffer a lot, others less so. The main (but not the only) symptoms of food poisoning are diarrhoea and vomiting, but the diarrhoea might only be slight and there might only be nausea rather than vomiting.

It is important to remember that the symptoms given in this programme refer to the majority of cases. Cases will occur where individuals are infected by a particular pathogen and yet show no symptoms, or even slightly different symptoms, from the 'classic' ones usually attributed to each pathogen.

---

5 Incubation periods are also averages. Just as with symptoms, they may not be true for all cases (although they are true for the majority). Before looking at the symptoms, incubation periods etc., of specific food-poisoning organisms, we should briefly discuss why this information is of value to us.

Environmental Health Officers (the EHOs of the Local Authority) investigate cases of food poisoning with a view to preventing a recurrence and to try to stop the outbreak spreading. To do this, the EHOs must be able to trace the original source of the outbreak.

The typical sequence of events is as follows:

(i) Someone is found to be suffering from food poisoning; their doctor informs the EHO. The patient is interviewed and information relating to what foods they have eaten, and where and when is collected. Samples of the patient's faeces are submitted to the Public Health Laboratory. Once an organism is found in the faeces, the EHO can tell which foods are the most likely cause of it. The EHO finds out if the patient has eaten those foods and, if so, where.

(ii) By visiting the establishment where the suspect food was eaten, the EHO can sample staff (to see whether there is a carrier) and food there to see if the same organism can be found. If it is found, at least one possible source of the outbreak has then been discovered.

(iii) Speed is of the essence, so the EHO must start to try to trace the source of the outbreak before a laboratory report is available. By taking details of symptoms from the patient, the EHO can guess the likely organism. By knowing the usual incubation periods for that organism, the EHO can trace back in time to discover what the likely food was. (For example, if symptoms indicate a *Salmonella* bacterium, the incubation period ranges from 6 to 72 hours, so the EHO is then interested in food eaten between 6 and 72 hours before the onset of symptoms).

Q Why should you, as a student of food hygiene, know the symptoms and incubation periods of food poisoning?

A There are three reasons. Firstly, the main point in learning food hygiene is to prevent food poisoning. You should therefore know something about it. Secondly, you may well be able to help with an investigation if your premises are unfortunately ever implicated in an outbreak. Finally, if you are taking an exam in food hygiene, it is likely that some of the questions will relate to 'food poisoning'.

---

6 You probably know that it is possible to become immune to some types of infectious disease (you build up an immunity). It is rare to get chicken-pox twice. It is also possible to be artificially immunised against some infectious diseases (e.g. the 'polio' vaccine given on sugar lumps). For reasons which are too involved to concern us here, it is not usual for anyone to become immune to food poisoning and vaccines are not available for the vast majority of this group of diseases.

NOTE: Because you will have to memorise the symptoms, incubation periods and sources of the common types of microbial food poisoning, the format of this programme now changes from that normally used in this book. This is to help you to memorise the necessary information. Any reader who wishes to study food poisoning more deeply should read *Food Poisoning* P A Alcock, published by H K Lewis and Co., London, 1983.

Let us first become familiar with the names of the organisms most commonly associated with microbial food poisoning.

Read the names below and try to become accustomed to them. Practise saying the names out loud, pronouncing them as indicated by the syllables in brackets.

Salmonella	— (sal-mon-ella)
Staphylococci	— (staff-i-low-cock-eye)
Clostridium	— (clost-rid-ee-um)
Bacillus cereus	— (bass-cill-us seer-ee-us)
Vibrios	— (vib-ree-os)
Campylobacters	— (camp-pie-low-bact-ers)

These are all bacteria. Two words are used to name specific types. *Salmonella typhi* is a different organism from *Salmonella paratyphi*. The first name (*Salmonella*) is the genus name (e.g. Terrier dog); the second name is the species (e.g. Cairn Terrier). Many different types of '*Salmonella*' exist, but there is only one *Salmonella typhi*.

By far the most common causes of bacterial food poisoning are: *Salmonella* (many types), *Clostridium perfringens* (*per-frin-gens*) and *Staphylococcus aureus* (*or-ree-us*).

The most common salmonella is *Salmonella typhimurium* (*tie-phee-muir-ree-um*) but nearly 2000 different species of salmonella exist, each with their own names, e.g. *Salmonella agona, Salmonella derby, Salmonella manchester,* etc.

We will now look at the diseases which these organisms produce. The table overleaf keeps all detail down to a minimum and therefore, makes it easier for you to remember.

Organism	Incubation Period	Symptoms	Foods Most Usually Involved
Salmonella	Usually 12–24 hours Can be 6–72 hours	Diarrhoea Vomiting (severe) Fever (possibly)	Poultry Shellfish Meat dishes Meat products
Staphylococcus aureus	Usually 2–4 hours Can be 1–6 hours	Vomiting	Cooked meats Cream cakes
Clostridium perfringens	Usually 10–12 hours Can be 8–24 hours	Severe abdominal pain Diarrhoea	Stews Soups Joints of meat (especially if re-heated)

Salmonella causes disease by being eaten in food and then invading the gut wall. A large number of these bacteria must be eaten before disease results. Illness can be fatal, especially to the young and the elderly and can be very severe, lasting, possibly, for a few weeks.

Staphylococcus aureus causes disease by first growing in food and producing exotoxin. It is the exotoxin (eaten with the food) that produces the disease symptoms. Illness is usually unpleasant but mild and recovery usually occurs within a few days at most.

Clostridium perfringens causes illness that is usually non-fatal but most painful, involving especially, abdominal pain. Clostridia form spores (see page 000) and will grow quite happily in stews, other made-up meat dishes, and in the centre of undercooked meat joints or re-heated foods.

Sources of organisms

Salmonellae frequently infect food animals at the farm. Raw poultry, raw red meat and duck eggs are common sources of these bacteria.

Staphylococcus aureus can frequently be found in the human nose. It is also found in cuts and skin lesions, which is why these must be covered with a waterproof dressing. Otherwise, the organism can be spread to cooked food and other ready-to-eat foods (especially cooked meat and cream) in which it grows well and produces toxin.

Clostridium perfringens is a soil organism. It can be found in root vegetables (soil contamination) and in raw meats. It is an anaerobe and will therefore only grow in the absence of oxygen. Foods most commonly involved, therefore, are stews, soups and the centre of joints, etc., where oxygen is excluded.

These are the three most common types of microbial food poisoning. The other varieties which can be found are:

Vibrios	— especially in raw fish, shellfish
Bacillus cereus	— especially in rice that has been boiled and then is 'flash' fried
Sonnei dysentery	— very infectious, although usually mild, and very common in nurseries
Campylobacters	— common in poultry

For the purposes of basic food hygiene knowledge, it is not really necessary for you to know any more about the organisms listed above. Again, interested readers should refer to *Food Poisoning* by P A Alcock, published by H K Lewis and Co., London, 1983.

You should, however, know a little about another species of *Clostridium* — *Clostridium botulinum* (*bot-you-line-um*). This is a spore-former (see page 34) which produces an exotoxin if it grows under anaerobic conditions (without oxygen). The toxin is in fact, one of the most powerful poisons known to humans. Cases of **botulism** are rare, but a few have arisen in the United Kingdom. Usually they are due to improperly processed canned foods. Canning processes are designed to kill the spores of botulism and, on the whole, modern canned foods are extremely safe.

A few special species of *Salmonella* exist — *Salmonella typhi* (*tie-phee*) and *Salmonella paratyphi* — which produce typhoid fever and paratyphoid fever respectively. These can be caught from food but contaminated water is the usual source. Neither is common in the United Kingdom. They produce a fever rather than food poisoning. It is possible to be vaccinated (immunised) against these diseases. (Paratyphoid fever can mimic severe gastro-enteritis in many cases.)

Viruses can be present in food or water supplies. Some (**Enteroviruses, Enteric viruses**) produce symptoms of gastro-enteritis. They can also be, and indeed most usually are, caught through the air-borne route (being breathed in like cold germs).

Brucellosis (*bruce-ell-o-sis*) and **tuberculosis** (TB) can be 'caught' by consuming untreated milk or cream. These diseases are not like food poisoning but are more like fever. They are not common in the UK as the vast majority of our milk and cream is heat treated which kills these organisms.

The protozoan and metazoan parasites (most usually called 'parasitic worms') can also be 'caught' from food. The pork and beef tapeworms can be 'caught' from eating inadequately cooked pork (especially bacon) or beef. Both are uncommon in the UK.

NOTE: Opinions differ on the point but I feel that students of the principles of food hygiene do not need to know more about 'food poisoning' than has been presented here. If, however, you are using this book as a classroom text, refer to your lecturer or tutor who may want you to study this topic in more detail. Otherwise, the most important points you should note are that food poisoning can KILL and that the only way to avoid it is by exercising good food hygiene practices as advocated in this book.

KEY FACTS

Differential diagnosis summary chart ('classical' food poisoning)

	Salmonella	*S. typhi (paratyphi)*†	*Staphy-lococcus*	*Cl. perfringens*	*Vibrio*	*B. cereus*	Viral	Chemical
Diarrhoea	C	R(V)	V	V	C	(C)*	V	R
Vomiting	C	R	C	R	V	(C)*	V	C
Nausea	V	R	C	V	V	(C)*	V	C
Abdominal pain	V	R(V)	R	C	C	(C)*	R	R
Taste/ burning	X	X	X	X	X	X	X	C
Dizziness	V	V	R	R	R	R	V	V
Headache	V	V	R	R	V	R	V	V
Fever	V	C(V)	R	R	V	R	V	R
Incubation Period (IP) (range)	6–72 hours	7–21 days (1–10 days)	1–6 hours	8–24 hours	4–96 hours	1–5* 6–16 hr	not accurately known	usually rapid

X, not known; R, rare; V, variably present; C, classic symptom.
*_B. cereus_ presents with either diarrhoea and pain in 6–16 hours *or* nausea and vomiting in 1–5 hours.
†*S. typhi* produces typhoid fever (enteric fever); usually this is water-borne. *S. paratyphi* produces paratyphoid fever which is often food-borne.
(Reproduced from *Food Poisoning* by P A Alcock, published by H K Lewis & Co., of London, 1983, with the permission of the Publishers.)

PROGRESS PAPER 17

Have a go at the questions below, and then compare your answers with the model answers. Write your answers on a separate sheet of paper.

1 What type of food poisoning is produced by a bacterium that is found in skin cuts?

2 What food-poisoning bacterium is most likely to be found in chickens and turkeys?

3 What food-poisoning bacterium is most likely to be found in duck eggs?

4 What type of bacterium produces vomiting within a few hours of eating food?

5 What type of bacterium produces severe abdominal pain as a main symptom of food poisoning?

6 In addition to food poisoning, name two other infectious diseases that can be caught from infected food.

7 What are the main symptoms of salmonella food poisoning?

8 What are the main symptoms of food poisoning caused by *Clostridium perfringens*?

9 What is the main symptom of food poisoning caused by *Staphylococcus aureus*?

10 A food consumer becomes ill with diarrhoea, vomiting and fever within 24 hours of eating a chicken meal. What is the most likely cause?

ANSWERS

1 Staphylococcal food poisoning (*Staphylococcus aureus*).

2 *Salmonella*.

3 *Salmonella*.

4 *Staphylococcus aureus*.

5 *Clostridium perfringens* (Note: this used to be called *Clostridium welchii*).

6 TB or brucellosis (from untreated raw milk, cream, etc).

7 Vomiting, diarrhoea and fever.

8 Abdominal pain and diarrhoea.

9 Vomiting.

10 *Salmonella*.

PROGRAMME 18

Unfit Food

1 The law in the United Kingdom makes it an offence to **sell**, or **offer** for sale, or **expose** for sale, or to have in your **possession**, food which is intended for human consumption and is unfit for human consumption.

Quite obviously it should be an offence to sell unfit food, but the UK law goes further than this, as you can see. The law does not define what is meant by the term 'unfit food' but my definition is:

> 'Unfit food is any food, the consumption of which would do the consumer harm in the short term and any food which is aesthetically unsuitable for consumption.'

This can be criticised on several grounds. Nonetheless, we do need something to work to, some sort of guideline, and I would suggest that my definition represents a useful guideline in practice. The definition does, however, require a little explanation.

Food that does a consumer harm is obviously 'unfit' to eat. I specify harm 'in the short term' as the long-term effect of eating too much cholesterol, for example, is harmful, but we would hardly say that the foods containing it are unfit. Some rotting foods could be eaten in some circumstances, with impunity, but it is aesthetically undesirable to most people so we classify such food as being unfit.

Q What about 'game' which is usually sold in a partially decomposing state — is that unfit?

A Not to someone who buys it knowing its condition. The game is sold in a 'hung' state as otherwise it would be too tough to eat. The consumers of game know this and they purposely buy it in a state of partial decomposition.

---

2 As the legal penalties for having unfit food in your possession (intending it for sale) are heavy, we had better ensure that we can recognise unfit food when we see it. The law states that an Inspector (the Environmental Health Officer) does not need to prove that you intended to sell the food: if it is in your possession, you must prove that it was not intended for human consumption. You must be very careful therefore, always to ensure that you recognise any food that is unfit and separate it from other foods prior to disposal. All unfit food should be stored in a properly built refuse area until it can be disposed of. If it gets near other foods, or near food preparation surfaces, etc., it will contaminate them.

Q How about food that is contaminated with food poisoning microbes — is that unfit?

A Yes, of course it is, but you must always remember that we cannot tell whether a food is contaminated with food-poisoning microbes or not. The problem is that the food could look, smell and even taste, perfectly normal. The 'rule' is that we can tell if a particular food is definitely unfit, but we cannot tell whether it is definitely fit. We must therefore, err on the side of safety and must seek advice from the Local Authority (Environmental Health Officer) in any cases of doubt.

---

3 In this programme, therefore, we shall be primarily concerned with signs of unfitness in food. We will be able to recognise whether a food is definitely unfit to eat. We will never be able to say that any food is fit unless we have a laboratory analysis carried out. So far as any discussion is concerned, this is THE most important point. We can definitely recognise unfit food but just because a food looks, tastes or smells normal may mean nothing at all. It could still be dangerous (perhaps fatal) to eat it. Bear this point in mind at all times. NEVER believe that you can 'pass' any food as being fit and safe. The best you will ever be able to do is to separate out food which is obviously and definitely unfit.

Q What 'tools' do you think we will need to use to decide whether a particular food is definitely unfit to eat?

A The very best 'tools' for this purpose are our senses of sight, smell and touch. NOTICE THAT TASTE IS NOT MENTIONED. Food which is rotting could be extremely dangerous even to taste — NEVER taste any food to see whether it is unfit; your nose will tell you as much as your tongue could in most cases.

---

4 We cannot consider all possible signs of unfitness in food in this short programme. Nor would this be possible in a whole book. The ability to detect food which is obviously and definitely unfit to eat is one which can only be developed after a lot of practice. What we can do is to learn the main things to look for. The best guide of all is this: **If it looks or smells 'off' — don't chance it.** It would be better to ask the Environmental Health Officer for an opinion.

In most cases you will already have a good idea about what to look for generally. Food which is badly rotting is obvious — its smell is very offensive. It is the food which is 'turning bad' ('on the turn', if you like) that causes most problems.

Q What do you think are the first signs of unfitness in raw meat (white and red)?

A Smell is probably the very best guide of all. Raw meats (white and red) should smell sweet — if they don't, suspect them as being possibly unfit. When raw meats start to 'go off', they become slimy to the feel. They soon start to smell and they look discoloured. Any presence of white or black mould spots should alert you to the unfitness of the meats.

Once meat has been cooked, unfitness is signalled by smell, presence of mould and (usually only in late stages) some sliminess or stickiness to the touch.

---

5 When wet (raw) fish is starting to go off, the eyes go opaque, the scales can be easily rubbed off and the skin feels very slimy. In later stages the smell of 'rotting fish' is unmistakable. Shellfish show their first signs of unfitness by their smell.

Cheeses are unfit when extensively mouldy. At the time of writing, it is still considered acceptable to scrape off the surface mould on a cheese block and to eat the rest. If current research into mycotoxins of fungi ever proves otherwise, this advice will change. Dried-up cheeses are obviously unfit.

Unfitness in milk and cream, eggs and other dairy produce is usually obvious — your sense of smell will be your best guide in these cases.

Q What are the most common signs of unfitness in fruit? (Think about any rotting fruit you may have seen.)

A Fruit is usually acidic and will therefore inhibit the growth of bacteria. Moulds will still grow in them, however, and a softening of the fruit, with mould growth, represents the very first sign of unfitness.

6 Vegetables usually go soft when rotting first starts. Some varieties (e.g. cabbages, sprouts and peas), smell most offensively and this smell could not go unnoticed. Some vegetables show mould growth after softening is first noticed.

We have now briefly considered signs of unfitness in the majority of types of food you are liable to come across. You have seen that such signs are usually rather obvious. All you really need to do is to keep an eye open and rely on your experience. Rarely will you be wrong so long as your err on the side of safety, and **treat everything that looks or smells out of the ordinary as being suspect.**

Q What is it that makes a food 'go off' and rot? Which agent(s) do the rotting?

A Two agents are primarily involved. In the first place, certain enzymes present in the food when it was 'alive' are released after slaughter, harvesting etc. These start to break down the dead cells of the once-living food. Those bacteria and fungi which are capable of rotting the food in question then play their part. The rotting process is carried to its extreme by microbes growing in or on the food. Different types of microbe can rot food at different rates. These 'spoilage organisms' have favourite foods. Spoilage bacteria usually rot meat and fish primarily, spoilage fungi get to work on fruit and cheese, etc. It should be noted, however, that spoilage bacteria and fungi often work together to rot food.

Although, as you know, 5 °C is the lower limit of growth for those pathogenic bacteria which are capable of producing food poisoning, this is not true in the case of spoilage organisms. Many varieties of spoilage microbe (both bacterial and fungal types) can grow below this temperature. These are the organisms which are responsible for rotting food stored in refrigerators. Some moulds can even grow (although very slowly) in freezers.

As with all microbes, the spoilage types grow best at warm temperatures. By keeping perishable foods cool we can delay the onset of spoilage as the low temperatures reduce the rate of growth of spoilage organisms. As soon as the food warms up again, the spoilage organisms grow quickly, which increases the rate of spoilage of the food.

7 It is not possible to exclude spoilage organisms from most foods. Such organisms are present in the air (especially fungal spores, i.e. mould spores), the water supply, and even in food when it is slaughtered, harvested, etc. Only careful storage methods, including low-temperature storage, can delay the spoilage process.

One method of food preservation can eliminate spoilage organisms virtually for ever — that is canning, so long as it is performed well. If a canned food is unfit, however, the consequences can be severe.

Q What (very dangerous) type of food poisoning is associated with canned foods?

A Botulism, produced by the anaerobic spore-former *Clostridium botulinum.* All commercial canning processes are designed to destroy the spores of this organism but even the most careful processes can go wrong occasionally.

---

8 We cannot afford to take any chances at all so far as canned foods are concerned. If we have any doubts about them we must treat them as being unfit for consumption. Sometimes it is necessary to open a can and to smell its contents to ascertain whether the food is unfit or not. As always this may not tell us very much but, if the contents smell 'off' you would be foolish to use the food.

Canned foods may, under some circumstances, provide us with a warning about the condition of the food inside. This arises if a microbe grows inside the food in the can and produces a gas. The can is sealed and so, as the microbes grow and produce more and more gas, the gas pushes the sides and ends of the can outwards. The ends of the can (and sometimes the sides also) bulge out. The can is said to be 'blown'. Such canned food must ALWAYS be considered unfit for consumption. You must always remember that not all canned foods do this, and that the contents of a normal looking can could still produce illness. If you do find a 'blown' can you are, of course, lucky in that you have had an early warning. Don't ignore that warning — put the can in a safe place (label it 'Do not use') and inform the Environmental Health Officer so that the source of the can and any other batches which might also be unfit can be traced.

Similarly, you may find a rusty can with contents that could be fit for consumption. Much depends on the extent of the rusting. If it has penetrated the tin-plate, microbes may have entered; if not, the contents might be fit. If you find a rusty can, the best procedure would be to ask the Environmental Health Officer for an opinion.

KEY FACTS

1 Unfit food is food which, if consumed, would do the consumer harm in the short term AND any food which is aesthetically unsuitable for consumption.

2 It is easy to tell whether food is definitely unfit (by smell and appearance), but it is impossible to tell whether any food is definitely fit. Apparently 'fit' food could be contaminated with pathogenic microbes and still look, smell, and taste perfectly normal.

3 If any food looks or smells 'off', 'don't chance it'.

4 All unfit food must be kept entirely separate from other foods and should be stored away from food handling and storage areas.

5 When food goes 'off' this is due to the combined action of spoilage bacteria and fungi. Most spoilage bacteria do not produce food poisoning and, similarly most food-poisoning bacteria do not spoil food.

6 If food has been spoiled by spoilage bacteria, this indicates that conditions have been suitable for the growth of bacteria. If the food was also contaminated with food poisoning bacteria (as well as spoilage types) they would have multiplied and the food would then be extremely dangerous to eat.

7 Excessive mould on cheese, and any amount of mould on other food, renders that food unfit to eat.

8 Always consider how a particular type of food looks and smells when fresh. If any food looks wrong or different from normal, the chances are that it has begun to spoil.

PROGRESS PAPER 18

As before, answer the following questions carefully. Remember to read the whole programme again if you cannot answer any of the questions or if, after having compared your answers with the model answers, you get any wrong. Of course, as always in this book, your answer need not be exactly like the model answer, so long as it is essentially correct. Write your answers on a separate sheet of paper.

1. What causes food to spoil?
2. What is a spoilage organism?
3. What 'tools' should be used to detect unfit food?
4. Can you say whether a food is definitely fit to eat?
5. Is it illegal to sell unfit food? Is it illegal to have it in your possession?
6. What are the main signs of unfitness in raw meat?
7. What are the main signs of unfitness in wet (raw) fish?
8. What is a 'blown' can, and what would you do with it?
9. Is mouldy food unfit?
10. If you have any doubt about a particular food, what should you do?

ANSWERS

1 The enzymes that are contained in the food cells and are released after death start the process of spoilage. Spoilage bacteria and/or fungi then start to grow if it is warm enough (but remember that spoilage organisms can grow below 5 °C) and the rate of spoilage is then proportional to the rate of growth of these organisms.

2 It is a bacterium or fungus that is able to spoil food by growing in or on it. These organisms bring about spoilage of the food by 'eating' the food while growing on it or in it.

3 Senses of sight, smell and touch (NOT taste).

4 No, not without a laboratory analysis. You can only say whether a food is definitely unfit to eat.

5 Yes, if you intend it to be used for human consumption. You must always keep fit and unfit food separate, in any case, as otherwise the unfit food may well contaminate the fit.

6 It smells 'off', looks slimy and may have mould growing on it.

7 It smells 'off', looks slimy, the scales rub off easily and its eyes are opaque.

8 It is a can which bulges at the ends or at the sides. The bulging is caused by microbes inside the can producing gas as they feed on its contents. You must always presume that the contents of the can may be highly dangerous. Put the can in a safe place, label it 'Do not use' and inform the Local Authority Environmental Health Officer who can try to discover whether there are any more of the same batch around (in other premises, at wholesalers, etc.). The can may be a 'one-off' (i.e. the only one in that condition) or it could be one of a batch in the same condition.

9 Not necessarily, according to current knowledge, although if mycotoxins from moulds are proved to be dangerous to health, this view would of course, change. Current opinion is that it all depends on the amount of mould and the food. Mouldy meat is unfit, as is mouldy fruit, etc. In the case of cheese, however, so long as the mould growth is not extensive, it is thought to be permissible to cut off the mouldy portion and to eat the rest. Mouldy bread is usually considered to be unfit as is mouldy confectionery. Usually such foods are totally unpalatable when they reach the stage of being mouldy.

10 Don't use it — call in the Environmental Health Officer for advice.

PROGRAMME 19

Food Preservation and Food Additives

1 Since the mid-1960s considerable changes have been observed with respect to the type and variety of foods eaten in the UK. Most noteworthy is the fact that more and more preserved and 'convenience' foods are consumed than ever before. Food-preservation techniques have reached a very high level of sophistication and the increasing use of food additives of various types, not all of which are directly concerned with preservation, has given rise to some public concern and much controversy. Many of the methods of food preservation used today are however, of ancient origin. Indeed some of the very best, and safest, preservation methods have been used since earliest times. It is both understandable and right that the public should question the use of food additives, that the safety of such additives should be assured and that other (non-chemical) preservation methods should also be considered from the health viewpoint. Despite justifiable reservations it must be noted that attempts to delay food spoilage (it cannot easily be prevented for ever) are essential in a world that is heading for mass food shortages on a scale never before imagined. It is with this thought in mind that you should study this programme. The topic of food preservation and additives is a vast one. For our purposes we shall concentrate on points of greatest concern to us from the hygiene viewpoint.

Q Name two common preservation methods used everywhere to delay food spoilage.

A The use of low temperatures (freezing), salting (brining), pickling and drying, are the most common methods of food preservation the world over. (NOTE: you were asked to name only two sources — any two of these four methods would do.)

2 All food-preservation methods have one aim in common — they are all intended to delay food spoilage. Such spoilage nearly always starts with enzyme attack on a food. The enzymes (which are chemical substances) were present in the food cells when the food was alive (as a plant or animal). On the death of these cells, the digesting enzymes are released.

Once enzymes of this type have started the spoilage process, microbes start to 'spoil' the food even more. Such microbes originate from many sources but most are already present in the food anyway. They have either been present in the food animal before slaughter or, in the case of plant type foods, they originate from the soil. The important point to note is that virtually all foods will be contaminated by microbes of a type that can bring about spoilage of the food (because they grow on the food, breaking it down to obtain energy and building blocks for their own 'bodies'). Such contamination will arise from source and there is very little that we can do about it. The only safe presumption to make is that all foods will contain spoilage organisms. Whether or not the foods spoil (rot) and how fast they do so, will depend on the nature of the food, the nature of the organisms involved and the way the food is handled, processed, stored or transported.

Q If most spoilage arises because of microbial action, how can we delay it?

A We can delay it by preventing the spoilage organisms from growing in the food. We must be careful to prevent further microbial contamination of the food, of course, but we can expect most foods to be contaminated with spoilage organisms when they first come into our hands.

---

3 Different types of food are more susceptible to spoilage than others. This is a matter of common observation. Most people would agree but few have ever really bothered to think just why it should be so. You should consider this for a moment before reading on.

If you think carefully about all we have said in previous programmes, you will recall that microbes (especially bacteria and fungi) prefer some foods to others. Bacteria and moulds are the 'food spoilers' (viruses of course, do not 'grow' in food at all). These microbes like certain conditions better than others. Bacteria prefer protein foods (meat, milk, etc.) whereas fungi prefer high carbohydrate foods. Therefore we can expect meat to be spoiled chiefly by bacteria and cheeses, bread, etc., to be spoiled chiefly by fungi (moulds). Jams and similar preserves are subject to spoilage by certain types of yeast and mould which can grow quite happily in these highly concentrated foods. Dried foods do not rot easily because of a lack of moisture (which microbes need in order to grow), fruits are too acidic for most organisms (although yeasts and some moulds can attack them) and so on. (NOTE: moulds are multi-celled fungi, yeasts are single-celled fungi).

Q What is the main principle of freezing as a method of food preservation?

A As in all types of food preservation, we should start to answer this question by considering what effect the process will have on any spoilage organisms which are present in the food. If we can stop them from growing in the food, we can effectively delay the food spoilage process. Freezing removes water from the microbe's grasp by solidifying it as ice. The microbes need liquid water to grow and therefore freezing preserves food by making the water in it unavailable for the microbes.

4 Freezing then, preserves food because the water is made unavailable to microbes by being converted to solid ice. Foods for freezing commercially are selected with care. Freezing can only delay spoilage; many of the organisms present in the food prior to the freezing process will survive to recommence growth on defrosting. Food will never come out of a freezer in a better state than when it went in. In most cases it will deteriorate gradually. Several methods of freezing are used commercially. 'Blast' freezing is common: usually, the food to be frozen is placed in a large refrigerated room equipped with large fans. Cold air is blown over the food for many hours. The choice of food to be frozen, the design of the chamber, the refrigeration plant and the food holder (air must circulate around each food batch) are all carefully controlled. The domestic type 'chest freezer' is an extremely inefficient freezing-machine. These should be used ONLY for holding food which has been frozen commercially under controlled conditions.

Liquid nitrogen is used as an alternative freezing process in which small batches of food (very carefully controlled as regards weight and size) travel through a tunnel in which extremely cold nitrogen is passed (nitrogen tunnel). The food batches pass through the tunnel on a conveyor and the freezing process can be completed in a few minutes. These are merely brief outlines of alternative freezing processes. It must be stressed that each process is complex and that each must be most carefully controlled. The most important thing is that the freezing process must be completed quickly. Fast freezing causes small ice crystals to be formed in the food, whereas slow freezing causes large crystals to be formed. The large crystals can break down the food substance when it defrosts. Fast freezing is essential so that the desirable small ice crystals will be formed in the food.

An alternative to freezing is to 'freeze dry'. This is actually a method of producing dehydrated (water removed) foods. The freezing process is performed in a partial vacuum so that the water in the food actually evaporates very quickly indeed, leaving a dried food as a result.

Q Once frozen food has been defrosted, is it permissible to re-freeze it?

A Strictly speaking, no, it is not. Much depends on the type of food, its original condition (especially its original degree of microbial contamination) and what has happened to it in the meantime.

The danger is that microbes will start to multiply again as the food is defrosted. It is always best to consume food soon after it is defrosted; it should not be re-frozen. Ice cream constitutes a special case. Once solid ice cream has risen above −2.2 °C (minus 2.2 °C, i.e. two point two degrees below zero), it cannot legally be sold unless it is heat-treated again (which is a commercial operation that only the manufacturers can carry out).

5 Freezers in catering and other establishments should ONLY be used to store food that has been frozen commercially. Such freezers should not be over-filled as cold air should be able to circulate freely around the food packs. Care must be taken to ensure that the freezer stays at about −18 °C (minus 18 °C) and not above. In the event of a breakdown, the food should be safe for a few hours, but again, once defrosted, it should be used or disposed of. This is a counsel of perfection in many cases and is not always necessary. It is wise to seek the advice of the Environmental Health Officer in individual cases.

Refrigerators only delay spoilage for a short time and should not be used for long-term storage. Both freezers and fridges should be defrosted regularly, well maintained and their actual temperature should be checked by means of an electronic thermometer. Foods must not be stored above the 'load line' in chest fridge/freezers because, above that line, the unit will not be reaching the required low temperatures.

Q Apart from freezing, what is the other common modern preservation method?.

A Canning, which has been extensively used since World War II.

---

6 Canning processes are complex. In essence, they work by the food in the cans being heated during processing to a high temperature for a sufficiently long period of time to kill any pathogenic or spoilage organisms that could be present in the food. Most important of all is that the temperature/time combination should be able to kill the spores of *Clostridium botulinum* (which produces the deadly botulism toxin). What temperature/time combination is used depends on the nature of the food and especially, its acidity. Highly acidic foods require to be heated to lower temperatures for shorter periods of time than other foods. As with freezing, the whole canning process is complex and must be controlled most carefully.

Once a food in the can has been processed by heat, it is protected from further contamination by the can itself. If, however, the can becomes damaged, or if it 'leaks' from the seams, microbes can enter. This is especially likely to happen after the cans come out of the cooking/processing retorts. They are usually cooled by water. If there is any fault in the can, water will be sucked in as the can cools. If the water is contaminated, the food inside the can will become contaminated also. Great care must be taken at processing plants to ensure that cooling water is entirely safe.

Some canned foods (notably some hams) are only partially heat-treated as full heat treatment would destroy the food. These MUST be kept refrigerated. The labels on such canned foods carry a warning to this effect and the food is usually described as 'pasteurised'. Fully heat-treated canned foods are capable of 'lasting' for a very considerable time (measured in years rather than months) and, on the whole, canning may be considered to be a safe and effective preservation method so long as the can is neither damaged nor rusty. In these cases advice should be sought from the Environmental Health Officer.

Q What is a 'blown' can? What causes it, and what should you do about it? (NOTE: we discussed this in Programme 18).

A A 'blown' can is one which bulges due (usually) to gas being produced by microbes growing in the can contents. A 'good' can should have dished-in (concave) ends. The contents of a 'blown' can could be highly dangerous — do NOT use the food — inform the Environmental Health Officer.

7 Raw milk may be contaminated with certain pathogenic, as well as spoilage, organisms. Virtually all milk sold in the UK must now be heat-treated to ensure that it does not harm a consumer's health. Three major heat treatment methods are used. They will all destroy tuberculosis (TB) and brucellosis (undulant fever) bacteria, which are the main dangers. Each method differs mainly in the degree to which spoilage organisms are killed.

'Pasteurised' milk is heated the least, and therefore has the shortest shelf-life. 'Sterilised' milk is heated more, so it keeps better. Best of all, so far as keeping-quality is concerned, is the 'UHT' (Ultra-heat-treated) milk which is heated to a very high temperature for a short time. Once the milk container is opened, the milk will soon spoil as it can then be contaminated with spoilage organisms. In any case, some spoilage organisms always survive the heat treatment process in small numbers.

Cheese is a preserved food of great antiquity. It 'keeps' for some time because it does not provide a good growth medium for anything other than slow-growing fungi. Cream should always be heat-treated (usually it is) as both TB and brucellosis could be contracted as a result of eating raw, untreated cream.

Q Why don't jams and similar preserves rot quickly?

A The high sugar content 'ties up' the water in them and makes it unavailable to microbes. (The concentrated jam, etc., is said to have a high 'osmotic pressure').

8 Other common methods of preservation are drying (dehydration), smoking, pickling and curing (brining). Each of these is used to varying degrees of success. Dehydrated foods do not spoil easily because no moisture is available to support microbial growth. They will last for years as long as they remain dry. Smoking is really a form of drying; it is not very effective as a preservation method and is used today as a flavouring and texturing process rather than for its preservation purposes. Pickling too is used mostly for its flavour effects, although the highly acid nature of the vinegar 'pickle' does delay spoilage very well.

Q What common food is processed by 'curing' (i.e. brining)?

A Bacon. Pork is made into bacon by being 'cured'. It is usually soaked in baths of curing brines for a few days. The brine contains sugar, table salt (sodium chloride), sodium nitrite and sodium nitrate. These latter substances have recently given rise to controversy. It has been been suggested that nitrites and nitrates (which are used in other 'cured' and vacuum packed meats, raw and cooked, apart from bacon) may be injurious to health. These substances are fairly effective as preservatives, however, although bacon should still be kept under refrigeration.

In the case of the familiar vacuum-packed (especially cooked) meats, the nitrites and nitrates very effectively inhibit the growth of botulism bacteria. It may be that, if the hazard of the nitrites and nitrates is removed, a hazard of botulism may appear in its place.

9 Salt, nitrates, etc., are examples of chemical preservatives. Several of these exist. Some are very specific and will prevent the growth of only certain classes of microbes (moulds, for instance). The use of these substances is, and should be, very carefully controlled.

Great difficulty arises, however, whenever attempts are made to ascertain whether a particular chemical preservative is 'safe' or not. The whole question of food-additive safety is one which is kept under constant review by the Ministry of Agriculture, Fisheries and Food and other bodies. Only approved additives may be used in food. The types of additive, how much can be used, and in what types of food they can be used, are all carefully controlled by law.

Q In addition to preservatives, what other uses do food additives have in food?

A They may be colours, flavours, flavour-enhancers (notably monosodium glutamate), texture-enhancers, antioxidants, and a whole lot more. The law carefully controls the use of such substances but research into possible hazards continues.

KEY FACTS

1 Food-preservation methods are intended to delay food spoilage. Some methods are more effective than others in that they delay spoilage for longer.

2 All food-preservation methods operate essentially by controlling the growth of spoilage organisms (bacteria and fungi).

3 The main preservation methods are:

(i) Low temperatures

(ii) Heat treatment and/or sealing

(iii) Use of chemicals

(iv) Water removal or control

4 Low temperatures operate by delaying the growth rate of spoilage organisms. Temperatures below 0 °C are needed. Freezing operates at about −18 °C and its main effect is to remove water (by solidifying it).

5 Heat treatments aim at killing as many of the spoilage organisms present in food as possible. Following such processes, the food must be entirely enclosed to stop any further spoilage organisms from getting access to the food. Sometimes (raw bacon, for example) the food to be preserved is merely sealed in a vacuum. This can reduce spoilage, but such foods should still be held in a refrigerator. The most common examples of preservation by heat treatment and sealing are canning and milk processing.

6 Chemicals are often added to food to delay spoilage. Such chemicals inhibit the growth of microbes. The traditional use of such preservative chemicals is found in the practice of salting (or brining) meats. Yet another traditional method of food preservation is found in the case of pickled foods where acetic acid (in vinegar) is the chemical used.

7 By removing, or controlling, water content, the growth of spoilage organisms can be delayed. Dried foods have all water removed and they have a long shelf-life as long as they are kept dry. Sometimes the water is merely 'tied up' so as to be made unavailable to microbes (as in salting and the use of sugar in preserves, e.g. jams).

8 Foods may have chemicals other than preservatives added to them. Additives to control texture, colours, flavour and so on, are often used. The use of such additives is not without its potential dangers and the use of food additives is carefully controlled by law.

PROGRESS PAPER 19

As in other programmes, we now have a short progress test. This is provided for your own sake, so please attempt to answer each question carefully, writing your answers on a separate sheet of paper. Check your answers against the model answers — if you get any wrong, or cannot answer a question, read the whole programme again. Attempt all the questions before looking at the model answers.

1 Why is it necessary to preserve food?

2 Which types of food require preservation?

3 Why do certain foods spoil quickly while others keep well for long periods?

4 Why is fruit not highly perishable?

5 Why is it potentially dangerous to drink raw milk?

6 What causes a can to 'blow'? What does a 'blown' can look like?

7 At what temperature should a chest freezer be operated?

8 Should defrosted frozen food be re-frozen?

9 Is it permissible to use just any preservative in food?

10 Should bacon be kept under refrigeration?

ANSWERS

1 To prevent it being spoiled. We must preserve food to prevent waste; this is especially important in a world where food supplies are dwindling. Correct food hygiene practices can, themselves, help to reduce food spoilage. This is an added benefit of good food hygiene.

2 Those which are perishable. Some foods are, obviously, more perishable (more liable to rot) than others.

3 Those which spoil quickly (highly perishable foods) are the ones which readily support the growth (multiplication) of spoilage microbes. It is the growth of such microbes in the food which causes it to rot.

4 It is highly acidic and only acid-tolerant organisms grow easily within it. These organisms tend to grow rather slowly.

5 The raw milk may contain the bacteria of TB or brucellosis, (or a disease called 'Q fever').

6 Gas produced by microbes growing in the contents of the can. A normal can has both ends dished inwards (concave), a 'blown' can bulges at the ends.

7 At −18 °C (minus 18 °C).

8 No, it should not. It should be used quickly. If in doubt, seek advice from the Environmental Health Officer.

9 No, all preservative use is controlled by law.

10 Yes, even though it is 'salted', it is still quite perishable and pathogens could grow within it.

PROGRAMME 20
Pests and Pest Control

1 In Programme 19 we said that one of the major aspects of food hygiene practice concerns the prevention of contamination of food by microbes. One of the most serious sources of contamination arises from pests. Rodents, insects, and even birds, carry a considerable variety of microbes in great numbers. These microbes are present both inside the pest's alimentary tract (gut) and on their bodies. Many pests habitually live, or forage, in waste materials, sewers, etc. where they inevitably pick up many pathogenic varieties of microbe. It is obviously essential to protect food from pests. Apart from the obvious waste which such pests create, the food will also become dangerously contaminated by pests. In addition, it is also necessary to protect the food environment from pest visitation. If preparation surfaces, utensils, shelves, etc. are visited by pests, contamination of those surfaces is inevitable.

Q How, do you think, can we prevent pests from contaminating food-preparation surfaces?

A The only way to prevent pests from contaminating food-preparation surfaces is to prevent them from gaining access to the food premises in the first place. It is a true maxim, so far as food safety is concerned, that 'prevention is better than cure', and certainly it is better to prevent pests from getting into food premises in the first place than attempt to kill them once they have gained a foothold.

---

2 The very first rule of pest control — the 'Golden Rule' if you like — is to prevent pests from gaining access to the premises at all. We must do all we can to avoid encouraging them. Removal of all food scraps; ensuring that areas under and behind all equipment are kept clean; the use of bins fitted with close-fitting lids, the use of a properly built and pest-proofed swill or refuse storage area — all these measures will go a long way to making premises unattractive to pests. The pests enter to find warmth, shelter, nesting materials and food. By ensuring that they cannot find any food, we can avoid attracting them in the first place. If rotting food is left within easy access, or if grease, fat, food scraps, etc., accumulate behind or under equipment or in dark and sheltered recesses, pests will be attracted as if to a magnet.

Q What else should we do to prevent pests from entering our food premises, apart from avoiding anything that could encourage them?

A It will be necessary to proof the premises against pest entry. We must make it very hard indeed for pests to enter the premises at all.

---

3 Pest-proofing is actually very much easier than most people imagine. Few food premises are routinely proofed against pests. Even fewer are designed properly — i.e. in such a way as to make it difficult for pests to enter. It is nothing short of amazing that this should be so. Pest-proofing is neither difficult nor unduly expensive. It is ridiculous to spend money eliminating pests from a food premises when they could be prevented from entering in the first place.

Rodents (especially mice) can enter through surprisingly small holes or gaps. The very first proofing measure that should be undertaken is to block such possible entry points. This requires a careful survey of the whole premises to disover possible entry points. This survey is carried out by the Local Authority Pest Control Operators. Private contractors could also be used but the Local Authority operatives are usually to be preferred. Having detected possible entry points, these can be sealed. Although rodents are gnawing creatures, they rarely enter a building by force (as it were), preferring to seek out ready-made access points. Nevertheless, any sealing or screening of such points, or sealing of gates to refuse areas, etc., must be done with substantial materials. Wire netting can be overcome by determined rodents if they are hungry enough and are determined to gain entry.

Q What do you think are the most likely entry points to a building for flying insects?

A Undoubtedly open windows and doors. Ideally, food premises should not have opening windows at all. Ventilation should be by mechanical means which makes it unnecessary to have opening window-lights anyway. Doors will, of course, have to be opened, but they need not be left open to present a welcome invitation to flies. It is possible to fit air-curtains to external doors and these are highly effective in preventing flying insects from entering. The air-curtain consists of fan driven ducts at the sides and top of the doors so arranged that a constant stream of air is passed across the door opening. This discourages flies from flying across the opening. If windows must be opened, they should be equipped with plastic mesh strung over a wooden frame enclosure. Such meshes are readily available and it is not difficult to have a wooden frame constructed so that a window can be opened and yet still be proof against fly entry.

---

4 It is reasonably easy to proof premises against the entry of flying insects, but less easy to prevent crawling insects from entering. Such insects are, of course, often very small (e.g. ants) and can enter through minute spaces. Nevertheless, we can protect our premises from these pests if we only exercise a little care. First of all we can repeat the general point made earlier, that it is better to prevent pests becoming a problem than it is to deal with them once they have become established. In other words, we must do all we can to avoid providing pests with a comfortable home, complete with food and shelter.

One of the reasons why it is essential to clean THOROUGHLY all around, under and behind equipment, is to discourage insect infestation. If insects do gain entry to the food rooms, they will feed quite happily on even small food accumulations, grease, etc., which is lodged behind equipment, under cupboards and so on. If we are to prevent insect infestation, it is absolutely essential to prevent accumulations of food, grease, etc. Thorough and proper cleaning, every nook and cranny, will go a long way to preventing insect infestation from arising in the first place.

Q How do you think can we discourage pests from gaining access to stored food?

A It is essential to make all food storage areas as proof against pest entry as possible. Remember that doors often fit badly and that even narrow gaps at top or bottom can allow small insects to enter. It is equally important to store bulked ingredients (sugar, flour, grains, etc.) in pest-proof containers fitted with close-fitting lids. Plastic containers of various sizes and shapes are available (even some the size of dustbins which are designed to be fitted with sealed lids). Such containers must be used to prevent pests from gaining access to food and food ingredients, if they do gain access to the premises.

---

5 Unfortunately, it is not unusual to find that insects, and even rodents, (notably mice) enter food premises with stores. Bags of grain, flour, etc., can provide pests with a free ride into the premises. It is essential to inspect stores carefully on reception to ensure that pests are not being delivered to the premises as well as new stock. It is equally important that all parts of the premises be inspected at least weekly to detect any signs of pest infestation. All pests are capable of reproducing at a very rapid rate, and even a small initial infestation can soon become serious if neglected.

Remember that pests usually hide in dark, inaccessible places. When searching for any signs of infestation, it is essential to look into and behind cupboards, behind equipment, and so on. Storage bins and containers should be moved so that any signs of infestation behind them can be easily seen. To survey even large premises for signs of infestation does not take up much time, and it is always time well spent.

Q How would you tell whether your premises had a mouse or rat infestation? (Think carefully and have a guess at this one.)

A You should be able to detect the droppings (which look like black or brown pellets and are small in the case of mice, but up to one inch long in the case of rats). The droppings are most likely to be found in inaccessible dark and sheltered areas, especially behind equipment and storage bins, etc.

In addition, you may be able to detect gnawing. If you foolishly store foodstuffs in their original containers (packets, boxes, etc.) rodents will be able to gnaw into them in order to get to the food inside. This is why hard, plastic containers should be used whenever possible. Nevertheless, rodents will gnaw at virtually anything and teeth marks are a sure sign of infestation. In addition, grease marks may be present on walls, pipes, etc., from the rodent's body.

---

6 Insect infestations are usually detected by seeing the insects themselves. Many insects leave a kind of webbing (like a spider's web) behind when they infest food ingredients such as flour. Such webbing provides a clue to their presence. If you detect an infestation of either insects or rodents, it is essential to act quickly. The faster the problem is dealt with the better. It is equally essential to try to discover where and how the pests gained entry. They may well have come in with stores, but you might have a fractured air-vent, drain, hole in a wall where pipes go through, etc. In all cases, it is wise to seek the advice of the Environmental Health Officer as soon as an infestation of any type is found. Under NO circumstances should a 'do-it-yourself' infestation-control programme be instituted. If success is to be achieved specialist advice is necessary. In all cases, Local Authority operators are to be preferred to any other. They are under the direct supervision of the Environmental Health Officer and have no interest in making a profit from the work. NEVER attempt to lay poisons or to spray insecticides yourself.

NOTE: It is my opinion, based on experience, that much danger can be caused by untrained personnel attempting to eliminate a pest infestation. For this reason, no details of poisons, insecticides, etc., will be given in this book. The ONLY safe procedure is to check for signs of infestation at least weekly and to call in the Environmental Health Officer at the first sign of trouble.

7 Flying insects can be controlled quite well by means of ultraviolet electrocution equipment. These consist of a bank of strip lights (they resemble 'fluorescent' lamps) in front of which is an electrified metal grid. Flies are attracted to the lamps and are electrocuted on touching it. They fall into a tray below which must be emptied regularly. It is important that these units be situated in appropriate areas and NOT merely distributed evenly throughout the premises. Once again, advice should be sought from the Environmental Health Officer.

Q We have mentioned rodents and insects — what else could be considered to be a 'pest'?

A Birds — especially pigeons. Birds do carry pathogenic microbes and they can sometimes gain entry to premises. It is necessary to proof eaves, etc. against bird entry where birds could gain access to the food storage and preparation areas themselves.

At this point we shall leave our brief discussion of pests as this is a specialist subject which should not be undertaken by non-specialists. More harm than good can be done unless specialist advice is followed and specialist treatments used where necessary. Much depends on individual circumstances (especially so far as pest-proofing is concerned) and readers are well advised to seek advice from their local Environmental Health Officer.

NOTE: If you are using this book as a guide to assist studies leading to the food hygiene exams (such as for the RSH or RIPHH), you will need a little more information than is provided here. You will need to know especially how to identify the most common types of insect pest. You should therefore ask your tutor or college teacher to provide you with this extra information.

KEY FACTS

1 Pests of many types (rodents, insects, birds) can carry a whole host of pathogenic organisms and can easily contaminate food premises. The only way to prevent such contamination is to prevent the pests from entering the food premises.

2 Pests can only be prevented from entering food premises if the premises are fully pest-proofed. It is of no value to 'treat' for pests (with poisons or insecticides) if they can gain easy access to the premises. If this is the case, then further pests will arrive to re-establish infestation.

3 Ideally, food premises should not have open windows or doors. If they do have open windows they must be fitted with fine mesh to stop insects entering. Doors should be self-closing and should not be left open.

4 Pests may enter food premises with incoming stores. All deliveries should be carefully examined to prevent this.

5 All waste foods should be removed to proper storage places. Waste food, cardboard, paper, etc., should be stored separately, in bins that have close-fitting lids to prevent insect access. The refuse storage area must be very carefully pest-proofed. Waste food and packages, etc. will attract rodents and insects and they must not be allowed to gain access to refuse areas. (Rodents use paper, boxes, etc., as nesting-material).

6 Pest proofing of a building is a detailed affair but it must always be done. It is always a waste of time, money and effort to attempt to control pests if the premises are not properly pest-proofed.

7 The use of poisons for rodents and insecticides for insects is always potentially dangerous as the poisons may get into food. Danger may also threaten the person who is using the poisons. Do-it-yourself treatments are always potentially hazardous and, in all cases, expert pest control operators will be able to get better results than any do-it-yourself treatments.

8 Pet animals must be excluded from food premises as they could easily contaminate food or the food environment.

PROGRESS PAPER 20

Have a go at the questions below! Check your answers against the model answers only after you have attempted all the questions. If you get any answers wrong, or cannot answer a particular question, go through the whole programme again.

1. Why are we concerned to keep pests out of food premises?
2. How can we prevent pests from contaminating food surfaces?
3. What is meant by the term 'pest proofing'?
4. What are the most likely entry points in a building for flying insects?
5. How can we prevent flying insects from entering a building?
6. Why should stores be checked on delivery to a food premises?
7. Name three indicators of a mouse or rat infestation in a food premises.
8. Name the three most common insect pests in food premises.
9. Is it hazardous for birds to be allowed into food rooms?
10. From whom should you seek advice concerning pest control?

ANSWERS

1 Pests carry pathogenic organisms in or on their bodies. We must keep them out of food premises in order to prevent them from contaminating food.

2 By preventing them from gaining entry to the food premises in the first place (i.e. pest proofing).

3 The term describes all methods of preventing pests from entering food premises.

4 Open windows.

5 Keep all windows/doors, etc., closed. Use netting at windows if they must be opened.

6 To detect whether any pests are being introduced into the premises with the stores.

7 Gnawed food, food packets, etc., droppings, and grease marks on walls, pipes, etc.

8 Flies, cockroaches and ants.

9 Yes, they may carry pathogens (especially in their droppings).

10 The Local Authority Environmental Health Officer.

Appendix

The law and food hygiene

It is not proposed to discuss the law relating to food hygiene and food control in this book. There are two reasons for this omission. Firstly, at the time of writing, the law is under review and may well be changed in some way. Secondly, although it is necessary for a food professional to know that legal rules apply to the handling, storage and sale of food, it is vastly more important to know how to ensure that food is safe and to follow safe practices always. If you follow the principles discussed within this book, you will automatically comply with the legal rules.

For examination purposes

For those readers who will be sitting an examination in food hygiene it may well be necessary to learn a little of the specific details of the law relating to food hygiene and food control because it could be the subject of an exam question. If you are to sit such an exam, you should ask your tutor or lecturer to provide details of the relevant law. Alternatively, enquire from your local council offices. You should speak to an Environmental Health Officer in the Environmental Health Department of your local authority. This officer will be able to provide the information you need. When seeking such information, make sure that you cover the following points especially:

(i) The legal responsibilities of food business owners, managers and supervisors in the food trade in general.

(ii) The legal responsibilities of food handlers (including cleaners, washers-up, bar staff, waitresses, etc., as well as those who prepare food).

(iii) The legal requirements relating to food premises (especially storage facilities, design of food rooms, surfaces, finishes, drainage, water supply, conveniences, washing facilities, equipment, first aid and servery equipment).

(iv) Details of legal requirements regarding hygienic practices and personal hygiene.

(v) Penalties for not observing the law relating to food hygiene, information about who can be prosecuted and details of how, and under what circumstances, food premises can be closed down.

(vi) An outline of the law relating to food composition (additives, etc.), what may and may not be added to food and food contamination.

(vii) Details of the law relating to the possession, use, sale or offering for sale, of unfit food.

(viii) Outline of consumer-protection law relating to food.

Test Papers

Instructions

Throughout this book you have been asked questions which were intended to do two things. Firstly, they were designed to make you think about the subject of food hygiene and its implications. Secondly, the questions were intended to help you measure your own progress of learning.

Now you have come to the end of the book, it is important for you to revise the material you have learned. Learning does NOT mean a process of committing facts to memory, but rather it involves an increasing awareness in understanding a subject. The test papers which follow will help you to revise that material from your studies which is of most practical importance. The papers will also help you to gauge your progress.

It is important that you answer the questions carefully. Think about each question and, if the answer does not come to mind quickly, do not despair. At the very least you can have a guess at the answer — your guess may well be right and you might surprise yourself with how much you have learned. Write your answers on a separate sheet of paper.

After answering each test paper, check your answers with the model answers which follow. Do not 'cheat', attempt all the questions before looking at the answers. Remember that your answers need not be exactly like the models; as long as you get the main points you can mark your answer as correct.

Those of you who will be sitting an exam in food hygiene will find that the test papers will be good practice. In these cases, you should allow yourself a maximum of 20 minutes ONLY to answer each test paper.

TEST PAPER 1

1 What are the advantages of high standards of food hygiene?

2 What are the possible consequences of poor standards of food hygiene?

3 Name two sources of pathogenic organisms.

4 Which group of bacteria are the most common causes of food poisoning in the UK?

5 What does a 'blown' can look like? What should you do if you find one?

6 At which temperature should frozen food be stored?

7 At what temperature should soup be kept in a *bain-marie* awaiting service?

8 At what temperature should a meat salad be displayed for sale?

9 What type of head-covering should be worn by a food handler?

10 What are the main signs of unfitness in fish?

11 Name the organism which produces food poisoning within a few hours of eating a contaminated meal.

12 What type of dressing must be used on a cut finger?

13 What are the two main signs of a rodent infestation?

14 Where should a food handler NOT wear overclothing?

15 How can the possibility of cross-contamination be avoided by means of kitchen design?

16 Are the staff, as well as the 'management' responsible for maintaining good standards of food hygiene?

17 What must be done before a sanitiser is used?

18 On what kind of surfaces, in a kitchen, must a sanitiser be used?

19 What are the main symptoms of food poisoning?

20 What should a manager do if a food handler reports sick?

21 What is a mycotoxin?

22 How should crockery be dried following washing?

23 What type of sanitiser should be used on food preparation surfaces?

24 Some viruses can cause a variety of food poisoning — true or false?

25 What kind of surface should be used for food preparation?

ANSWERS TO TEST PAPER 1

1 Protection of food consumers (prevention of food poisoning); increased shelf-life of food; protection of business reputation; protection from legal prosecution.

2 Legal prosecution, damage to business reputation; decreased food shelf-life; food consumers may suffer food poisoning (which can be fatal).

3 You were asked to name only two sources — any two of the following would do): man, raw foods, water supply (sometimes), pests, animals, soil, air.

4 The salmonellae.

5 The can bulges (its ends are not concave). The contents may be dangerous to eat. Do not use the can. Label it as not to be used, and inform the Environmental Health Officer.

6 At −18 °C (minus 18 °C). (This is the general temperature for most frozen foods but some do not need such a low temperature. If in doubt, read the instructions on the packaging.)

7 Above 65 °C.

8 Below 10 °C (preferably below 5 °C).

9 Any type which entirely encloses the hair.

10 Scales rub off easily, the flesh is flaccid, the eyes are opaque.

11 *Staphylococcus aureus.*

12 A waterproof dressing.

13 Droppings and gnawed food packets.

14 Overclothing should not be worn outside the food premises, nor in conveniences.

15 Separate areas for the preparation of raw and ready-to-eat food are needed. A work-flow should be possible, passing from raw to ready-to-eat preparation. Raw vegetable preparation must be entirely separated from other food handling areas.

16 Yes, good standards are everyone's concern.

17 The surface on which a sanitiser is to be used must first be degreased (washed with a hot water/detergent solution).

18 Upon any surface with which food is liable to come into contact.

19 Diarrhoea and vomiting.

20 Lay the food handler off work and inform the Environmental Health Officer.

21 A toxin produced by some fungi (especially some moulds). Some mycotoxins are thought to be implicated as possible cancer-producing substances.

22 It should be air-dried (allowed to dry naturally). If this is not possible, disposable paper towels should be used.

23 A chlorine-generating agent.

24 True (some produce gastro-enteritis).

25 A surface that is smooth, impervious to moisture and capable of being readily cleaned, (e.g. stainless steel).

TEST PAPER 2

1. At what temperature should ice cream be stored?
2. What is the 'danger zone' of temperature?
3. What is the main sign of unfitness in raw meat?
4. What should a food handler do with a cut finger?
5. Name three possible ways in which cross-contamination can occur.
6. What material should sinks be made of?
7. What is the 'two sink method' of washing up?
8. What should handbasins not be used for?
9. How should a stainless-steel preparation table be cleaned?
10. What kind of material would you recommend for use as a kitchen floor?
11. Why is it important to have a good standard of lighting in a food room?
12. What kind of ventilation should be used in a kitchen?
13. What should be done with windows in a food area if they must be opened?
14. In what kind of container should refuse be stored?
15. What should be done to discourage infestation by insects in a food room?
16. Is it necessary to ensure that food delivery vehicles are kept clean?
17. Could 'unfit' food cause disease in a consumer?
18. Where should handbasins be located in food premises?
19. What type of food poisoning (invasive or toxic) is produced by *Staphylococcus aureus*?
20. What is an exotoxin?
21. What type of material should be used for food-room walls?
22. What is the best method of hand-drying?
23. What symptoms of illness should a food handler report?

24 A customer suffers diarrhoea, vomiting and fever about 48 hours after eating a meal. What is the most likely cause?

25 Why are flies hazardous to food?

ANSWERS TO TEST PAPER 2

1 Below –2.2 °C (minus 2.2 °C).

2 From 5 °C to 65 °C, pathogenic bacteria multiply most readily within this temperature range.

3 Bad odour; fit meat smells 'sweet'. Unfit meat loses colour and feels clammy or slimy.

4 Apply a cream antiseptic after having washed the cut. Cover it with a waterproof dressing and consult a doctor if the cut is serious or if it fails to heal normally.

5 (You were asked to name three possible ways only, any three of the following would suffice): using the same slicing machine for raw and ready-to-eat foods; using the same knife, other utensil or surface, etc.; the food handler's hands.

6 Stainless steel.

7 Fill one sink with hot water and detergent to degrease items in this sink. Fill a second sink with hot water and sanitiser for use as a sanitiser rinse.

8 Handbasins should not be used for anything except hand-washing.

9 Firstly remove all food scraps and gross contamination, wash with hot water and detergent, wash thoroughly with hot water and sanitiser and leave to air-dry.

10 Material used must be smooth, impervious to moisture and capable of being easily cleaned. Preferably, it should have as few joints as possible. A granolithic floor is best for heavy-duty use; alternatively heavy-duty vinyl sheets could be used in areas subject to light use.

11 For safety and to see clearly during cleaning and food preparation.

12 Mechanical ventilation (extractor fans).

13 They must be screened by fine mesh to prevent the entry of flying insects.

14 A container which can be easily cleaned and which has a close-fitting lid.

15 Maintain food rooms in a thoroughly clean state, ensure that food, grease etc., does not accumulate under equipment, in crannies, etc.

16 Yes, contamination can occur from an unclean delivery vehicle.

17 Yes, it all depends upon why the food is unfit.

18 In positions that are easily accessible to all food handlers wherever they may be working.

19 Toxic.

20 It is a toxin which is excreted out of certain bacteria (*Staphylococcus*, Clostridia, *Bacillus cereus*) following growth of the bacteria in food.

21 A material which is smooth and capable of being readily cleaned. Sheet plastic panels are best, but plaster and paint would be adequate in areas not subject to steam. Corners, etc., must be protected from percussion damage.

22 Hot-air dryer.

23 Diarrhoea (however slight), abdominal pain, vomiting, nausea, fever, 'cold' symptoms, sore-throat, coughing.

24 A Salmonellae.

25 They carry pathogenic organisms in and on their bodies and can easily contaminate food, equipment and surfaces with these pathogens.

TEST PAPER 3

1 Why is it dangerous to have rodents in a food premises?

2 What are spoilage organisms?

3 What is meant by 'work-flow'?

4 A food handler licks his fingers. What should he do next?

5 A food consumer suffers severe abdominal pain, followed by diarrhoea, approximately 12 hours after consuming a meal. What is the likely cause?

6 Why is it important for food handlers to wear clean, washable, overclothing?

7 Is it permissible to eat food from a rusty can?

8 What food is most often associated with salmonella food poisoning?

9 What kind of material should be used for a food-preparation surface?

10 What is the 'load line' of a refrigerator?

11 What should you do before using a sanitiser on a work surface?

12 Which types of surface do not require to be sanitised? (i.e. washed only).

13 At what temperature should cream cakes be stored awaiting sale?

14 Name any four methods of food preservation.

15 From whom should you seek advice if you discover a rodent infestation in your premises?

16 What should be done with a chicken after it has been removed from an oven if it is to be used in a chicken salad?

17 What must be done with a frozen chicken before preparation?

18 What is the maximum, approximate, weight of turkey that should be cooked?

19 Fill in the missing words below:

Heat food thoroughly, keep it . . . .

Cool food . . . . , keep it . . . .

20 What kinds of animal can be allowed into food premises?

21 May a food handler wear jewellery while at work?

22 What is meant by the term 'cross-contamination'?

23 What should a food handler with long hair do?

24 What should food handlers do with their finger nails?

25 What kind of shoes should a food handler wear at work?

ANSWERS TO TEST PAPER 3

1 Rodents carry pathogenic organisms in and on their bodies and they can, therefore, contaminate food, equipment, surfaces, etc.

2 Organisms that are capable of spoiling (rotting) specific foods. They may or may not be pathogenic.

3 It is a design concept whereby a food processing unit is so arranged that the order of preparation is from raw food to ready-to-eat food. It reduces the risk of cross-contamination.

4 He should wash his hands carefully, immediately.

5 *Clostridium perfringens.*

6 To prevent their own clothing from contaminating food.

7 It is most unwise to do so. Much depends on the degree of rust. If the can is punctured (even minutely), microbes might have entered.

8 Poultry.

9 A material that is smooth, impervious to moisture and capable of being easily cleaned (e.g. stainless steel).

10 It is the marked upper limit for loading a chest type or tiered refrigerator/freezer. If food is stacked above the 'load-line', the food will not be held at a low enough temperature.

11 Remove gross contamination (food scraps, etc.) then degrease it by washing it with hot water and detergent.

12 Surfaces with which food will not come into contact.

13 Below 10 °C (preferably below 5 °C).

14 Canning, freezing, dehydration (drying), salting (brining), smoking, use of chemical preservatives. (Any four of these will do for the answer.)

15 The Environmental Health Officer of the Local Authority.

16 Cooled quickly and thoroughly to below 10 °C. (It could be cut into pieces.)

17 It must be thoroughly defrosted.

18 About 7 kg (15 lbs). We are concerned to get maximum heat-penetration right through to the centre of the food.

19 Hot; quickly; cool.

20 None, except a guide dog within a public area.

21 No jewellery should be worn except a plain gold ring or necklace worn inside the clothing.

22 It is a process whereby pathogens from raw food are passed (either directly or indirectly) to ready-to-eat food.

23 Tie it back and ensure that it is entirely enclosed by a head covering.

24 Keep them short and clean (do NOT bite them and do not wear nail varnish).

25 The most important point is that a special pair of shoes must be kept for use in the food premises only.

TEST PAPER 4

1 Should frozen poultry be defrosted in an oven?

2 What equipment would you recommend to inhibit the growth of bacteria in food?

3 You have received a consignment of food and are doubtful about its fitness. From whom should you seek advice?

4 What piece of equipment would indicate that a refrigerator was not working properly?

5 How do bacteria multiply?

6 What advice should be given to food handlers about their finger nails?

7 What action should a manager take on discovering that a member of staff has symptoms of food poisoning?

8 What is the best way to dry crockery?

9 What do bacteria need in order to multiply?

10 What precautions must be taken with respect to frozen poultry prior to cooking?

11 What is a 'symptomless carrier'?

12 What should be done with cracked plates and cups?

13 What is likely to occur if the same slicer that is used for slicing raw meat is then used to slice boiled ham afterwards?

14 Which organisms are likely to be found in duck eggs?

15 When should food handlers wash their hands?

16 How can a kitchen be designed to reduce the risk of 'cross-contamination'?

17 What food is liable to be contaminated with campylobacters?

18 Should you wear your protective clothing when visiting conveniences?

19 Should a sweets trolley be kept in a warm restaurant all evening?

20 Are all microbes harmful?

21 Is it dangerous to smoke in a food room if you are a food handler?

22 Is it permissible for a food handler to wear a diamond ring while handling food?

23 How should boiled ham be displayed for sale in a retail shop?

24 Name the two indicators of a rodent infestation in food premises.

25 What kind of foods do moulds prefer?

ANSWERS TO TEST PAPER 4

1 No, defrosting will not be efficient and it is likely that the outside will start to dry or burn before defrosting is complete.

2 A refrigerator capable of reaching below 5 °C.

3 The Environmental Health Officer.

4 A thermometer.

5 By binary fission (that is, they grow to a predetermined size and then split into two).

6 Do not bite them, keep them short and clean, and do not use any nail varnish.

7 Exclude them from the food premises immediately, and inform the Environmental Health Officer without delay.

8 Allow it to air-dry naturally.

9 Food, moisture and warmth (their primary, main requirements).

10 Ensure that it is thoroughly defrosted.

11 An individual who is infected with a pathogenic organism but does not show (suffer) any symptoms.

12 They should be thrown away (cracks allow microbes to lodge inside them, and make cleaning impossible).

13 The microbes which will be present on the raw food (from source) will contaminate the slicer blade and will then be passed on to the ready-to-eat boiled ham.

14 Salmonellae.

15 Whenever they are likely to be contaminated with pathogenic organisms (e.g. before handling any food, after using the toilet for any reason, after touching the body (scratching, etc.), after using a handkerchief and after having handled any raw foods).

16 Use separate areas of the kitchen, preferably separate rooms, for raw food and ready-to-eat foods. Ensure work-flow is operated so that food passes from the raw stage, through processing, to ready-to-eat foods (no back-flow). Ensure raw vegetable preparation is entirely separate from all other food preparation areas.

17 Poultry especially.

18 No, because it is liable to pick up contamination from the conveniences.

19 No, the sweets, (especially if containing cream) are a good growth medium for any bacteria or fungi which may contaminate them. Such sweets should be held below 10 °C until consumed.

20 No, in fact many varieties are useful to man. Most are neutral.

21 Yes, you can touch your lips and carry pathogens from your mouth to food. Ash may fall onto food.

22 No, there is a danger that the diamond may dislodge and fall into food. Furthermore, a food handler wearing a diamond ring is less likely to wash hands regularly. Dirt, and microbes, may become lodged behind the ring and in the ring setting.

23 In a refrigerator at a temperature below 10 °C (preferably below 5 °C) and not touching, or close to, any raw food.

24 Droppings and gnaw marks on foods, food packets and containers.

25 Carbohydrate and sugary foods and cheeses.

TEST PAPER 5

1. How do bacteria multiply?
2. Above what temperature do pathogenic microbes stop growing?
3. Below what temperature do pathogenic microbes stop growing?
4. What type of surface should be cleaned by a three-stage cleaning method?
5. Is each food handler in a premises responsible for food hygiene?
6. Will 'unfit' food always harm a consumer?
7. What are the main symptoms of Salmonella food poisoning?
8. What are the main indicators to suggest a rodent infestation in food premises?
9. Name the main signs of unfitness in fish.
10. Name the items of clothing which a food handler should wear only inside a food room.
11. What is the best material to use for making food equipment?
12. What is meant by 'pH control' in food preservation?
13. What is meant by 'osmotic control' in food preservation?
14. What is the difference between UHT milk and pasteurised milk?
15. What is special about pasteurised canned hams?
16. Apart from the prevention of food poisoning and protection from possible prosecution, what other two advantages can be gained from the maintenance of a high standard of food hygiene?
17. How should boiled ham be displayed for sale in a retail shop?
18. Is a good standard of hygiene essential in all food premises?
19. How should cream cakes be displayed for sale?
20. Why should a vegetable preparation area be kept entirely separate from other food preparation areas?
21. What is meant by the term 'cross-contamination'?
22. What type of sanitiser should be used for sanitising a food preparation table?

23 When must food handlers wash their hands?

24 Is it permissible to use a washing-up sink to wash hands?

25 Could birds contaminate food if they gained access to a food room?

ANSWERS TO TEST PAPER 5

1 By binary fission. They grow to a predetermined size and then divide into two.

2 65 °C

3 5 °C (many types cease at 10 °C).

4 A surface with which food is liable to come into contact.

5 All food handlers are responsible for their own hygiene.

6 No, not always. It depends on what has made the food unfit, but it is NEVER worth taking a chance.

7 Diarrhoea, vomiting and fever.

8 Droppings, gnawed food and food packets.

9 Glazed eyes, bad odour and scales rub off easily.

10 White coat or overall, head-covering, and shoes.

11 Stainless steel.

12 Employing an edible acid (e.g. pickling vinegar) to inhibit microbial growth.

13 Employing a highly concentrated solution (e.g. jams and preserves) to inhibit microbial growth.

14 UHT milk is heated to a higher temperature so that more spoilage organisms are destroyed.

15 They must be kept under refrigeration (below 10 °C but above 0 °C) until consumed.

16 Enhancement and protection of business reputation and increased shelf life of perishable foods.

17 It must be protected from the risk of contamination (notably cross-contamination) and be kept below 5 °C.

18 Yes, no matter what type of food is sold.

19 They must be protected from possible contamination and be held below 5 °C.

20 Because root vegetables are contaminated with soil. Soil commonly contains *Bacillus* and *Clostridium* spores. Such spores may be swept into the air and be carried by it to contaminate food in other preparation areas.

21 It is the process whereby pathogenic microbes from raw foods contaminate ready-to-eat foods (either directly or indirectly).

22 A chlorine generator.

23 Whenever they may be contaminated (e.g. after visiting the toilet, after handling raw foods, etc., and before handling any foods).

24 No, the hands will contaminate the sink, which will then contaminate utensils, etc., washed in the sink.

25 Yes, in fact some birds can carry bacteria of a type that causes food poisoning.

TEST PAPER 6

1. Name two advantages of maintaining high standards of food hygiene.
2. When should food handlers wash their hands?
3. What advice would you give to a newly recruited female food handler with respect to her finger nails?
4. Is it permissible for food handlers to wear rings on their fingers?
5. Name two symptoms of illness which a food handler should report.
6. Why is it forbidden for a food handler to smoke in a food room?
7. What kind of handkerchief should a food handler use?
8. What should food handlers do if they sneeze in a food room?
9. Which food poisoning organism produces vomiting within a few hours of eating a meal?
10. Which food poisoning organism is most likely to be caught as a result of contamination of food from a cut on a food handler's finger?
11. Name two common ways in which cross-contamination can arise?
12. Should it be illegal to sell unfit food?
13. Unfit food can be stored in the same fridge as fit food — true or false?
14. Which form of bacterial food poisoning is characterised by severe abdominal pain?
15. Apart from microbes, what else can cause food poisoning?
16. What is a 'symptomless carrier'?
17. What is meant by 'work-flow' in kitchen design?
18. Name the three main topics which constitute food hygiene practice.
19. What is a 'blown' can? What causes it to 'blow'?
20. What should you do if you find a 'blown' can?
21. Name two common insect pests of food premises.
22. What is the first line of defence against insects as far as food premises are concerned?

23 Is it permissible to use the same slicing-machine for cooked and raw meats?

24 What is an exotoxin?

25 What kind of dogs are allowed in retail food shops?

ANSWERS TO TEST PAPER 6

1 (You were asked to give only two advantages — any of the following two would suffice); protection from prosecution; protection of food consumers; protection and enhancement of business image; increased shelf life of food.

2 Whenever the hands are liable to be contaminated (e.g. after visiting the toilet, after handling raw food, and always before handling any food).

3 Keep them neat, short, well-manicured, free of nail polish, and unbitten.

4 Yes, but only a plain gold ring (one only). Rings containing precious or other stones (such as diamonds) must not be worn as dirt will lodge in the setting.

5 Diarrhoea (including just bowel looseness), vomiting, nausea, abdominal pain, sore throat, cold and 'flu symptoms and coughs (any two of these will suffice for the answer — you were asked to name only two).

6 Because ash may enter food and, while smoking, the fingers often touch the lips and pick up contamination from them. Such contamination can be carried to food.

7 A disposable paper handkerchief (tissue), which is used once only and then discarded into a bin with a tight-fitting lid.

8 Trap the germs in a disposable handkerchief (tissue), dispose of the handkerchief in a bin with a close-fitting lid, and wash their hands carefully immediately afterwards.

9 *Staphylococcus aureus.*

10 Staphylococcal food poisoning.

11 Using the same surface or utensil for raw and then ready-to-eat foods, by contact between raw and ready-to-eat foods and by food handlers handling raw then ready-to-eat foods. (You were asked for two examples only).

12 Yes, and it is illegal to do so.

13 False, unfit food must be entirely separated from fit food otherwise serious contamination could occur.

14 *Clostridium perfringens* food poisoning.

15 Toxic chemicals in food, additives added in too high a quantity, inherently toxic foods (poisonous toadstools, for instance), and food allergies.

16 Someone who is infected with a pathogenic organism (who is 'carrying' it) but who shows no symptoms.

17 The organisation of work within a kitchen which arranges that all processes go from raw food, through heating and other processing, to ready-to-eat food. It is an essential method of reducing the risk of cross-contamination.

18 Contamination control, temperature controls, and decontamination control (cleaning).

19 A can which is bulging (its ends are not concave, i.e. not dished inwards). The effect is produced as a result of gas being generated inside the can (usually from microbes growing in the can's contents).

20 Do not use it, put it aside and mark on it clearly that it is not to be used. Inform the Environmental Health Officer.

21 (You were asked to name only two — any of the following will do): cockroaches; flies; ants.

22 Insect-proof the premises.

23 It may be. The risk is that if the slicer is used for raw meat, it will pick up pathogens from that meat. If the slicer is then used for slicing cooked (ready-to-eat) meat, dangerous contamination will be created. If, however, you slice the ready-to-eat meat first, or properly and carefully sanitise the slicer between slicings, danger could be averted. Because of the risk, however, it is always better to use separate slicers — one for raw and the other for cooked meats.

24 A chemical poison excreted from certain types of microbe.

25 Guide dogs only (when accompanied by a blind person).

TEST PAPER 7

1. Why should fruit not be cooked in copper pans?
2. Can you tell whether food is safe to eat by looking at it or smelling it?
3. What conditions in a kitchen lead to condensation?
4. What is the best way of drying washed crockery?
5. What is the best method of drying the hands?
6. What is a pathogen?
7. What should a food handler do with a sore on the hand?
8. What type of receptacle should be used to store waste food?
9. Can viruses cause food poisoning?
10. What is a mycotoxin?
11. What is an anaerobic bacterium?
12. At what temperature should a gateau filled with cream be displayed for sale?
13. How should canned pasteurised ham be stored?
14. What is the most important thing to do with frozen poultry before cooking it?
15. Where should raw meat be prepared?
16. Would you recommend sliding-doors for a kitchen cupboard? (Explain your answer).
17. Where should buckets of dirty washing water be disposed of?
18. What is the most common bacterium causing food poisoning?
19. What should a food handler do immediately before starting work?
20. What should be done with cracked cups and plates?
21. Where should outdoor clothing be kept in food premises?
22. At what temperature should ice cream gateau be stored?
23. What precautions should be taken with meat cooked the day before it is to be sold?
24. Name two diseases that can be caught from raw milk.
25. What is a bacterial spore?

ANSWERS TO TEST PAPER 7

1 The acid in the fruit may dissolve the copper from the pan which, if eaten with the fruit, could cause chemical food poisoning.

2 No, you cannot. Most organisms which produce food poisoning do not produce any changes in the food at all.

3 Steam production and lack of adequate ventilation.

4 Allow it to air-dry naturally.

5 Use a hot-air blower dryer.

6 An organism which is capable of causing disease.

7 Cover it with a waterproof dressing.

8 A container that is capable of being easily cleaned and has a close-fitting lid.

9 Yes, some can. (They may be food-borne, airborne or water-borne.)

10 A toxin produced by some fungi (especially moulds) during growth.

11 A bacterium which cannot grow in the presence of air. (It does not use oxygen for growth).

12 Below 10 °C (preferably below 5 °C).

13 Within a refrigerator, below 5 °C.

14 Ensure that it is thoroughly defrosted.

15 In an area or on a surface which is specifically reserved for raw meat preparation and handling.

16 No, food scraps can become lodged in the grooves (where they are difficult to clean out).

17 Down a drainage gully and NOT down a handbasin or sink as these could become contaminated by the dirty water.

18 The Salmonellae.

19 Wash the hands thoroughly.

20 They should be thrown away.

21 Within an area specifically reserved for such storage, away from food rooms.

22 Below −2.2 °C (minus 2.2 °C), because it contains icecream.

23 It must be thoroughly and rapidly cooled to below 5 °C and be stored below 5 °C until consumed.

24 (Any two of the following will do). TB, brucellosis, Q fever.

25 It is a protective coat that some types of bacteria can form around themselves and which renders them resistant to heat, chemicals and drying. (Only species of *Clostridium* and *Bacillus* can form spores).

TEST PAPER 8

1 Name three advantages of maintaining high standards of food hygiene.

2 Name two sources of pathogenic organisms.

3 What is meant by the term 'cross-contamination'?

4 What is the ideal temperature for the growth (multiplication) of pathogenic bacteria?

5 At what temperature should a frozen food cabinet be operated?

6 At what temperature should a stew awaiting service be kept?

7 How should ham and salad sandwiches be displayed for sale?

8 Name the stages of the three-stage cleaning period.

9 What is meant by the term 'work-flow'?

10 Name the main signs of unfitness in fish.

11 Is it permissible for a food handler to go outside (to visit a shop, for instance) while wearing overalls?

12 Is it permissible for a food handler to wear sandals at work?

13 If you see a nail-brush on a handbasin, should you use it to scrub your finger-nails?

14 Which are more likely to cause food poisoning — bacteria or viruses?

15 Can viruses spoil food?

16 Name three types of infectious disease which can be caught from raw milk.

17 What kind of shoes should a food handler wear when in a food room?

18 What kind of head covering should a food handler wear?

19 What advice should you give new food handlers regarding their finger nails?

20 How should corned beef be displayed for sale in a retail shop?

21 Why should food premises be equipped with two meat-slicing machines?

22 How do bacteria multiply?

23 What is an exotoxin?

24 What is a mycotoxin?

25 Can good food hygiene standards help to increase food shelf-life?

ANSWERS TO TEST PAPER 8

1 (You were asked for only three advantages, any of the following would do): protection of food consumers; protection of business reputation; protection from legal prosecution; increased food shelf-life.

2 (You were asked for only two sources — any of the following would do): rodents; insects; humans (food handlers or customers); raw foods; air; water (possibly: note that tap water in the UK is treated in order to kill pathogens).

3 It is the process whereby pathogenic organisms on or in raw foods are passed (either directly or indirectly) to ready-to-eat foods.

4 (NOTE: you were asked for the ideal temperature, NOT the range). The answer is 37 °C.

5 −18 °C (minus 18 °C).

6 Above 65 °C.

7 Protected from possible contamination, and below 10 °C.

8 Remove gross contamination (such as food scraps), degrease by means of washing with hot water and detergent, and apply hot water sanitiser solution.

9 It is an arrangement of work whereby food passes from the raw stage, through preparation, to the ready-to-eat stage. It is intended to reduce the risk of cross-contamination.

10 Eyes opaque, smell and scales that rub off easily.

11 No, she could pick up contamination from outside and carry it into the food rooms.

12 No, you could easily hurt your feet badly if something fell on them.

13 No, the nail brush may have been contaminated. Each food handler should have their own nail brush which is kept clean and regularly sanitised.

14 Bacteria.

15 No, they only multiply when inside live host cells. (Cells of food are dead).

16 TB, brucellosis and Q fever.

17 Shoes used only in the food premises (if worn outside they may pick up contamination which would then be transferred to the food premises).

18 Head-covering which completely encloses the hair.

19 Keep them short, well-manicured, clean, unbitten, and free from nail varnish.

20 Protected from risk of contamination (especially cross-contamination) and at a temperature below 5 °C.

21 So that one can be used to slice raw meat, and the other for ready-to-eat meat. This is one method of reducing the risk of cross-contamination.

22 By binary fission (they grow to a predetermined size and then split into two).

23 A chemical toxin which is excreted by certain bacteria (e.g. Clostridia and Staphylococci) and causes toxic food poisoning.

24 A toxin produced by certain fungi (especially moulds).

25 Yes, this is one advantage of good food hygiene.

TEST PAPER 9

1 Name two advantages of maintaining a high standard of food hygiene.

2 Is it important for a food handler to bath regularly?

3 Can food premises be closed if hygiene standards are bad?

4 Can rodents carry food poisoning organisms?

5 Is it illegal to use a food ingredient that is unfit?

6 What must a handbasin not be used for?

7 What must a sink not be used for?

8 What is meant by the term 'cross-contamination'?

9 Give three examples of how cross-contamination can occur.

10 What is involved in three-stage cleaning?

11 What is the difference between a detergent and a sanitiser (NOTE: 'sanitiser' is frequently, but wrongly, called 'disinfectant').

12 What is meant by 'work flow'?

13 Food animals are frequently infected with Salmonella. What is the source of infection of these animals (i.e. from where do the animals become infected)?

14 What is the best material for using to make food room equipment?

15 What kind of surface should be used for a kitchen floor?

16 What kind of surface should be used for the walls of a kitchen?

17 Is it correct for the wall-to-wall, and wall-to-floor, junctions in a kitchen to be at right angles?

18 Is it necessary for food-delivery people to observe good hygiene practices?

19 Complete this sentence: 'Once food is cooked, it should not be . . .'

20 Name three indicators of possible rodent infestation.

21 If food (e.g. vegetables) is displayed for sale outside a shop, what precautions should be taken against possible contamination by animals?

22 Does freezing kill bacteria?

23 What is the preferred (optimum) temperature for the growth of pathogenic bacteria?

24 Should a food handler wear the same shoes inside a food room as are worn in the street?

25 Where should handbasins be located in food premises?

ANSWERS TO TEST PAPER 9

1 (You were asked to name only two advantages, any two of the following would do): protection of consumers; protection from risk of prosecution; protection of and enhancement of business reputation; increased shelf-life of food.

2 Yes, food handlers must maintain high standards of personal hygiene.

3 Yes, if the conditions would be likely to cause a danger to health, the local authority may apply to a court for a closure order.

(NOTE: 14 days' notice must be given but an emergency order, requiring only 3 days' notice may be obtained if conditions are such as to cause an 'imminent' risk of danger to health).

4 Yes, which is why they are so dangerous to food.

5 Yes, it is illegal to do so.

6 It must not be used for any purpose other than hand-washing.

7 It must not be used for any purpose other than washing food, equipment or utensils.

8 It is the process by which pathogens on raw food may contaminate ready-to-eat food.

9 (You were asked for only three examples, any three of the following would do): using same surface for raw and ready-to-eat foods; using the same equipment (e.g. slicer) or utensils for raw and ready-to-eat foods; raw food touching ready-to-eat food; food handlers carrying pathogens from raw to ready-to-eat foods.

10 Remove gross contamination (food scraps, etc.), then degrease with hot water and detergent and, finally, apply sanitiser solution.

11 A detergent is a degreasing (cleaning) agent, whereas a sanitiser is designed to kill microbes.

12 It is an arrangement of work processes so that raw food passes through various stages of production to a ready-to-eat state. It is designed to help prevent cross-contamination.

13 From the farm, usually by their feedstuffs.

14 Stainless steel.

15 A surface that is smooth, impervious to moisture and capable of being easily cleaned (a granolithic surface is best).

16 A surface that is smooth and capable of being easily cleaned. Plastic-type wall-boards (specially made for the job) are best, but plaster and paint would suffice in areas where condensation is unlikely to be a problem.

17 No, because they cannot be cleaned. Such junctions should have wide-angle coving.

18 Yes, they are just as capable of endangering food.

19 . . . it should not be reheated.

20 Droppings, gnawed food, food packets and grease marks on pipework/walls, etc.

21 It is a legal requirement that they be at least 45 cm (18 inches) above the ground.

22 No, it does not with any certainty. Some will die, but many will survive.

23 37 °C. (You were asked for the optimum temperature not the range of temperatures.)

24 No. The shoes will pick up contamination from the street.

25 In positions that are conveniently accessible to all food handlers.

TEST PAPER 10

1. What kind of surface would you recommend for a kitchen floor?
2. What surface would you recommend for the walls of a food room?
3. What would you do if you found a rusty can of food in your stores?
4. Would the food inside a rusty can be fit for consumption?
5. What should a food handler do immediately before entering food premises?
6. Which food-poisoning organism is likely to be found in the human nose?
7. What are the main symptoms of food poisoning caused by *Clostridium perfringens*?
8. Which food-poisoning organism would you suspect caused vomiting in a consumer within a few hours of eating a cooked meat salad?
9. Which foods are most commonly contaminated with *Salmonella* from source?
10. Which types of food are most commonly associated with *Staphylococcus aureus* food poisoning?
11. Which types of food are most commonly associated with food poisoning caused by *Clostridium perfringens*?
12. In addition to bacteria and viruses, what other organisms cause harm to a consumer who has eaten contaminated food?
13. Can food additives cause danger to consumers?
14. Why should copper dispensers not be used for dispensing fruit juices?
15. Name one commonly used food preservative.
16. Is mouldy food dangerous to eat?
17. Where should waste food awaiting disposal be stored?
18. Is it permissible to store waste in a food room?
19. What conditions do bacteria need in order to multiply?
20. The lower limit of temperature for growth of pathogens is 5 °C. Is this also true for other microbes?
21. Which group of organisms cannot produce spoilage in food?

22 Where could you find a *Trichinella* parasite?

23 A food handler should report symptoms of a sore throat to the management — true or false?

24 Cuts on the hand of a food handler should be covered in elasticated plasters — true or false?

25 The most common fault that an examinee makes in a written exam is to fail to read the question properly — true or false?

ANSWERS TO TEST PAPER 10

1 A surface which is smooth, impervious to moisture and capable of being easily cleaned. Ideally a granolithic surface is best. This cannot be used on timber floors (floorboards) in which case, heavy-duty vinyl sheet should be used.

2 A surface that is smooth and capable of being easily cleaned. Plastic wallboards are best (several branded makes are available). In a room where no steam is produced, a plaster and paint would suffice, but this surface must be protected at edges, etc. to avoid percussion damage.

3 Seek advice from the Environmental Health Officer.

4 It depends on whether or not the can has been holed by rotting through the metal. If the can is badly rusted, it must be disposed of and the food must not be used.

5 Change into protective overclothing (don't forget shoes) and wash the hands thoroughly.

6 *Staphylococcus aureus.*

7 Severe abdominal pain and diarrhoea.

8 *Staphylococcus aureus.*

9 Raw meats (especially poultry), duck eggs and, possibly, shellfish.

10 Cooked (ready-to-eat) meats, cream and foods containing cream, possibly milk (raw, untreated), custards, etc.

11 Rolled meat joints, cooked hams (it is anaerobic near the bone), stews and similar foods providing anaerobic conditions.

12 Fungi, metazoan and protozoan parasites.

13 Yes, especially if present in the wrong (too high) concentration. (Legislation specifies which additives can be used in what foods and in what concentrations.)

14 The acid in the fruit juices may dissolve the copper. Copper consumed in the juices may produce chemical food poisoning in a consumer.

15 (You were asked to name only one common preservative so any one of the following would do): sugar, in jams, etc.; salt; vinegar.

16 It depends on the type of mould and how mouldy it is, but the food will probably be unfit to eat.

17 In a container that has a close-fitting lid and is capable of being easily cleaned.

18 Only for a very short time and then only if it is in a proper container. Waste should only be stored in a properly constructed waste-disposal area.

19 Warmth, moisture, suitable food and a suitable chemical environment.

20 No, spoilage organisms can grow below this (down to about −7 °C, i.e. minus 7 °C).

21 Viruses, metazoan and protozoan parasites cannot spoil food.

22 In raw (or improperly cooked) pork.

23 True.

24 False, they should be covered with waterproof (unventilated) dressings.

25 True — so please, whenever you do a written exam **Always read each question carefully, think about what it means, before you answer.**

PERSONAL MESSAGE TO READERS

I would like to wish each of you good luck with any exams you take and a prosperous — and safe — career in the food industry. Remember what you have learned, and, equally important, always apply it. The health of your consumers depends on you.

I will be pleased to answer any queries and may be contacted through the publishers. (Please enclose a stamped, self-addressed envelope for a reply.)

P.A. ALCOCK

Glossary

Glossary

Aerobic

Requiring oxygen (from the air) in order to perform metabolic (life) processes. Aerobic organisms will only grow in the presence of oxygen. (See also *Anaerobic* and *Facultative Organism.*)

Anaerobic

The opposite of aerobic. Anaerobic organisms will NOT grow in the presence of oxygen (air) and some are killed by exposure to it. The term means 'without air'. (See also *Aerobic* and *Facultative Organism.*)

Available Water

Microorganisms need water in order to be able to grow; many varieties will die if they are dried. The mere fact that water is present within a particular environment does not mean that the organisms will be able to use it. The water must be in such a form that organisms can transfer it from the environment into themselves (available water). Water may be unavailable because it is frozen or bound up in concentrated sugar or salt solutions.

Bacteria

A group of microorganisms which consist of a single cell (although in some cases a number of individual bacteria may be grouped together in a cluster or chain). (See also *Spores — Bacterial.*)

Binary Fission

A method by means of which many types of microbe reproduce (notably bacteria). In this process the microbe grows to a certain size and then splits into two. The two 'daughter' cells then grow to a certain size and again split into two.

Cell

The smallest unit of life. Cells are like bags of chemicals and inside a cell the processes of life are performed. A human being consists of billions of cells, each one contributing in its own specific way to the life of the human. Many microorganisms (notably the bacteria) consist of only one cell.

Challenge Dose

The minimum number of disease-causing microorganisms necessary to produce symptoms of disease. If the body is 'challenged' by a smaller number than this dose, symptoms will not result. This minimum number is different for different microorganisms. The main point to note with respect to food poisoning is that we need to ingest this minimum number of food-poisoning organisms, or food in which the minimum number of toxin-producing organisms are actively growing, before food poisoning results.

Clean/Cleanliness

There are TWO types of 'cleanliness'. (See *Visually Clean* and *Microbiologically Clean.*)

Cross-contamination

An undesirable, and potentially dangerous, process by which microorganisms are transferred from one area to another. The term is commonly applied to the process whereby potentially dangerous microorganisms are transferred from raw food to ready-to-eat food via surfaces, equipment, hands, slicing machines and so on. The presence of such organisms on raw food does not matter because the food will be cooked before consumption. The presence of the organisms on ready-to-eat food DOES matter because such food will not be treated in any way liable to kill the organisms. For this reason cross-contamination is dangerous and is responsible for many outbreaks of food poisoning.

Detergent

A substance used to enable water to mix with and remove grease and fat ('washing-up liquid' is a detergent). Water alone will not be able to 'cut through' grease and fat, it can only do so when a detergent is added to the water.

Endotoxin

A toxin (poison) released when certain varieties of bacteria die inside the human body. When the bacterial cell dies it breaks apart and the endotoxins within it are released. The effect of the endotoxin may be severe and if a massive number of bacteria die inside the body at the same time death of the victim could result. (Fortunately, death by 'endotoxic shock' is rare, but it must borne in mind as a type of fatal food poisoning.) (See also *Exotoxin.*)

Enzymes

These are chemicals which are produced by all kinds of living cells. Many different kinds of enzyme exist, and they each have their own particular function. Specific kinds of enzyme are produced by certain food-spoilage bacteria. These enzymes are excreted out of the bacterial cells and poured over the food they are rotting. It is these enzymes that actually cause the rotting process by partially digesting the food.

Exotoxin

A toxin (poison) produced by certain bacteria which is excreted from the bacterial cell. It is the exotoxins of the staphylococci which produce staphylococcal food poisoning. As the staphylococci grow in a suitable food they excrete an exotoxin into it. Anyone eating this food will then suffer food poisoning if a sufficient quantity of the exotoxin has been poured into it by the growing staphylococci. (See also *Endotoxin.*)

Facultative Organism

An organism that can grow using oxygen (in the air) when it is available, but that can also grow without oxygen when it is not available (i.e. it is both aerobic and anaerobic). (See also *Aerobic, Anaerobic.*)

Food Handler

Anyone who is engaged in ANY of the processes which go to make up or are ancillary to food processing (e.g. a cook, a washer-up, waitress etc, is a 'food handler', even though they might not handle food directly).

Food Hygiene

An exercise in applied microbiology. It consists of a series of techniques, procedures and rules, all designed to help ensure that food is safe to eat. (It is directly concerned with the prevention of microbiological food poisoning and the increase in food shelf-life.)

Food Poisoning

An illness produced by the consumption of inherently poisonous food (e.g. certain toadstools), or of food that is contaminated by poisonous chemicals, or of specific kinds of microorganism (especially certain types of bacteria).

Fungi

A group of microorganisms. Most fungi are multi-celled (e.g. moulds, toadstools, etc.) but the yeasts are single-celled. Most fungi are spoilage organisms rather than food-poisoning organisms BUT some produce a toxin (mycotoxin) that is thought to be capable of causing some kinds of cancer. (See also *Spores — Fungal.*)

Gastro-enteritis

A common term for a condition characterised by vomiting and diarrhoea. The condition may be a type of food poisoning or it may, in many cases, be produced by particular varieties of virus breathed in or eaten in food. (See also *Gastric 'Flu.*)

Gastric 'Flu

A common, but incorrect, name for 'gastro-enteritis'.

Incubation Period

The time between someone being infected by a particular disease-producing organism and the first signs of illness (i.e. the first onset of symptoms).

Metazoan Parasites

Multi-celled parasites (e.g. the intestinal worms and tapeworms). (See also *Protozoan Parasites.*)

Microbiologically Clean

A surface, utensil, etc. which not only looks clean (visually clean) but which is also as free from contamination by microorganisms as is reasonably possible under practical conditions. (See also *Visually Clean.*)

Mould

A kind of multi-celled fungus.

Mycelium

The thread-like 'body' of fungi. It is not found in yeasts, which are single-celled fungi.

Osmotic Pressure

The pressure produced in a solution due to the presence of dissolved solids. The more solids (e.g. sugar and salt) that are dissolved in a liquid, the more concentrated the solution is, and the higher is the osmotic pressure. Jams and salted foods are 'preserved' because they are highly concentrated. The high osmotic pressure produced prevents bacteria from absorbing water from them (i.e. the water is made unavailable).

Pathogenic

Capable of producing disease.

pH

This is a measure of the degree of acidity or alkalinity of a solution. pH 1 is very acid, pH 7 is neutral, and pH 14 is very alkaline.

Protozoan Parasites

Single-celled parasites (e.g. parasitic amoeba). (See also *Metazoan Parasites.*)

Sanitiser

The technically correct name for 'disinfectant'. Sanitisers are chemical substances that are capable of killing SOME microorganisms. Different sanitisers are more or less effective at killing different kinds of organism.

Spoilage Organism

A microorganism that will spoil (rot) food. Most spoilage organisms do not cause disease, they merely spoil food.

Spores — Bacterial

Special forms of certain bacteria which enable them to withstand severe, adverse conditions. Bacterial spores are able to withstand treatment by many types of sanitiser and are very heat resistant (you would have to boil them at 100 °C for 4 to 5 hours or more to kill them). Bacterial spores are entirely different to the spores of fungi (which are the equivalent of 'seeds' and which are only slightly resistant to either chemicals or heat). Note that only species of bacteria belonging to the *Bacillus* and *Clostridium* genera are capable of changing themselves into spores. (See also *Spores — Fungal.*)

Spores — Fungal

The 'seeds' produced by certain types of fungi (usually released into, and distributed by, air currents). (See also *Spores — Bacterial.*)

Surface Tension

A property of water by which it forms a kind of 'skin' at its interface with air. It is this property that causes water to form globules when spattered onto a surface. The surface tension of water must be broken down if the water is to wet a surface properly, by spreading evenly over it. Detergents will lower the surface tension of water and allow the water to wet a surface fully.

Temperature Control

By keeping perishable foods either below 5 °C or above 65 °C it is possible to prevent the growth of any food-poisoning bacteria that may be present in the food.

Temperature Danger Zone

The (danger zone) is between 5 °C and 65 °C. Within this zone of temperature it is possible for those bacteria which can produce food poisoning to grow. By keeping perishable foods outside this zone it is possible to control the growth of any food-poisoning bacteria that might be in the food.

Toxin

'Toxin' is the technical term for 'poison'. (See *Endotoxin* and *Exotoxin.*)

Unfit Food

Food may be unfit to eat either because it could be harmful to anyone who ate it or because it has been changed in flavour, consistency or nature to such an extent that it has become unpleasant to eat.

Virus

Viruses are the 'odd men out' in nature. They can be thought of as being either very simple organisms or very complex chemicals. All viruses are parasitic inside specific host cells. When outside a host cell, they are merely like chemical crystals and perform no life activities at all. When inside a host cell viruses enslave it and cause it to reproduce more virus particles.

Visually Clean

A state whereby a surface, utensil, etc. looks clean. Such a surface or utensil may still be contaminated by bacteria or other microorganisms. (See also *Microbiologically Clean.*)

Yeasts

Single-celled fungi.

Index

Key Facts Index

Progress Paper Index

NOTE: revision test papers commence on p. 187